BY HIS LIGHT
Character and Values in the Service of God

Based on addresses by
RABBI AHARON LICHTENSTEIN

•

Adapted by
RABBI REUVEN ZIEGLER

KTAV PUBLISHING HOUSE
Jersey City, NJ
YESHIVAT HAR ETZION
Alon Shevut, Israel

5763 / 2003

Library of Congress Cataloging-in-Publication Data

Ziegler, Reuven.
  By his light : character and values in the service of God / based on
addresses by Rabbi Aharon Lichtenstein ; adapted by Rabbi Reuven Ziegler.
    p. cm.
Includes bibliographical references and indexes.
  ISBN 0-88125-796-6
  1. Spiritual life--Judaism. 2. Ethics, Jewish. 3. Jewish way of
life. I. Lichtenstein, Aharon. II. Title.
  BM723.Z54 2003
  296.3'6--dc21

                          2002155631

                    First edition, March 2002
                  Second edition, February 2003

                       Yeshivat Har Etzion
              Alon Shevut, Gush Etzion 90433, Israel
                       www.haretzion.org
                  Email: office@etzion.org.il
      Tel.: 011-972-2-993-1456 ext. 5 (Israel); 212-732-4874 (USA)
      Fax: 011-972-2-993-1298 (Israel); 212-732-4886 (USA)

   Questions and comments about the book: develop@etzion.org.il
   Visit Yeshivat Har Etzion's Virtual Beit Midrash: www.vbm-torah.

             Manufactured in the United States of America

                         Published by
                 KTAV Publishing House, Inc.
                      930 Newark Avenue
                    Jersey City, NJ 07306
                    Email: info@ktav.com
                        www.ktav.com
                      (201) 963-9524
                    Fax (201) 963-0102

CONTENTS

ספר זה מוקדש לזכר הבחור היקר

YAAKOV LEVI MATANKY

יעקב לוי ז"ל בן הרב אריה ומרים אסתר מטנקי

שנקטף בדמי חייו, ב' מנחם אב תשס"ב

Yaakov was an outstanding *talmid* of

Yeshivat Har Etzion (5760 - 5761)

who was taken from us much too soon,

but whose memory will live on forever

in the hearts of his family,

teachers and friends.

שמאי אומר עשה תורתך קבע. אמור מעט ועשה הרבה.

והוי מקבל את כל האדם בסבר פנים יפות. (פרקי אבות א:טו)

PREFACE

It is a privilege and a pleasure to present before the reading public this collection of discourses by Rabbi Aharon Lichtenstein, one of the premier Torah educators and thinkers of our day. For both those who have already experienced his profound and powerful teaching and those who have not, this is an opportunity to be enlightened by the depth and breadth of his learning, and inspired by the scope and beauty of his vision. It is our hope that sensitive readers will be stirred by the book's teachings and motivated to incorporate them into their personal lives.

The issues explored in this book are of concern to anyone seeking to fashion his or her religious personality. Its major theme perhaps is encapsulated best in the dual import of the verse, "*Bekhol derakhekha da'ehu*, In all your ways, know Him" (*Mishlei* 3:6). Firstly, this verse indicates that there is more than one way for a person to serve God. Concomitantly, it calls upon us to make each of our actions into part of our service of God, instead of regarding whole areas of our life as being religiously neutral. The advocacy of a theocentric life—and specifically one that, despite its focus on the single goal of serving God, nevertheless recognizes multiple paths and entails multiple demands—is a hallmark of Rabbi Lichtenstein's thought. Indeed, it characterizes Rabbi Lichtenstein's life; anyone who knows him can attest that he is a living exemplar of the ideals set forth in this book.

Beyond the actual positions espoused, these presentations are noteworthy for their methodology: the recognition of complexity, the openness to a plurality of approaches, the eschewing of simplistic black-and-white positions, the attempt to view issues in a broad perspective ("to see life steadily and see it whole," in a phrase much beloved of Rabbi Lichtenstein), the bringing to bear of a wide range of thought and experience on the problems addressed, and the sensitivity to nuance. The result is a treatment that, while passionate in aspiration, is nevertheless balanced and moderate in judgment. It is also striking in its intellectual honesty. Although Rabbi Lichtenstein articulates a specific vision of Judaism, he nevertheless is honest enough to acknowledge the legitimacy of other positions. And while these essays are exhortatory and not only analytic, Rabbi Lichtenstein's strong advocacy of certain positions does not blind him to their risks and potential pitfalls, which he confronts squarely.

The balanced and multifaceted nature of these essays stems from the proposition that the Jewish value system, like life itself, is indeed complex and dialectical. The essays' style, therefore, is a manifestation of a way of looking at the world in general and at Judaism in particular. Thus, apart from its specific messages, the book conveys a world-view, a manner of approaching the questions of life and religious existence. It encourages the reader to fathom the complexity of human experience and to view his or her individual, communal and historical contexts in a wider perspective.

This breadth of vision—employed in the perception of both experience and values—is perhaps the defining quality of Rabbi Lichtenstein's thought. It manages to encompass both religious and humanistic elements, drawing them into closer relation. Rabbi Lichtenstein brings to these essays not only a staunch commitment to Halakha and a firm grounding in rigorous Torah study, but also a deep spirituality, a profound moral sensitivity and a keen awareness of both the challenges and opportunities of the contemporary era, which distinguish his teachings from much current discourse. He harnesses the crystalline forces of intellect—subtle and acute powers of analysis, orderly patterns of thought and presentation, and literary sensitivity to the relationship between substance and form—to an overflowing capaciousness of spirit and a vigorously pulsating faith that course through his words and animate his educational endeavors.

• • •

This book's title, *By His Light*, is inspired by a number of Biblical verses. The first two verses (*Tehillim* 89:15-16) enumerate qualities associated with God, which, by extension, man should seek to imitate. As such, these verses are fitting for a guide to the development of *Character and Values*:

Righteousness and justice are the base of Your throne;
Kindness and truth shall go before You.
Happy is the nation that acknowledges You;
O Lord, they shall walk *by the light of Your countenance.*

Beyond individual qualities, these verses express a general tendency: the need for our path in life to be illuminated by divine light, all our decisions informed by religious considerations.

The ideal religious personality sketched in the pages of *By His Light* is, in fact, guided by a passionate quest for the divine, from which he or she derives strength and inspiration. The book's title thus echoes another verse as well (*Tehillim* 36:10):

With You is the fountain of life;
by Your light do we see light.

As indicated by the Rambam in the opening to his *Sefer Hamadda,* the next verse (36:11) clarifies that this quest for the divine should be expressed in both spiritual and moral terms:

Bestow Your kindness upon those who know You,
And Your righteousness upon the upright in heart,

The psalm thus points to knowledge of God and uprightness of heart as the ends of the religious pursuit.

Yet the opening verse of this psalm (36:1),

To the conductor, to *the servant of God*, to David,

places the yearning for sanctity and goodness within its proper framework. The book's subtitle, which speaks of *the Service of God*, thus provides a necessary complement to its title, for the spiritual aspirationism implicit in the phrase *By His Light* is grounded in an overriding sense of duty and discipline. While the title expresses human grandeur, man's capacity for emulating the divine, the subtitle indicates the necessity of submission to God's will, viewing oneself as a servant of God. The interplay between these two themes—duty and aspiration—is central to the book, and, indeed, is basic to Rabbi Lichtenstein's outlook on life.

The phrase *Character and Values* highlights the book's emphasis on inwardness and character development, while signaling that these are constituent parts of *the Service of God*. Furthermore, this cultivation of character is to be rooted in the traditional components of *avodat Hashem*—namely, Torah study and mitzva observance—and expressed concretely via both specifically-defined acts of worship and the broader area of *devar ha-reshut*, encompassing the entirety of one's life.

Clearly, then, the layers of meaning contained in the title indicate the multiple thrusts of the book's message. In Chapter Eleven, Rabbi Lichtenstein notes that if a thinker acknowledges a multiplicity of values and desires to maintain a balance between them, then he will find it necessary to weight a presentation in one direction in order to rectify the imbalance he perceives in his audience towards the opposite direction. Since many of the addresses in this book employ this educational technique, it is important to note which audience Rabbi Lichtenstein is addressing in each of them. As the head of a *yeshivat hesder*, an advanced Torah institution whose students also participate in Israel's military defense, and as a *rosh yeshiva* at Yeshiva University, Rabbi Lichtenstein is a leader of the Religious Zionist community in

Israel and the Centrist Orthodox community in America, and his speeches gathered here address audiences of those communities. (One can distinguish between these two groups, which, though similar, face a different set of issues in their daily lives.) More importantly, the overall balance that Rabbi Lichtenstein advocates makes it crucial to treat the book as a whole, and not to regard any part in isolation as expressing the entirety of his broad-ranging and nuanced position.

Although most of these addresses focus on individual spiritual growth, the book concludes with a vision of a community animated by the ideals espoused throughout the preceding chapters. In this sense, the final chapter is the most inclusive one and constitutes a coda to the volume as a whole.

• • •

It is important to note that although Rabbi Lichtenstein sanctioned the publication of this book, he did not have a hand in selecting and preparing its chapters, nor did he review the book's contents before publication. Nevertheless, I believe the book accurately conveys his ideas, and I hope that his trust is not misplaced. Although these adaptations hew closely to Rabbi Lichtenstein's original wording, those familiar with his own writings will immediately note that the style here is somewhat simpler, if less elegant. This difference in styles reflects the book's origin in oral presentations, as well as an attempt on the part of the editor to make it accessible to a broader audience. For the same reason, Hebrew terms are explained (generally in parentheses) the first time they appear in each chapter, and a glossary is appended at the end of the book. For further treatments of some of the issues raised in this book, readers are encouraged to refer to Rabbi Lichtenstein's own two-volume collection of essays, *Leaves of Faith* (Ktav, 2003). The challenge presented by those essays (in comparison with the essays in this book) is more than matched by their rewards.

All these speeches, with one exception, were taped and then transcribed word-for-word. Chapters 7, 8 and 9 were originally delivered in Hebrew; the rest of the discourses were delivered in English. After reviewing the transcripts against the tapes, I adapted them for print by breaking them into subsections, translating Hebrew quotes and terms, editing for style and occasionally abridging or reorganizing. Chapter 8 is an exception to this rule: it is based on a student's summary of an address by Rabbi Lichtenstein, but nevertheless was included because it covered a more comprehensive range of themes than other lectures on the same topic that had been recorded. The titles of all the chapters and sub-chapter divisions are my own. Endnotes containing references and cross-references are my additions, while substantive endnotes derive from Rabbi Lichtenstein's lectures.

The following people prepared the initial transcripts of these lectures: Rabbi Eli Clark—chapters 5, 10 and 12; Rabbi David Debow—chapter 6; Aviad Hacohen—chapter 9; Reuven Lavi—chapter 2; Hillel Maizels, Saul Adler and Mordy Friedman—chapter 11; Shira and Avi Shmidman—chapters 2, 3 and 4; Ramon Widmonte—chapter 1.

The *sichot* which form the basis of Chapters 1-4 were delivered as a unit; the rest of the addresses included in this volume were delivered independently of each other. The following is a list of the original venues and dates of these speeches:

- Chapters 1-4 were delivered to first-year foreign students at Yeshivat Har Etzion in Winter 5747 (1986-7).

- Chapter 5, "Determining Objectives in Religious Growth," was an address at Yeshiva University's Gruss Institute in Jerusalem in 5744 (1984).

- Chapter 6, "Being *Frum* and Being Good," was an address to Yeshiva University Rabbinic Alumni in Cheshvan 5747 (1986).

- Chapter 7, "*Bittachon*: Trust in God," was delivered to a conference of senior educators of the National-Religious school system in Israel in the wake of the Yom Kippur War. This adaptation is based on a transcript of that lecture published in Elul 5735 (1975) by the Israeli Ministry of Education.

- Chapter 8, "I Am with Him in Distress," was delivered at Yeshivat Har Etzion on *Asara Be-Tevet* 5746 (1985).

- Chapter 9, "If You Remain Silent at this Time," was delivered at Yeshivat Har Etzion on *Ta'anit Esther* 5744 (1984).

- Chapter 10, "*Teshuva*: Repentance and Return," was delivered at the Gruss Institute in Jerusalem in Tishrei 5748 (1987).

- Chapter 11, "A Pure Heart," was delivered at the Gruss Institute in Jerusalem in Tishrei 5763 (2002).

- Chapter 12, "Centrist Orthodoxy: A Spiritual Accounting," was an address to the Educators' Council of America in Cheshvan 5746 (1985).

The fact that all of these speeches (apart from Chapters 7 and 11) are from the mid-1980's is not meant to exclude Rabbi Lichtenstein's earlier or later thought. Rather, this is due to the simple biographical fact that those were the years when I was first exposed to Rabbi Lichtenstein. When selecting speeches for inclusion in this collection, I found that these addresses, which I had heard years before either live or on cassette, were the ones that remained most vivid in my memory. It is my hope that the powerful impact these speeches made on me at the time will be felt by a new generation encountering them for the first time.

Prior to the publication of this book, the majority of these adaptations were distributed on the Internet by Yeshivat Har Etzion's Israel Koschitzky Virtual Beit Midrash (http://www.vbm-torah.org) as part of a series entitled, "Developing a

Torah Personality." Several thousand readers subscribed, and we received many enthusiastic responses. Especially gratifying were the responses of those readers who had used the material in educational settings: classrooms, youth groups, adult education and private study circles. We welcome feedback: please write to develop@etzion.org.il with your questions or comments. Also, if you do utilize these essays in an educational setting, please drop us a line to let us know about your experience.

Many people deserve thanks for their help or guidance in preparing this book: first, Rabbi Eli Clark, who initiated the enterprise of transcribing Rabbi Lichtenstein's English lectures and who provided many helpful editorial comments for this volume; the other transcribers listed above, especially Avi Shmidman, who had a number of tapes professionally transcribed; Mrs. Naomi Tabory, for her sharp eye; Debra Berkowitz, for preparing the source and name indices, and for overseeing all technical matters with characteristic graciousness and efficiency; Yoseif Bloch, for preparing the subject index; Andrea Riffkin and Rabbi Mordechai Friedman, for helping prepare the glossary; and Drs. David Shatz and Joel B. Wolowelsky, for their always beneficial advice. This book was first printed in a limited edition by the Etzion Foundation in 5762 (2002), and is now being published for the general public in a revised and expanded edition. Special thanks to Perry Davis and Dassi Lewis, for seeing the first edition to print; the board of the Etzion Foundation, for underwriting publication of the first edition; Dr. Mayer Brayer, for his support and encouragement throughout the project; and Ktav Publishing House and its president, Bernard Scharfstein, for being so professional, forthcoming and enthusiastic in their handling of this revised edition. *Acharon chaviv*, a world of thanks to my wife Yael and to my parents, Rabbi Zvi and Sandra Ziegler, for their constant love and support.

Finally, the publication of this book is a way of saying thank you to Rabbi Lichtenstein for formulating and embodying the vision presented herein, for his unstinting educational efforts, and for being an inspiration and a lodestar to his students. It is rare for a *talmid* to have the opportunity to repay his *rebbe* in some small measure for all that he has received from him; I, and all those involved in the preparation of this volume, are thankful for the opportunity. In his discussion of the commandment to love God, the Rambam (*Sefer Ha-mitzvot, aseh* 3), based on the *Sifri* (*Vaetchanan*, 32), says that if you love someone, you want others to love him as well. We hope that we have accomplished something analogous in this book.

This volume is published on occasion of Rabbi Lichtenstein's thirtieth year as co-*rosh yeshiva* of Yeshivat Har Etzion. His many students and admirers wish him decades more of *harbatzat Torah* in good health; may he continue to go "from strength to strength."

וקוי ה' יחליפו כח יעלו אבר כנשרים ירוצו ולא ייגעו ילכו ולא ייעפו.

(ישעיהו מ:לא)

... ואוהביו כצאת השמש בגבורתו.

(שופטים ה:לא)

Reuven Ziegler

Chanuka 5763

Alon Shevut

CHAPTER ONE

To Cultivate and to Guard:
The Universal Duties of Mankind

W hen seeking to shape our personalities according to Torah values, we must relate to at least three levels of expectation and responsibility. These can be regarded as concentric circles, moving from the broader to the more specific:

1) the universal demands placed upon one simply as a human being;
2) the demands of a Jew;
3) the responsibilities of a *ben-Torah*, one who makes Torah study a central part of his life and embodies its values.

I wish to deal now with the first level.[1] What are the basic, cardinal, universal values for which every person should strive?

TWO TASKS

L et us open a *Chumash* (Pentateuch) to the chapter describing the creation of man and see what task was assigned to him.

> The Lord God took the man and placed him in the Garden of Eden to cultivate it and to guard it. And the Lord God commanded the man, saying, "Of every tree of the garden you are to eat; but as for the tree of knowledge of good and evil, you must not eat of it; for as soon as you eat of it, you shall die." (*Bereishit* 2:15-17)

In the seventh chapter of *Sanhedrin,* the *Gemara* derives the seven universal Noachide Laws from the last two of these verses. However, I would like to address the first of these verses: God placed man (Adam) in the garden *"le-ovdah u-leshomrah,"* to work or cultivate the garden and to guard it. Here we have two distinct tasks. One, *"le-shomrah,"* is largely conservative, aimed at preserving nature. It means to guard the world, to watch it—and watching is essentially a static occupation, seeing to it that things do not change, that they remain as they are. This is what Adam was expected to do, and part of our task in the world is indeed to guard that which we have been given: our natural environment, our social setting, our religious heritage.

In a sense, we are expected also to be a *shomer* (guard) of the Torah itself. What do *Anshei Kenesset Ha-gedola,* the sages of the Great Assembly, mean when they instruct us to "Make a fence around the Torah" (*Avot* 1:1)? They mean to guard it, to watch it. Similarly, *Chazal* speak of *"Asu mishmeret le-mishmarti,* Set a guard around My guard" (*Mo'ed Katan* 5a, *Yevamot* 21a). We often use the term *shomer mitzva* to describe someone. This doesn't just mean that he does what the *Shulchan Arukh* says, but also that he guards it; he sees to it that the mitzva as an entity, as a reality, remains pure; he envisions himself as having a sense of responsibility towards it. All this is included in the term *"le-shom-rah"* (to guard it).

At the same time, there is the task of *"le-ovdah"* (to cultivate it), which is essentially creative: to develop, to work, to innovate. This applied even in the Garden of Eden, which, according to some of the *midrashim,* was already a perfect environment.

Here we have, then, two foci of our primary obligation: a) to guard, to have a sense of responsibility in relation to that which we have been given; and b) to work and to develop. Although Adam was commanded specifically to till and guard the Garden of Eden, I think that we would not be stretching things too far if we were to understand that this mandate applies far beyond that particular little corner of the Garden where Adam and Eve were placed. What we have here is a definition of how man is to be perceived in general: as a *shomer* and as an *oved*.

PART 1:
Le-shomrah—To Honor, Protect and Preserve

WHO IS THE MASTER?

As I said, the mandate to guard relates in part to the natural world; the concern for ecology has some basis in this. To some extent, this mandate extends to the society one is in. But to a great extent, it applies in relation to oneself. One must guard the human personality itself and everything appended to it, one's *dalet amot* (four cubits) which he assumes to be his own private domain.

Now, this is of great importance and needs to be stressed, because we are dealing here with a fundamentally religious perception that runs counter to the notions prevalent within the widely secular society in which we find ourselves. The essence of modern secular culture is the notion of human sovereignty; individual man is master over himself, and collective man is master over his collective. This creates problems as to where the line is to be drawn between individual and collective man, and that issue is the crux of much of modern socio-political theory—when the state can and cannot interfere. But the common denominator of all these discussions is that they think fundamentally in terms of human sovereignty, the question being whether you speak of humanity or of a particular person.

From a religious point of view, of course, *eilu va-eilu divrei avoda zara*—both approaches are idolatrous. Here one establishes individual man as an idol, and there one idolizes, in humanistic terms, humanity as a whole. The basis of any religious perception of human existence is the sense that man is not a master: neither a master over the world around him, nor a master over himself.

"THE EARTH IS THE LORD'S"

Of course, this is not to say that the notion of private property does not exist. It certainly exists within religious thought generally, and within Judaism specifically; the notion of private property is a very central concept in Halakha, and large sections of the Talmud are devoted to it. Rather, what this means is that the notion of property is never absolute. It is always relative; ultimately, *"La-Hashem ha-aretz u-melo'ah*, The Earth is the Lord's and all that it holds" (*Tehillim* 24:1). But within the world in which we exist, we can say that relative to Shimon, Reuven has been granted ownership, or that relative to the individual, the community has been granted authority.

In this manner, one can understand the *gemara* in *Berakhot* (35a-b) which points out a seeming contradiction between two verses in *Tehillim*: on the one hand, "The Heavens belong to the Lord, but the Earth He gave over to man" (115:16), and on the other hand, "The Earth is the Lord's and all that it holds" (24:1). The *gemara* answers: "This is not really a difficulty. One verse is speaking of the reality before a person has recited a *berakha* (blessing), and the other verse is speaking of the reality after a person has said a *berakha*."

A person who partakes of the world without reciting a *berakha* has, so to speak, stolen from God; he has committed an offense of *me'ila* (misusing that which has been consecrated to God). However, when he pronounces a *berakha*, this does not mean that the item is now absolutely his. It is not like purchasing a loaf of bread from a storeowner, who then disappears from the picture. Heaven forbid! "Mine is the silver and mine is the gold, says the Lord of Hosts" (*Chaggai* 2:8). Rather, the *gemara* teaches that, at an operational level, there are two different levels of one's mastery over the object, in terms of the permissibility for one to use it. Initially, you cannot partake in any way. But once you say the *berakha*, you have in effect recognized God's ownership. You recognize His hegemony, you accept the fact that you live subject to Him, you have acknowledged His sovereignty, and now you partake of the world with His permission. Through our reciting a *berakha*, God grants us permission the way a medieval king might have delegated a fief to a particular person.

Regarding some forms of *kodashim* (sacred items), the *gemara* says, "*Mi-shulchan gavo'ah ka zakhu*, They have acquired it from Heaven's table" (see *Beitza* 21a, *Bava Metzia* 92a). What the *gemara* says in a narrow halakhic sense is true in a broader sense of our ability to partake of the world. We are guests at God's table. This means that whatever we have in the world, we have as *shomerim* (guards)—it has been given to us to guard and we are never truly masters.

Now, of course, there are different kinds of *shomerim*. There are those who have only responsibilities and no rights, such as a *shomer chinam* (unpaid guard) and a *shomer sakhar* (paid guard). On the other hand, a *sho'el* (borrower) and a *sokher* (renter) have both *chiyyuvim* and *kinyanim* (liabilities and rights). In the sense that we too have both *chiyyuvim* and *kinyanim*, we are analogous to a *sho'el* or *sokher*. (However, the analogy is not exact, since, unlike a *sho'el*, we do not have rights against the Owner; we merely have rights to use the property, given the Owner's continuing consent.) And if this is true regarding property, it is equally true of our own selves.

OWNERSHIP OF ONESELF

I mentioned earlier the prevalent secular conception of one's "ownership" of himself. One hears this argument in various contexts, especially with regard to the question of abortion: it's a

woman's right, it's her own body, she can do what she wants, etc.
Years back, I was asked to testify before a subcommittee of the
Knesset which dealt with abortions.[2] Among other things, I mentioned that, leaving aside the significant question of whether it is
the woman's body only or whether the fetus has some rights as
well, there is a more fundamental problem. Even if we were to
accept that indeed it is the woman's own body, we totally reject
the conception that she then can do with it as she pleases. This is
a completely anti-halakhic perception. It rests on a secular
assumption that, as it were, "My Nile is my own; I made it for
myself" (*Yechezkel* 29:3), as if we are the source of our own existence and therefore the masters of our own being. This is assured-
ly not the case. In absolute terms, a person does not own himself.

In fact, there are prohibitions that apply to how a person
relates to himself. Just as one is forbidden to injure or curse others,
so is he forbidden to injure himself[3] or to curse himself.[4] Similarly,
the mitzva of "*Ve-nishmartem me'od le-nafshoteikhem*, Take utmost
care of yourselves" (*Devarim* 4:15) specifically prohibits a person
from taking unnecessary risks, even though he will not affect any-
body else. The very notion that a person should be free to do what
he wants with relation to himself is at absolute odds with our conception. We believe that you are never an independent entity, nor
do you "own" yourself; you are always a *shomer* appointed by God.
That applies to your "property," to your own self, and certainly to
your relationship to what surrounds you.

HONOR GUARD

Let us now further refine our understanding of the duty of "*le-
shomrah*." It has not only a negative aspect, namely, that a
person does not have the right to dispose of objects arbitrarily or
even to deal with himself as he wishes. It has also a positive aspect:
there is an obligation to be a *shomer*, and not merely in order to

avoid damage. Although this is essentially a passive activity, there nevertheless is an active aspect to it as well. The Rambam says:

> The guarding of the Temple is a positive commandment. This applies even though there is no fear of enemies or bandits, for its guarding is in order to honor it. A palace with guards is not comparable to a palace without guards. (*Hilkhot Beit Ha-bechira* 8:1)

Even though there is no fear of invasion, nevertheless the *Mikdash* (Temple) must have *shomerim*. Why? They serve as an honor guard. *Le-havdil*, the Swiss Guards do not protect the Vatican from enemies, nor do guards stand outside Buckingham Palace out of fear that someone is going to enter. Rather, guards are stationed out of a sense of *kavod* (honor) for the *palterin shel melekh* (palace of the king); there is a sense of elevation, of nobility, of something unique that requires guarding.

Now, this sense of *palterin shel melekh* which requires guarding is presumably part of the mandate Adam initially received. When he was placed in the Garden "*le-ovdah u-leshomrah*," against whom was it being guarded? The animals were part of the Garden, and there was nobody else around, no one to invade. Rather, you guard something which you value and appreciate; you hover over it constantly. While, of course, the *Mikdash* is *palterin shel Melekh* in a very special sense, the world as a whole is also *palterin shel Melekh*: "The heaven is My throne and the earth is My footstool" (*Yeshayahu* 66:1). In this sense, we must all cultivate a concern for and a sensitivity to the natural order as a whole, to that Garden of Eden into which we have been placed. This is part of *kevod Shamayim*, *yirat Shamayim* and *malkhut Shamayim* (the honor, fear and sovereignty of Heaven). In fact, our responsibility with respect to the orders of creation—natural, human, social and personal—is now heightened, since, subsequent to Adam's sin, there are indeed real dangers which threaten them.

There is a term which *Chazal* (the Sages) always apply in relation to *shomerim: achrayut*, responsibility. In our capacity as *shomerim*, we must live with a sense of responsibility, obligation and demands. What is demanded is not simply a kind of passive awareness, but rather the application of consciousness. What does a *shomer* have to do? He must be alert. His human self must be asserted, that part of him which can watch, which is intelligent, which guards. One guards with intelligence. When he combines his intelligence, sensitivity and awareness of the importance of what he is guarding with a sense of duty and readiness—that is what being a *shomer* is all about.

PART 2:
Le-ovdah—The Work Ethic

The sense of duty I mentioned above with regard to *"le-shom-rah"* applies likewise to the first component of Adam's mandate—*"le-ovdah."* It is not enough to guard; one needs also to develop and to create. Let us be mindful that this applied even in what seemingly had been a perfect world! "And God saw all that He had made and found it very good" (*Bereishit* 1:31). If all is wonderful and perfect, what need is there for *"le-ovdah?"* There are two possible answers. Although the difference between them is of great significance in many areas, I would prefer not to focus on the clash between them, but rather to see them both as being correct.

MAINTAINING THE WORLD

The first answer is that, indeed, the world was created perfect—but part of that perfection, and one of the components within that order, is human activity. Part of "And He found it very good" is man, not existing simply as a biological being enjoying the world, but rather as a functional being who contributes, creates and works. The need for man to work is not part of the curse subsequent to the sin; man was originally placed in the Garden in order to cultivate it. The curse was that man would have to battle with an unwilling earth: "Thorns and thistles shall it sprout for you. . . . By the sweat of your brow shall you get bread to eat" (*Bereishit* 3:18-19). But the fact that one needs to work at all is part of the primeval, primordial order, irrespective of any element of sin. This had been intended from the beginning. Simply put, this is indeed a perfect order, provided that man does his part. If man does not, then one of the pieces of the picture has fallen out, and the world is no longer perfect.

According to this approach, both "*le-ovdah*" and "*le-shom-rah*" are designed to maintain the world at its present level, and this entails two components: passively guarding against damage and actively working in order to replenish. We need to work so that the natural processes repeat themselves; if you do not contribute your share, the seasons come and go, but nature does not replenish itself.

PERFECTING THE WORLD

The second approach assumes that "*le-ovdah*" is a mandate to go beyond the original state of creation. "*Le-ovdah*" is not meant simply to maintain the original standard; rather, we have been given the right and the duty to try to transcend it. While the former approach asserts that man was asked to maintain the world as God had created it, this answer claims that man was empowered and enjoined to create something better, as it were.

Although this approach is audacious, we find it advanced by *Chazal* in several places. Perhaps the most celebrated is the *midrash* (*Tanchuma*, *Parashat Tazria*) which speaks of the encounter between the Roman governor Turnus Rufus and Rabbi Akiva. Turnus Rufus asked Rabbi Akiva, "If God wanted man to be circumcised, then why did He not create him that way?" Rabbi Akiva responded, "Bring me some wheat." Then he said, "Bring me a loaf of bread." He asked, "Which do you prefer to eat, the bread or the wheat?" "Naturally, the bread," Turnus Rufus replied. Rabbi Akiva retorted, "Do you not see now that the works of flesh and blood are more pleasant than those of God?" There is a certain audacity here, but these are the words of Rabbi Akiva! What you have here is an assertion of human ability and grandeur, and of human responsibility to engage in this kind of improvement.

The extent to which this particular view is accepted depends on whether one adopts, to a greater or lesser degree, a humanistic perspective. Humanists talk a great deal about man placing his imprint upon the world, improving it, building it, and so on. When I say humanists, I am not talking only about secular humanists; I mean religious humanists within our world as well. Rav Yosef Dov Soloveitchik and Rav Meir Simcha of Dvinsk, for example, talk a great deal about the need for man to create.

Historically, this debate has found expression in some very strange contexts. In late seventeenth-century England, there was a vigorous debate about the hills and valleys. Some assumed that in the Newtonian world of mathematical precision, a perfect world presumably would be perfectly shaped. How, then, to explain the indentations of hills and valleys which seem to mar what should be a perfectly round globe? People with a more Romantic perspective said that it's nicer this way, with some variety; who would want the whole world to be as flat as the New Jersey Turnpike? Others gave a more theological interpretation: really, a perfect world would be a perfect globe without any ups and downs, but God made the mountains and the valleys so that man should have the challenge of flattening everything. To us, this debate seems curious, but the basic notion is clear.

The debate about the role of art similarly reflects these two basic positions about man's relation to the world. Plato claimed that artists misrepresent reality. He believed that the ultimate reality is the world of ideas, of which our world is just a kind of reflection or image. Now, says Plato, what does the poet or the artist do? He has the image of the image, and is now two steps removed from reality, instead of being one step away. So he banished all of them from his ideal republic. One response was given to this by Plotinus. The best known statement of this response in English is Sir Philip Sidney's "The Defense of Poesy," an essay written in the late sixteenth century. Sidney says that Plato's perception is wrong: the poet does not imitate nature, he goes beyond nature. The natural world, he says, is brass, but the poet's world is gold.

THE IMPORTANCE OF WORK

For our purposes, however, both of these approaches to the value of labor can be regarded as correct. What is important is the sense of human responsibility and the recognition of the importance of building the world and improving society. To us, work is indeed a central value. *Chazal* have numerous statements to this effect. For example, just as there is an obligation to rest on Shabbat, there is also an obligation that "Six days shall you labor and do all your work" (*Shemot* 20:9); the two are somewhat interrelated (see *Avot De-Rabbi Natan*, version B, chap. 21, and *Mekhilta de-Rabbi Shimon bar Yochai* on *Shemot* 20:9).

In a famous statement, the Rambam spoke of this in a halakhic context. The *gemara* (*Sanhedrin* 25b) says that a dice-player (i.e. a gambler) is disqualified from giving testimony in court. Two reasons are offered for this. One opinion is that he is a sort of thief, because of the halakhic principle that "*asmakhta lo kanya.*" Whoever gambles does so because he assumes he is going to win, and if he knew that he would lose he wouldn't gamble.

Thus, he gambles based upon an *asmakhta*, relying on an implicit condition. Therefore, the loser does not really transfer ownership of the money, and the winner does not legally acquire it. The second opinion disqualifies a gambler because "*eino osek be-yishuvo shel olam*," he is not involved in developing the world constructively. The *gemara* then brings a practical distinction between these two opinions. According to the first reason (*asmakhta*), even a person who gambles only occasionally is ineligible to give testimony. However, according to the second approach, only a professional gambler is disqualified—someone who has no other profession, but rather spends his entire day at the racetrack, or doing something similarly non-constructive.

The Rambam rules according to the latter opinion, but he takes the occasion to generalize:

> One who plays dice with a gentile does not transgress the prohibition of stealing, but he does transgress the prohibition of occupying oneself with worthless things, for it is not suitable for a person to occupy himself all the days of his life with anything other than matters of wisdom and the developing of the world. (*Hilkhot Gezeila* 6:11)

I won't deal now with the reason the Rambam thinks that the problem of *asmakhta* doesn't apply to this case. What is relevant to us is his definition of the two things a person should be engaged in: *divrei chokhma* (matters of wisdom) and *yishuvo shel olam* (the developing of the world).

WHY WORK?

This notion of the significance of work *per se*, of engaging in *yishuvo shel olam*, of "*le-ovdah*," has several bases. First, in a purely psychological sense, in terms of mental health, one's self-fulfillment comes through work. For instance, the *mishna* (*Ketubot* 5:5, 59b) says that if a woman marries, she is expected to perform certain tasks in the house, but if she brings servants with her, she does not have to do them. The *gemara* (*ibid.*) adds that the more servants she brings, the less she has to do, because they will take care of the needs of the household. However, beyond a certain point, this does not apply; her husband can demand that she do something—anything—because, Rabbi Eliezer says, "Idleness leads to lewdness;" it leads to a loose, lascivious life. Rabban Shimon ben Gamliel offers a different reason: "A husband who takes an oath that his wife should do no work, should divorce her and pay her *ketuba*, since idleness leads to *shi'amum*." *Shi'amum* can be understood either as insanity or as boredom, ennui, a sense of spiritual degradation. Even if she's as wealthy as Midas, she has to do some kind of work, lest idleness lead to psychological and spiritual problems.

There is also, of course, a social basis to our emphasis on work. The fact is that work needs to be done. A society in which people work is, in terms of its basic structure and values, very different from one in which they do not. The *midrash* at the beginning of *Lekh Lekha* asks: When God told Avraham, "Go forth from your native land . . . to the land which I will show you" (*Bereishit* 12:1), how did Avraham know when he had arrived at the right place? From a mystical point of view, one might assume that he was attracted by the *kedusha* (sanctity) inherent within the land. But the *midrash* gives a very non-mystical explanation:

> Rabbi Levi said: When Avram walked through Aram Naharayim and Aram Nachor, he saw the people there eating, drinking and acting loosely. Avram said to himself, "I hope that I do not have a portion in this land." When he arrived at the cliffs of Tyre (what is now called Rosh Ha-nikra, at the northern border of Israel), he saw people busying themselves with weeding during the season for weeding, hoeing during the time for hoeing, etc. He said to himself, "I hope that I will have a portion in this land." (*Bereishit Rabba* 39:8)

When Avraham saw people lounging around, eating and drinking and having a good time, he knew that he had not yet arrived. But when he saw people performing agricultural tasks that needed to be done, he sensed that he had come to the promised land. That is what attracted him. This was not a land whose people were devoted to the quest for pleasure but rather to commitment, work and responsibility. These are the things that define a culture.

There is a third basis as well to the emphasis on work, and this is more specifically religious in nature. A person who works is a partner to God in *ma'aseh bereishit* (creation). In this respect, he is imitating God. Usually we speak of imitating God by being merciful, or by performing acts of *chesed* (kindness), but the *midrash* also tells us:

> Rabbi Yehuda ben Rabbi Simon said: [The verse states,] "After the Lord your God you shall walk" (*Devarim* 13:5) . . . [What does this mandate of *imitatio Dei* entail?] At the beginning of the world's creation, the Holy One occupied Himself first with planting, as it says, "And the Lord God planted a garden in Eden" (*Bereishit* 2:8); so too, when you enter the Land [of Israel], occupy yourselves first with planting—and thus it says (*Vayikra* 19:23), "When you enter the land and plant all fruit-bearing trees. . ." (*Vayikra Rabba* 25:3)

Of course, the trees are symbolic of man's contribution to this world, to nature—something which is planted by human agency, rather than something which appears spontaneously. There are numerous other *midrashim* in this general vein.

THE REDEMPTIVE QUALITY OF WORK

The thrust of all this is that there is significance to work, quite apart from the need to pay your bills. There is, if you will, a certain redemptive quality to work, in psychological, social and religious terms. This notion is not uniquely Jewish. When most people hear about the importance of work, they immediately think of the Puritans and the Puritan work ethic. The Puritans, of course, were very much influenced by Judaism. Certainly, however, there are famous propagators of this general view in circles which are neither Jewish nor Puritan.

In Thomas Carlyle's early work *Sartor Resartus*, he describes his own spiritual crisis. He speaks first of what he describes as "The Everlasting No," the voice of cynicism and skepticism, but even beyond that of *ennui*, of a sense of the lack of purpose, meaning, direction and substance in life. From there he moves on to describe "The Center of Indifference," which is still a very low-key type of existence, and then progresses to "The Everlasting Yea," that which is assertive and positive in relation to the world and human existence. At the heart of the chapter on "The Everlasting Yea" is the notion of work. For Carlyle, the great prophet of work is the late eighteenth-century, early nineteenth-century German writer Goethe. In a famous line, Carlyle says, "Close thy Byron; open thy Goethe!" Work is central to "The Everlasting Yea" precisely because of its redemptive capacity.

In that context, one can view work as part of the collective human responsibility to establish human hegemony and to impose a certain character on nature as a whole. The ennobling conception of work, the sense of challenge, the work ethic (in contrast to a sybaritic, hedonistic existence) can also be found in a secular context. But for us, this is not simply a question of engaging in a great Romantic quest to place the world under human imprint. This is part of what we are doing for God, part of our relationship to Him: we are His guards and we are His laborers. This presents matters in a totally different perspective.

A Divine Mandate

Our attempt to place the human imprint on nature is part of God's mandate: "Fill the earth and master it, and rule over the fish of the sea, the birds of the sky, and all living things that creep on earth" (*Bereishit* 1:28). But whereas that mandate in the first chapter is formulated in terms of rights, in the second chapter (*"le-ovdah u-leshomrah"*) it is formulated in terms of obligation— it is part of our responsibility, part of our task.

This notion of the centrality and importance of work, as opposed to pursuing a life of leisure and hedonism, runs counter to the message that is inundating the Western world. The implicit idea in all the crass advertising you see is that, ideally, you shouldn't work at all; ideally, you would retire when you're eighteen. Small wonder that many people have reached the conclusion that the less they work, the better off they are. The notion of leisure has suddenly become a problem in sociological and moral terms. There is a whole literature about the problem of leisure, precisely because work is perceived as a necessary evil, and not as spiritually redemptive.

For us, however, the sense of effort, of striving, above all of working (in Milton's phrase) "as ever in my great Taskmaster's eye," is very central. *"Le-ovdah u-leshomrah,"* the sense of the importance of work and a work-oriented life, is part of the universal mandate; it is part of what we, as *benei-Torah*, understand to be central to our being.

Glatt Kosher Hedonism

I mention this point particularly to an American audience. In recent years, one observes on the American scene a terribly disturbing phenomenon: the spread of hedonistic values, but with a kind of glatt-kosher packaging. There was a time when the problem of hedonism for religious Jews didn't often arise, because even if you wanted to have the time of your life, there wasn't very much that you could do. The country clubs were all barred to Jews, there weren't many kosher restaurants, there were no kosher nightclubs, etc. In the last decade or two, a whole culture has developed geared towards *frum* Jews, where the message is enjoy, enjoy, enjoy, and everything has a *hekhsher* (kosher certification) and a super-*hekhsher*. The message is that whatever the gentiles have, we have too. They have trips to the Virgin Islands, we have trips to the Virgin Islands. Consequently, there has been a certain debasement of values, in which people have a concern for the minutiae of Halakha (which, of course, one should be concerned about), but with a complete lack of awareness of the extent to which the underlying message is so totally non-halakhic and anti-halakhic.

Don't misunderstand me—I am not opposed to people enjoying themselves to some extent. I am not arguing for a totally ascetic approach to life; I don't live that way myself, and what I don't practice I certainly am not going to preach. In a sense, I don't practice it because I don't really think that it is demanded. (There certainly were *gedolim* [great rabbis] who did advocate it, but others disagreed.) The question is something else entirely. The question is not whether there is room in human life for a person to have a certain measure of pleasure. Rather, the question is what is his basic perspective? How much does he involve himself in this? Does he see himself as basically being born to enjoy or to work?

There is nothing wrong with a person wanting to enjoy, to have a good meal. But if you open up the food critic's column in a newspaper, it is simply *muktzeh machmat mi'us* (untouchable because of being revolting)! A person who is morally sensitive finds it impossible to read those columns. They begin discussing, for example, the advantages of one airline food over another: here the food was a little bit underdone, there a little bit overdone, the vegetables were a little too fresh, not fresh enough; they begin to go into the finest details. It is astonishing that a person should devote so much time and effort and energy to these questions, and should assume that his readers are going to do so as well, when it is all merely a matter of knowing exactly what the food will be like when you happen to fly. To assign that kind of attention to this kind of nonsense?

To some extent, this feeling has permeated our world: a whole culture of enjoyment has begun to take hold. This is something which is recent, and with which anyone who is a *ben-Torah*, certainly, should in no way identify or associate. That whole culture advocates that man is born for pleasure, but unfortunately has to work if he wants to enjoy. In contrast, we have to know that "*Adam le-amal yulad*, Man is born to do labor" (*Iyyov* 5:7).

MATTERS OF WISDOM

I've addressed myself here to one major question, namely, the sense of a person's existence in the service of God, and the responsibilities and obligations which attend upon that existence: obligations *vis-a-vis* God, the world and oneself. The importance of work, and of constructive contribution through involvement in the world and society, is very, very clear, and is a cardinal element in our basic worldview. There is, though, another aspect to this question, which at this point I will simply mention. The Rambam said above that a person should engage in only two things—*divrei chokhma* and *yishuvo shel olam*. What he does not describe there is the breakdown between these two.

Surely, this is a very major question for us, and it is a significant and legitimate question at a universal level as well. To what extent should one engage in work—and by work I mean not simply making money, but rather constructive activity—and to what extent should he pursue wisdom? A gentile, too, has a certain dimension of *talmud Torah*: "Rabbi Meir says: Even a gentile who occupies himself with the Torah is like a High Priest" (*Sanhedrin* 59a). The *gemara* later understands this in terms of more universal wisdom, the Seven Noachide Laws. Even secular advocates of the work ethic have had to deal with the relation between work and other cultural, aesthetic or moral values. How much more so for us, for whom Torah study is so central—"You shall meditate upon it day and night" (*Yehoshua* 1:8). Thus, while our position is clear regarding work versus hedonism, the question of work versus Torah study is entirely different, and will be treated independently in the next chapter.

APPENDIX TO CHAPTER ONE:
Does the Torah Supplant or Supplement Universal Values?

At the beginning of this chapter, I proposed that we deal with three levels of duty incumbent upon us: as human beings, as Jews, and as *benei-Torah*. I then discussed the first of these, namely, our general responsibilities as humans. However, this entire discussion entails the assumption that, subsequent to the Jewish Nation's *keritat berit* (formulation of a covenant) with God, we are still bound by the more general norms that preceded it. It is this assumption I would like now to address.

NATURE AND GRACE

A *berit* (covenant) is something special and unique; by definition, it delineates a particular relationship between God and a specific community. What then happens to more universal elements? Do these fall away because of the exclusivity of the new relationship? Or do we regard the new relationship as being superimposed upon the old, but not at odds with it?

Even according to the latter approach, at times there may be a conflict between a universal value and a specific one. Fundamentally, however, this approach regards the specific covenant as complementing and building on top of the universal covenant, rather than replacing it and rendering it obsolete. According to this approach, we do not believe that what existed until now was merely scaffolding which was needed until the building was complete, but now that the building is finished, everything else is insignificant. Instead, we assume that whatever commitments, demands and obligations devolve upon a person simply as a member of the universal community, will also apply to him within his unique context as well; but in addition, there are also new demands.

This question has been raised extensively within the Christian context, where it is referred to as the issue of "nature and grace." Does the order of grace—which is the more specific relationship of a given community towards God—do away with the order of nature: natural values, natural morality and natural religion? Or is the order of nature fundamentally sound, significant and normative, but in addition to it comes the order of grace? Broadly speaking, within the Christian context, the more rationalistic and humanistic thinkers have stressed that the universal component remains in force. Those who espoused a more anti-humanistic and anti-rationalistic line generally felt that anything which human reason develops, anything which is universal, anything which is not part of the specific order of revelation, is absolutely meaningless and not binding. In fact, they felt it may even be injurious, because it leads a person to think that these kinds of universal values are significant, whereas in reality the order of nature was good for one phase of human history but has been totally replaced by the order of grace.

THE TEST OF SHABBAT

Translating this into our categories, I recall years back hearing a talk by *mori ve-rabbi* Rav Yitzchak Hutner *zt"l* regarding the relationship between *berit Avraham* and *berit Noach* (God's covenants with Avraham and Noach). As he put it, did *berit Avraham* come "on top" of the foundation of *berit Noach*, or was it meant to replace it? Rav Hutner wished to learn from Rabbeinu Yona (*Berakhot* 49a) that the latter was the case, and he took Shabbat as the test case. Jews, of course, are commanded not to work on Shabbat. However, *Chazal* interpreted the verse, "Summer and winter, day and night shall not cease" (*Bereishit* 8:22) as teaching us that *Benei Noach* (descendants of Noach, i.e. general humanity) are always obligated to work; in fact, a gentile who refrains from *melakha* (labor) on Shabbat is punished! (See *Sanhedrin* 58b.) Evidently, concluded Rav Hutner, the universal value of "[They] shall not cease" has been countervailed within our more specific Jewish context. Thus, the new *berit* is meant to replace the old.

I do not adopt this general approach; in fact, I think quite the contrary is true. Whatever is demanded of us as part of *Kenesset Yisrael* does not negate what is demanded of us simply as human beings on a universal level, but rather comes in addition. (Regarding Shabbat, let me just briefly note that the sanctity of Shabbat does not abrogate the universal value of work, but rather adds an additional element to the picture.)

RENEWING OR COMPLETING THE TORAH

Similarly, I believe *mattan Torah* (the giving of the Torah) also needs to be understood in a dual fashion. At one level, *mattan Torah* was a wholly new departure; there was nothing like it before. One can indeed speak of "*Nittena Torah ve-nitchadsha halakha*"—the Torah was given and the law was renewed.[5] In this vein, the Rambam states that although some *mitzvot* (such as the seven Noachide laws) were given before *mattan Torah*, we are obligated by them only because they were reiterated at Sinai.[6] As examples, he cites the prohibitions of eating *ever min ha-chai* (a limb from a live animal) and *gid ha-nasheh* (the sciatic nerve), and the commandment of circumcision. Although these appear previously (with regard to Noach, Ya'akov and Avraham respectively), our obligation is based solely on the fact that they were reinforced through *mattan Torah.*

In another sense, however, one can regard Torah not as a totally new chapter in human history, but rather as the pinnacle of the earlier development. Although in one perspective Torah can be seen as unique and relating only to *Kenesset Yisrael,* there is another perspective in which one can view Torah as being the highest stage in human development. The Rambam elsewhere seems to speak in these terms, using a very telling phrase. When discussing the evolution of Torah, he says:

> Six precepts were given to Adam . . . An additional command-ment was given to Noach . . . So it was until the appearance of Avraham, who, in addition to the aforementioned command-ments, was charged to practice circumcision. Moreover, Avra-ham instituted the Morning Prayer. Yitzchak tithed and insti-tuted the Afternoon Prayer. Ya'akov added [the prohibition of eating] the sciatic nerve and he inaugurated the Evening Prayer. In Egypt, Amram (Moshe's father) was commanded additional *mitzvot,* until our master Moshe arrived and the Torah was *completed* through him. (*Hilkhot Melakhim* 9:1)

The phrase, "*nishlema al yado,* it was completed through him," suggests that there were various stages and that Moshe is the pinnacle, not that Moshe's Torah simply disposes of every-thing which had preceded it.

CAN THE TORAH PERMIT WHAT UNIVERSAL LAW FORBIDS?

The major text dealing with the relationship between Jewish law and universal law is the famous *Mekhilta* at the beginning of *Mishpatim* which addresses the issue of one who kills a gentile. In *parashat Noach,* there appears a general directive to humanity:

"Whoever sheds the blood of man, by man shall his blood be shed" (*Bereishit* 9:6). However, a verse in *Mishpatim* (*Shemot* 21:14) seems to indicate a Jew is put to death only if he murders a fellow Jew. How are we to understand this?

> Issi ben Akiva says: Before the giving of the Torah, we were prohibited to murder. After the giving of the Torah, instead of being more stringent, are we now more lenient!? (*Mekhilta De-Rabbi Yishma'el, Parasha* 4, *s.v. Ve-khi Yazid*)

Issi ben Akiva finds it inconceivable that something which previously had been forbidden to general humanity would now be permitted to Jews by the Torah. The *gemara* applies this reasoning with regard to various laws, asking simply, "Is it possible that there is anything at all which is permitted to a Jew, yet nonetheless is prohibited to a non-Jew?"[7]

The principle elucidated by Issi ben Akiva does not necessarily negate the possibility that the new *berit* abolishes the old one. One may argue that indeed the new *berit* supplants the old, and the Jew can approach God only through God's covenantal relationship with *Kenesset Yisrael*—but in terms of its content, the new *berit* must be more demanding than the old one.

Even if this is so, it does not matter much for our purposes. When trying to understand what are the normative demands made upon us, there is not a great difference between saying that the old *berit* is gone and the new one comprehends all of the contents of the old, and saying that there exists a dual level of responsibility. Practically speaking, both positions agree that whatever is demanded of a person on a universal level is *a priori* demanded of a Jew as well; Torah morality is at least as exacting as general morality. The only difference is whether we formulate the demand as emanating from a general covenant or from the specific *berit*. Thus, part of what is demanded of a *ben-Torah* is simply, on an initial level, what is demanded of every person as a human being.

DEREKH ERETZ KADMA LA-TORAH

B roadly speaking, this is what is intended by the celebrated
phrase, "*Derekh eretz kadma la-Torah*" ("Civility preceded
the Torah"). *Chazal* (*Vayikra Rabba* 9:3) understood this in historical terms: the Torah came twenty-six generations after the pre-
cepts of *derekh eretz* had already been in effect. But there is another meaning to this phrase, which refers to logical or axiological
priority. The Maharal (*Netivot Ha-Torah, Netiv Derekh Eretz*)
understands it in this sense. The *ben-Torah* in you is built on the
spiritual person in you; if it is the other way around, then you are
walking on your head, so to speak.

Let me emphasize that this has nothing to do with the question of what is more valuable. If we say that something is prior to
something else, it does not necessarily mean that it is more important. For example, there are two ways we can understand *Chazal's*
requirement that someone who wants to be a *ben-Torah* must be
"*yirato kodemet le-chokhmato*—his fear [of Heaven] must precede
his wisdom" (*Avot* 3:9). It is entirely conceivable that *Chazal*
intend to say that ultimately the *yira* is really more important than
the *chokhma* (as important as the *chokhma* may be). However, we
can also understand this as referring to logical precedence; and
what serves as the basis is not necessarily the most important element. Although foundations must precede a building both tem-
porally and logically, no one would imagine that they are more
important than the building.

Chazal themselves may have been divided on this question, as
would appear in the following dialogue:

> While Rabbi Simon and Rabbi Elazar were sitting, Rabbi
> Ya'akov bar Acha passed in front of them. The one said to the
> other, "Let us stand before him, because he is a man who fears
> sin." The other said, "Let us stand before him because he is a
> scholar." He replied, "I tell you he fears sin and you tell me he

is a scholar!?" [In other words, I praise his fear of sin, and you think that being a scholar is greater?] (*Shabbat* 31b)

The one who believes that *chokhma* is more important than *yira* does not negate the fact that *yira* must precede *chokhma*. The kind of *chokhma* which may be more important than *yira* is only one which is rooted in *yira*. *Chazal* say (e.g. *Ta'anit* 7a) that *chokhma* which is not rooted in *yira*, God forbid, is not an elixir of life but rather a potion of death.

So, in speaking of "*Derekh eretz kadma la-Torah*," we should not in any way prejudge what is more or less important, simply because one precedes the other. The question of importance is a totally independent issue. But as far as *kedima*—what provides the matrix, the context, the foundation—one can speak of the logical and not only the temporal priority of *derekh eretz* over Torah.

A MENSCH AND A BEN-TORAH

Thus, our specific Jewish commitment rests on our universal commitment, and one cannot address oneself only to the specific elements while totally ignoring the general and the universal ones. Therefore, in delineating what a *ben-Torah* should be striving for, the initial level of aspiration is a general one: to be a *mensch*, to hold basic universal values, to meet normative universal demands.

This point has no bearing upon the question of the temporal sequence via which a person attains his values. I mentioned before that *Chazal* say there was a period stretching over millennia during which the world had *derekh eretz* and didn't have Torah. This does not mean that, moving from the macrocosm to the microcosm, one therefore should practice the same while educating his children, saying, "We'll devote the first ten or so years to making a *mensch* out of him, and then when he is bar-mitzva we will see to it that he becomes an observant Jew as well." Obviously, within the world in which we live, this is not an advisable option. If you want your child to be a *ben-Torah* and a *shomer mitzvot,* you have to imbue him with values of Torah and *yirat Shamayim* from a very early age. But this still means that as he grows and matures, he must be given to understand that he needs to address himself to various levels of obligation, one being universal and the other specific to him as a Jew.

NOTES

1   The second level of responsibility is addressed in Chapter Three and the third level in Chapter Four.

2   This was later printed as, "Abortion: A Halakhic Perspective," *Tradition* 25 (1991), pp. 3-12, and appears on Yeshivat Har Etzion's Israel Koschitzky Virtual Beit Midrash: http://www.vbm-torah.org/halakha/abortion.htm.

3   See *Bava Kama* 90b-91b and Rambam, *Hilkhot Chovel U-mazik* 5:1.

4   Rambam, *Hilkhot Sanhedrin* 26:3.

5   *Shabbat* 135a, *Bava Batra* 110b.

6   *Commentary on the Mishna, Chullin* 7:6.

7   See, for example, *Chullin* 33a and *Sanhedrin* 59a.

CHAPTER TWO

In All Your Ways, Know Him: Two Modes of Serving God

In the previous chapter, we discussed the importance assigned to work in our worldview. Even prior to his punishment, Adam was placed in the garden in order to work it, thus teaching us that constructive labor is part of what a person ordinarily ought to be engaged in. This mandate can be viewed from various perspectives: as a facet of *gemilut chasadim*, helping others and improving the world; as simply fulfilling that which God has demanded of us, working as His agents; as essential for one's psychological well-being and moral self-development; and as placing the human stamp upon the world. Various schools of thought have stressed each of these, and I think all of them are correct. Our *hashkafa* (outlook) stands foursquare behind the so-called "work ethic," which emphasizes the moral, psychological, religious and social importance of work. In terms of two poems by Tennyson, if our choice is whether to join the indolent Lotos-eaters or "to strive, to seek, to find, and not to yield" with Ulysses, there is no question as to where we would stand.

However, all of this is correct and important insofar as one is dealing with the contrast between indolence and work. But of course, those are not the only choices open to us, and the question confronting us as individuals who have to make concrete decisions is: How do we want to spend our lives? How do we want to earn a living? How do we balance a profession with *tal-*

mud Torah, or with *avodat Hashem* (service of God) in a narrow
sense? I say "in a narrow sense" because when we think of what
kind of life the Torah wants us to lead, we have to think in two
contexts, and then try to understand the relationship between the
two. These two contexts are serving God through *devar mitzva,*
that which we have specifically been commanded to perform, and
serving Him through *devar reshut,* the broad area of choice in
one's life.

DEVAR MITZVA: LIMITED AND UNLIMITED

We all know that there are many *mitzvot* we are obligated to
perform. Some of these are clearly delineated, to the point
where adding to them is of no substance; in fact, it may even be
problematic. If a person decides that instead of sitting in a *sukka*
for a week, he will sit for ten days, then he transgresses the prohibition of *bal tosif* (adding to *mitzvot*). Even if a person does not
violate a prohibition, the quantitative addition is often neutral.
For example, if a person decides that instead of eating one *ke-zayit*
of *matza* he will eat two, then according to most opinions he has
not accomplished anything.

However, there are *mitzvot*—and these are among the most
critical *mitzvot*—which do not have any prescribed bounds and
which therefore may be viewed as laying claim to the totality of
our being. Some of these *mitzvot* which have no specific limits
relate to states of mind—*mitzvot* of the heart such as *ahava* (love
of God), *yira* (fear of God), *deveikut* (clinging to God), etc. All of
these *mitzvot* have no particular focus in terms of a specific activity. Consequently, at least in theory, they need not conflict with
anything else, so that you don't have to ask yourself whether they
preempt any other sphere of human activity.

In theory, a person can love or fear God no matter where he
is and what he is doing. In practice, this is not always the case,

because a person whose attention is focused upon some other activity may find it difficult to concentrate upon *ahava* and *yira*. A person may find that in order for *ahava* and *yira* to be not merely subliminal but rather consciously perceived, he may have to abandon some other activities in order to concentrate purely upon these. But at any rate, in theory there need not be any conflict between these unbounded *mitzvot* and anything else.

There are, however, some *mitzvot* which really are in conflict, at a practical level, with other interests. This conflict can take two forms. For example, the Rambam (*Hilkhot Melakhim* 3:9) discusses two possible conflicts between governmental decrees and Halakha. The first entails a clash between governmental demands which are legitimate in and of themselves, but which in practice may entail foregoing the fulfillment of a mitzva. In this case, he says, *"Divrei ha-rav ve-divrei ha-eved, divrei ha-rav kodmin*—The words of the Master (God) take precedence over the words of the servant." The second type of conflict is created by a decree which specifically bans the fulfillment of a particular law. This type of decree, says the Rambam, is totally null and void.

The type of clash I wish to discuss is not of the latter kind, which is direct, frontal and inherent. Rather, I am referring to a clash of the first kind, where, practically speaking, a person cannot do both things. Here, one may clearly encounter a conflict between certain more general interests and the specific focus on *avodat Hashem*. And this, I repeat, is with regard to certain obligations which are limitless, primarily the three central areas delineated by the *mishna* in *Avot* (1:2): "The world stands on three things: on Torah, on *avoda* (divine service), and on *gemilut chasadim* (acts of kindness)." The *Mishna* (*Pe'a* 1:1) lists *talmud Torah* (Torah study) and *gemilut chasadim* as the two general categories "which have no [maximal] measure," and similarly we find *avoda* placed in the same category: "to serve Him with *all* your heart and *all* your soul" (*Devarim* 11:13). Since these three areas are without limit, each, in effect, can make a total claim upon a person.

Thus, as general categories, these three areas encompass the totality of one's being; and even if you translate them into specific activities, there are different views in the *Gemara* as to whether these activities themselves are limited. For example, what does *avoda* mean? In the broader sense, it means simply to serve God, and that is a total kind of commitment. If you want to translate it more specifically, it means either the sacrificial service in the Temple or the service of the heart, namely, *tefilla* (prayer). With regard to *tefilla*, different views appear among *Chazal* (*Berakhot* 21a). Rav Elazar believes that *tefilla* is limited in scope, while Rav Yochanan says, "Would that a person pray the whole day!"

This raises another question: If each of these three areas makes a total claim upon us, how do we reconcile these claims with each other? How do we draw the lines between these areas? Leaving this question for a later chapter,[1] I would like to focus on the claim which this triad as a whole makes upon us. How does this triad stand in relation to other areas of human life? Does it negate the value of work and of other human pursuits?

DEVAR RESHUT: ALL FOR THE SAKE OF HEAVEN

Here we come to the question of *devar reshut*. On the one hand, we spoke of the "three things upon which the world stands" in terms of specific *mitzvot* and fulfillments. But on the other hand, there is also an ideal which is based on the verse, "*Be-khol derakhekha da'ehu*"—"In *all* your ways know Him" (*Mishlei* 3:6). A person should serve God in all walks of life; everything he does should be oriented ultimately towards *avodat Hashem*. This means that a person can be an *oved Hashem* in the broader sense of the term, not only by fulfilling *mitzvot* specifically defined as such, but also in the much larger area of *divrei reshut*. These too some-how must become part of the totality of one's *avodat Hashem*.

The Rambam[2] made a point of this when discussing the state-ment, *"Ha-kol bi-yedei Shamayim chutz mi-yirat Shamayim*, All is in the hands of Heaven except for the fear of Heaven" (*Berakhot* 33b). Following Rabbeinu Bachya, he says that indeed a person controls only *yirat Shamayim*, but the term *yirat Shamayim* encompasses the whole range of human activity. Whatever a per-son does expresses his *yirat Shamayim* or lack thereof. The Rambam speaks of this extensively in *Shemona Perakim* and *Hilkhot De'ot*:

> A person must direct every single one of his deeds solely towards attaining knowledge of God. His sitting down, his standing up, and his speech should all be directed toward this goal. . . Even when he sleeps, if he sleeps with the intention of resting his mind and body so that he does not become sick—for he is unable to serve the Lord when he is sick—his sleep shall become a service of God. Concerning this, *Chazal* commanded (*Avot* 2:12), "Let all your deeds be for the sake of Heaven." That is what Shlomo said in his wisdom (*Mishlei* 3:6): "In all your ways know Him, and He will make your paths straight." (*Hilkhot De'ot* 3:2-3)

The particular formulation of the Rambam, both here and in *Shemona Perakim*, bears his own personal stamp. The Rambam interprets the saying, "Let all your deeds be for the sake of Heaven," in terms of knowing God. The verse which he quotes at the end, "In all your ways know Him," provides him with a certain measure of support. However, the concept *per se* is not dependent upon accepting his specific formulation. There are surely many who find Rambam's formulation to be excessively intellectualistic, too narrowly focused upon knowing, as opposed to other ways of relating to God, such as the affective or the conative.

However, this dispute about interpreting "for the sake of

Heaven"—whether it refers to knowing God, or submitting to God, etc.—is irrelevant with respect to our present discussion. Regardless of how one defines the term, it denotes that the totality of a person's existence is oriented towards his relationship with God, towards *avodat Hashem.*

DIVINE SERVICE VIA ONE'S PROFESSION

On the one hand, the approach of *"Be-khol derakhekha da'ehu"* seems to extend the demands of *avodat Hashem,* and therefore to delegitimize other ultimate goals. On the other hand, it also serves to give some legitimization to those other areas. In effect, it tells you that when you are outside the immediate area of Torah, *avoda* and *gemilut chasadim,* when you are outside the *beit midrash* and the synagogue, you are not necessarily beyond the purview of *avodat Hashem.* You can be an *oved Hashem* in the field of business or in any other profession—"in *all* your ways." This is central to our whole perception of human endeavor. In a sense, *devar reshut* is only a relative term; no area of life is truly neutral. The Rambam even speaks of sleeping as being part of one's *avodat Hashem.* But within this broad realm of *"be-khol derakhekha,"* one's profession is singled out as being more directly a form of *avodat Hashem,* although it may not be a fulfillment of a mitzva narrowly defined.

The view that one's *umanut* (profession) is a kind of mitzva has halakhic implications. For example, the *gemara* (*Shabbat* 19a) says that a person should not set out on a boat trip less than three days before Shabbat. However, the *gemara* continues, this is permitted for a *devar mitzva.* What if a person wants to take a business trip? Rabbeinu Tam (cited by the Mordekhai, *Shabbat* 1:258) says that this is considered a *devar mitzva,* and this is the halakha quoted by the Rema in the *Shulchan Arukh* (*Orach Chayyim* 248:4).[3]

To take another example, the *gemara* twice offers the same *midrash* on each word of the verse, "You shall inform them of the path which they shall pursue and the action which they shall perform" (*Shemot* 18:20). This exegesis begins, "Rav Yossi says: 'You shall inform them' refers to *beit chayyeihem*." In one place, Rashi explains *beit chayyeihem* as referring to *talmud Torah* (*Bava Kama* 99b). In the other place, however, Rashi explains it as teaching one's child a trade by which to earn a living (*Bava Metzia* 30b).

From all the above, we see that work is not just significant in its own right, but can also be considered as an important part of the totality of one's *avoda*. More specifically, it can be seen as a kind of *devar mitzva* in the narrow sense, over and above the sense in which all human activity has some significance as part of *avodat Hashem*.

Thus, we have two levels of *avodat Hashem*. One is more specifically and narrowly defined: this is the *devar mitzva*. One is more broadly defined: this is *devar reshut*, the area of "*Be-khol derakhekha da'ehu*." The former is more directly and immediately related to God, and is restricted to the area narrowly perceived as "religious." It poses both limited demands (e.g. Shabbat and *kashrut*, etc.) and all-encompassing demands (Torah, *avoda*, *gemilut chasadim*). However, the latter level—"*Be-khol derakhekha da'ehu*"—informs us that everything a person does can and should be directed to God.

These two levels of *avodat Hashem* can, in a sense, be regarded as complementary. Nevertheless, it behooves us to examine the differences between them and to determine whether one takes precedence over the other.

ASPIRING TO TORAH ONLY

King David says: "One thing I ask of the Lord, only that do I seek: to dwell in the house of the Lord all the days of my life, to gaze upon the beauty of the Lord and to frequent His temple" (*Tehillim* 27:4). Enthusiasts of work are scandalized by this verse. How can he say, "*one* thing?" Is that all David wants to do? What about building the country, developing society or expanding the economy? This is a good question, but the verse remains a verse. Clearly, one has to try to understand what wish King David expresses in this verse, and how we are to understand the importance of a profession in light of it.

One way of explaining this verse is to say simply that labor is very good if it is contrasted with indolence; but if it is contrasted with "gazing upon the beauty of the Lord and frequenting His temple," then a person is much better off doing the latter than working for General Motors. This explanation is indeed correct. Nonetheless, it does not free us from trying to understand what attitude a *ben-Torah* should therefore have towards working for General Motors or the equivalent thereof.

The *Yerushalmi* records:

Rabbi Shimon bar Yochai says: Had I been present at Mount Sinai at the time the Torah was given to Israel, I would have asked God to create for man two mouths—one to engage [exclusively] in Torah and one to take care of all of a person's other needs. (*Shabbat* 1:2)

This is a different way of formulating "One thing I ask of the Lord." Rabbi Shimon desired a personality which could concentrate wholly and solely upon "gazing at the Lord's beauty," upon engaging in Torah, upon the immediate and direct contact and consultation with the Almighty. One mouth would constantly engage in Torah, and more mundane concerns would be taken care of by a second, more profane, mouth.

This remains, of course, in the nature of a wish, but its importance as a wish is very central. It presents a direction, an ultimate goal. Granted, a person who goes to work can be doing something legitimate and constructive. But if he spends so much of his time doing things which are not immediately part of the *devar mitzva* of *avodat Hashem* (even though they can be integrated within *avodat Hashem* in the broader sense), is this regarded with favor?

COMBINING TORAH WITH WORK

In the previous chapter, I quoted the Rambam (*Hilkhot Gezeila* 6:11) who said that a person should spend all his time engaged in only two things: *divrei chokhma* and *yishuvo shel olam* (matters of wisdom and developing the world). This, of course, leads to the question of establishing the appropriate ratio between *chokhma* and *yishuvo shel olam*. This question is taken up in a famous *gemara*:

> Our Rabbis taught: "You shall gather in your grain" (*Devarim* 11:14)—what is to be learnt from these words? Since it says, "This book of the Torah shall not depart from your mouth" (*Yehoshua* 1:8), I might think that this injunction is to be taken literally. Therefore the Torah says, "You shall gather in your grain," which implies that you should combine Torah study with a worldly occupation. This is the opinion of Rabbi Yishmael.

> Rabbi Shimon bar Yochai says: Is that possible? If a person plows in the plowing season, and sows in the sowing season, and reaps in the reaping season, and threshes in the threshing season, and winnows in the windy season, what is to become of the Torah? Rather, [this means that] when Israel performs the will of God, their work is done by others, as it says, "Strangers shall stand and feed your flocks" (*Yeshayahu* 61:5). But when Israel does not perform the will of God, they perform their own work, as it says, "*You* shall gather your grain." Not only this, but the work of others is also done by them, as it says, "You shall serve your enemy" (*Devarim* 28:48).

Abbaye said: Many have acted in accordance with Rabbi Yishmael, and did so successfully, others have followed Rabbi Shimon bar Yochai, and did so unsuccessfully. (*Berakhot* 35b)

The verse Rabbi Yishmael uses to describe normal human existence, "You shall gather in your grain," is almost a curse in the eyes of Rabbi Shimon bar Yochai. He regards it as a heavy burden which conflicts with one's need and desire to become a *talmid chakham*, to become an *oved Hashem* in the more specific and narrow sense of the term.

TORAH AND WORK—WHICH IS PRIMARY?

Indeed, we have here a dispute between *Tannaim*, and likewise there is also a dispute among the *Rishonim*. The *mishna* (*Avot* 2:2) says, "*Yafeh talmud Torah im derekh eretz, she-yegi'at sheneihem meshakachat avon*—Excellent is the study of Torah together with a worldly occupation, for exertion in both of them causes the thought of sin to be forgotten." How is this to be understood? Which is the main element—*talmud Torah* or *derekh eretz*—and which is secondary? Which is the main focus of a person's activity, and which is a mere accompaniment? This is the subject of a disagreement among the *Rishonim*, which appears in several places.[4]

Rabbeinu Tam believes that whenever the Talmud says, "A with B," this means that A is simply an accompaniment, but the main item is B. Thus, when the *gemara* (*Yoma* 85b) says that "Yom Kippur atones with *teshuva* (repentance)," it means that *teshuva* is primary and Yom Kippur secondary. In our case, he says that *derekh eretz* is primary, and *talmud Torah* is a nice addition. However, Rabbeinu Tam's grand-nephew Rabbeinu Elchanan (son of the Ri) disagrees in all of these places. He believes that the first element—whether *talmud Torah* or Yom Kippur—is primary.

The dispute between Rabbeinu Tam and Rabbeinu Elchanan is really a sharper form of the argument between Rabbi Yishmael and Rabbi Shimon bar Yochai. Here again we encounter different perceptions concerning how a person is normally expected to live. Rabbeinu Tam, however, seems to go far beyond Rabbi Yishmael's position. While Rabbi Yishmael recognized the legitimacy of labor, Rabbeinu Tam considers it to be the *ikkar* (primary component). Thus, Rabbeinu Tam is the opposite extreme of Rabbi Shimon bar Yochai, who negated the value of work entirely.

However, we must be more precise in our understanding of Rabbeinu Tam's position. It is inconceivable that Rabbeinu Tam, of all people, thought that working in the fields or collecting garbage is the *ikkar*—the main thing in human life and the purpose of one's existence. Not that these things may not be valuable and good, but could they be the *ikkar*?

One therefore needs to differentiate between two senses of the term *ikkar*. It can be meant in an axiological sense, in terms of value: What is most important? It can also be meant as something which is central not in qualitative, axiological terms, but rather in quantitative terms: How does the Torah expect, how do *Chazal* expect, a person to spend the bulk of his day? I believe we must interpret the argument between Rabbeinu Tam and Rabbeinu Elchanan in the latter sense: How does God expect a person to spend his day?

ALLOCATING TIME BETWEEN TORAH AND WORK

The Rambam had some very pointed comments on this question. On the one hand, he was sharply critical of people who don't work and just try to feed upon the public treasury, even if they are spending their time learning Torah.

> One who makes up his mind to study Torah and not to work but to live off charity, profanes the name of God, brings the Torah into contempt, extinguishes the light of religion, brings

evil upon himself, and deprives himself of life in the hereafter. (*Hilkhot Talmud Torah* 3:10)

But this very same Rambam presents the average man working three hours a day—just enough to sustain himself—and learning Torah nine hours a day (*Hilkhot Talmud Torah* 1:12). Although the Rambam himself was able to live like this only at certain stages of his life, this was the kind of existence he expected one to live.

It is precisely the kind of life described by the Rambam that Rabbeinu Tam says is not expected of us. If, instead, a person works nine hours a day and learns three hours, he should not feel that he is not living up to God's expectations. Rather, he should feel that he is leading the kind of life which perhaps is not the pinnacle of human existence, but is the kind of solid, decent *avodat Hashem* of "*Be-khol derakhekha da'ehu*" that God expects of a person.

Rabbeinu Elchanan and the Rambam reject the notion that *derekh eretz* is what occupies most of one's time and Torah is merely a component within the remaining time. But their argument with Rabbeinu Tam about time allotment has nothing to do with the question of values. The quantitative factor is by no means a reflection of what we value most in our lives. If a person sleeps eight hours a day and prays two hours, does that mean he thinks sleeping is four times more important than praying? If he works in an office for eight hours a day and spends only an hour with his children, does it mean that he thinks that his children are relatively unimportant?

THE IDEAL: MAXIMIZING TORAH

For various reasons which a person does not always control, he may be devoting much more time to less valuable activities than to more important ones. Of course, the test of his true priorities is demonstrated by what he would do if he could somehow be freed of all these secondary pressures. What is a person's real aspiration? For what does he truly long?

Ideally, a person wants to be in a position to devote as much of his life as he can to his ultimate goals, and as little as possible to the things he does only because he has to, not because he wants to. There are things he does because of their inherent value, and there are things which he does only because of their instrumental value. So, although we know that "*Im ein kemach ein Torah*, If there is no flour, there is no Torah" (*Avot* 3:17), and Rabbeinu Tam posits the legitimacy of a life spent primarily in pursuit of *kemach*, this surely does not obliterate the qualitative and axiological difference between *kemach* and Torah.

Rabbeinu Tam, too, knows the verse, "One thing I ask of the Lord." Who is the author of this verse? King David! Was he the model of a person who spent all his time "gazing on the beauty of the Lord and frequenting His temple?" Not at all. He ran a country and commanded an army, but nevertheless saw himself rooted in *avodat Hashem* and his ultimate aspiration in coming close to God.

In practical terms, this translates into trying to find those opportunities which enable you to maximize the time devoted to the significant things in your life. This is an important consideration for a person who is choosing a career. I don't want to get involved for the moment in the question of whether one should look for a secular career or a Torah career. Even if a person is choosing a secular career, certainly one of the factors to bear in mind is giving priority to a career which will enable him to have more "free leisure time" during which he can learn Torah and pursue spirituality, as opposed to one which is more demanding of his time. I'm not saying that this should be the *only* factor, but it should be one factor. (I will not try to list all the factors here, but clearly among those factors should be issues such as what society needs, where one's talents lie, what professions are inherently valuable, etc.) In terms of one's ultimate aspirations, one should aspire to more Torah and less *kemach*. But this doesn't mean that a person should aspire to zero *kemach*, for reasons that I specified in the previous chapter.

The Rambam expresses this idea at the end of *Mishneh Torah*:

[At the time of the Messiah,] there will be neither famine nor war, neither jealousy nor strife. Blessings will be abundant, comforts within the reach of all, and the one preoccupation of the whole world will be to know the Lord. (*Hilkhot Melakhim* 12:5)

Since there will be no political, military, economic or social pressures, people will be free to devote themselves to what is of ultimate importance. Of course, to most people this is merely an aspiration: King David was not able spend all his time engaged in the "one thing" he requested; Rabbi Shimon bar Yochai had only one mouth. But the questions nevertheless remain: How should a person make career choices? What kind of self-image should he have when making the choice?

I repeat: as a general guideline, a person should be looking for a kind of life which will enable him to approach Rabbeinu Elchanan's as opposed to Rabbeinu Tam's ideal. And he should be content to have a standard of living which will enable him to devote more time to *avodat Hashem* in the direct sense, as opposed to the broader, indirect sense. But to say this is not to delegitimize the importance of *umanut* and of "*le-ovdah u-leshomrah*."

WITH ALL YOUR STRENGTH

Two final points deserve emphasis. "*Be-khol derakhekha da'ehu*" means that regardless of what sphere of activity a person is engaged in, he can give expression within that sphere to his relationship with God. This takes two forms: *why* he does something, and *how* he does it.

The first of these means that a person can do something whose ultimate goal is to help him serve God, even though his spiritual self does not come into play as he engages in it. The Rambam says that "*Be-khol derakhekha da'ehu*" can apply to sleeping, if one sleeps in order to have the strength to serve God, to be able to learn, pray and perform *gemilut chasadim* the next day. This transforms sleeping, recreation and relaxation into part of one's *avodat Hashem*, even though one is not thinking of God while he is doing it.

Secondly, in many areas of human life a person's moral and spiritual self does find expression, even when he is engaged in a "secular" activity. The *gemara* says:

Four matters require strengthening, and they are: Torah, good deeds, prayer and *derekh eretz*. (*Berakhot* 32b)

Rashi explains:

What do we mean by "require strengthening?" That one should continually strengthen himself in them with all his might. . . If he is a craftsman, he should be strong in his craft; if he is a trader, he should be strong in his trade; if he is a warrior, he should be strong in his martial skills. (*ad loc.*)

Regardless of what a person does, he should try to act in the spirit of the work ethic, namely, *be-khol kocho*, with maximal effort. This is a religious value.

In *parashat Vayetze* (*Bereishit* 31:6), Ya'akov says to his wives, "You know that with all my strength (*be-khol kochi*) I served your father." The Rambam (*Hilkhot Sekhirut* 13:7) quotes this passage as the source of the law that a laborer should always work with maximal effort. Even if a person is engaged in an activity which in and of itself does not have an immediate moral element, nevertheless, how one relates to that activity can reflect a moral, amoral, or immoral view.

The Rambam, of course, addresses a situation where you work for somebody else, in which case it is simply theft if you are slack in your duty. But the question of whether or not a person is doing things *be-khol kocho* applies not only to interpersonal relationships with one's boss, but also to one's relationship with "The Boss." The Almighty has commanded us to engage in *yishuvo shel olam*—doing something constructive within society—but one can do that either half-heartedly or with full dedication.

Therefore, a person who works as an *oved Hashem* should ask himself two questions. 1) In what activity am I engaged? There are activities which are more directly related to *avodat Hashem* and there are those which are less so. 2) How do I approach these activities? It is entirely conceivable that a person may be more spiritually engaged in a less inherently spiritual activity, than a person who is engaged in an inherently spiritual activity but performs it in a very lackadaisical manner.

The *gemara* (e.g. *Berakhot* 28b) speaks of *yoshevei beit ha-midrash* and of *yoshevei keranot*, those who dwell in the *beit midrash* and those who dwell at street-corners. What is a *yoshev keranot*? Someone who hangs around the candy store, the pub, or whatever the current equivalent may be. He is defined by merely hanging around, by being a loafer. It is possible for a person to be seated in the *beit ha-midrash* as a *yoshev keren*, and it is possible for a person working in a store to be the equivalent, in a sense, of a *yoshev beit ha-midrash*.

The significance of effort is very considerable in our *hashkafa*. This can find expression even in inherently trivial areas. For example, the world of sports is, in a certain sense, trivial; mature adults are running around trying to put a ball through a hole. Nevertheless, moral qualities can and do come into play: cooperation, teamplay, an attempt to get the maximum out of yourself, etc. The inherent effort of the person himself, or the loneliness of the long-distance runner in his isolation, are very significant moral elements. While one need not accept the British belief that the battle of Waterloo was won on the playing fields of Eton, there is no question that within the essentially trivial world of sports, real moral greatness and real moral degradation can be seen. If you see someone on the basketball court who wants only to shoot and score, and defense means nothing to him, this is not simply disturbing to another basketball player, but is morally repugnant.

TORAH AND FLOUR

Ideally, a person should strive to live a life within which there is coincidence between the two, namely, to be applying himself maximally within an area which is objectively important—subjective *avoda* within the objective *avoda*. But that is not always possible; the majority of people must spend most of their time engaged in *kemach*, not Torah. *Kemach* can be a matter of necessity on either a personal economic level or on a collective social plane. Serving in the army is also *kemach*, but on the level of collective necessity. However, regarding the pursuit of *kemach* on the personal plane, one has to honestly confront the question: How much is really necessary and how much derives simply from the desire to have a fancy lifestyle?

Is a person really driven to a particular career because he thinks that it is necessary and important for society? Does he feel that he has a personal contribution to make? Will it bring out the better parts of himself, helping him grow? Is he doing it just for the money or is he doing it out of a sense of mission and commitment? Although not every occupation can generate the same sense of mission, it is important that a person feel that what he is doing is necessary from the social and collective point of view. This should be a major factor in a person's career choice. Then, after choosing a career, he must ask himself whether he is giving it his maximal effort. Regardless of what he is doing, he must work with the sense of being an *oved Hashem*—"*Be-khol derakhekha da'ehu.*"

THE ATTITUDE TOWARDS WORKING PEOPLE

The final *mishna* in *Menachot* (13:11, 110a) points out that the same phrase, *rei'ach nicho'ach* (a sweet savor), is used with regard to sacrificial offerings of different value—cattle, birds and flour. From here it derives a principle: "*Echad ha-marbeh ve-echad ha-mam'it, u-bilvad she-yekhaven adam et da'ato la-Shamayim*—It matters not whether a person offers much or little, so long as he directs his heart to Heaven." This *mishna* is quoted in a *gemara* which every person should learn and apply; it should be hung on the wall of every *beit midrash*:

> A favorite saying of the Rabbis of Yavneh was: I am God's creature and my fellow man (i.e. a non-scholar) is God's creature. My work is in the town and his is in the field. I rise early for my work and he rises early for his work. Just as he does not presume to do my work, I do not presume to do his. Will you say, I do much and he does little? We have learnt: "It matters not whether a person does much or little, so long as he directs his heart to Heaven." (*Berakhot* 17a)

The Rabbis of Yavneh say that one should have a sense of the worth not only of people who sit in a *beit midrash*, but also of those who are "in the field," engaged in building society, culture, economy, country, government—any of the various walks of life whose development is essential if the world of "*le-ovdah u-leshom-rah*" is to be sustained. This is a very clear and direct critique of the kind of condescension towards *balebatim* (people in non-Torah professions) which unfortunately one sometimes encounters in yeshiva circles. Sometimes, yeshiva students tend to regard themselves as the salt of the earth, while considering other people to be of secondary value. This kind of arrogance has no place in a *beit midrash* and must be shunned by any *ben-Torah*. A *ben-Torah* must believe that Torah is important, but that people engaged in other walks of life are also part of God's world, and are fulfilling their mission of "*le-ovdah u-leshomrah*" within that world. He is doing his work and I am doing my work, but what is important is the quality, intensity and scope of a person's dedication to Heaven. Whatever a person does can be geared ultimately to fostering his relationship with God.

Does this mean that therefore it is irrelevant whether a person is *marbeh* or *mam'it*, as long as he directs his heart to Heaven? Surely not! Surely not if we are talking about *avodat Hashem* generally, and certainly not if we are talking about *talmud Torah*. Rather, this phrase means that even if a person finds himself in circumstances where he needs to be *mam'it*—after all, God did not create the world as one tremendous *kollel*—he should attempt to serve God in whatever he is doing, and others should value his efforts. But to the extent that a person can be a *marbeh*, of course he is supposed to be a *marbeh*!

LABORING IN TORAH

One's ultimate aspiration should be to focus on Torah, not *kemach*. This receives expression on two planes. Emotionally, even when one is a *mam'it*, he longs to be a *marbeh*. Practically, it means that he should try to maximize his Torah study and his direct *avodat Hashem*.

On the one hand, *talmud Torah*, like other *mitzvot*, has a certain minimum. The *gemara* (*Nedarim* 8a) says that one can fulfill the daily requirement of Torah study merely by reciting *Keriat Shema* twice daily. The Vilna Gaon (*Pea* 1:1) goes even further, asking: Why recite the whole *Shema*? One word will suffice to fulfill the mitzva of *talmud Torah*! But this is true only at one level of the mitzva. *Talmud Torah* is not just a daily obligation, but a general direction in a person's life. "You shall meditate upon it day and night" (*Yehoshua* 1:8). Through God's revealed word, we can come to know Him, approach Him, relate to Him. This is a value, a goal to be maximized as far as one can. In the words of

the *mishna*, "These are the things which are without measure."
As the Ran points out:

> It would seem that [by reciting *Shema*], one has not necessari-
> ly fulfilled his obligation [to learn Torah], for every person is
> required to learn Torah continually, day and night, *kefi kocho*—
> according to the best of his ability. It says in the first chapter of
> *Kiddushin* (30a): "Our Rabbis taught, *Ve-shinantam* means
> that the words of the Torah shall be clear-cut in your mouth,
> so that if anyone asks you something, you should not show
> doubt and then answer him, but rather you should be able to
> answer him immediately," and reciting *Shema* twice daily does
> not suffice to attain this level. (Ran, *Nedarim* 8a)

This is an axiom that has guided *Kenesset Yisrael* for all generations: one must try to learn Torah *kefi kocho*. True, there are
other avenues of life which are important and valuable; true, work
is a very constructive endeavor—but that means work as opposed
to indolence, and not work as opposed to Torah. In fact, Torah
study itself is work; we frequently refer to *amalah shel Torah*, the
labor of Torah. Rashi, quoting the *Torat Kohanim*, says:

> "If you will follow My statutes" (*Vayikra* 26:3)—I might think
> this refers to keeping the *mitzvot*, therefore the verse continues,
> "and if you will keep My commandments." Since the latter part
> of the verse refers to mitzva observance, what does "If you will
> follow My statutes" mean? That you should labor in Torah.

Unfortunately, *balebatim* very often have the notion that they
are the ones who work, while those in the *beit midrash* are *bat-
lanim*, idlers. A person who knows what learning is all about
knows that Torah is the real *amal*.

CONCLUSION

Of course, there are other legitimate demands, and here the
crucial question comes up. When the Ran says "*kefi kocho*,"

what does that mean? Is it a function of one's psychological ability, his intellectual ability, his economic ability? Probably it means all three. As much as a person can, he should try to engage in Torah, and as I said before: pay attention to the *kemach*, recognize its importance and significance, but don't confuse *kemach* with Torah.

It remains an unresolved dispute whether ideally one should have only Torah and not *kemach*, as Rabbi Shimon bar Yochai felt. Everyone, however, agrees that a person should strive to reach the kind of existence within which Torah and direct *avodat Hashem* are maximized and other things are minimized. This is the *kefi kocho* that the Ran is talking about. Now, to say this does not in any way delegitimize the importance of constructive endeavors in *yishuvo shel olam*, nor show disrespect to those engaged in them. As I said, these people are doing something valuable, and really may be engaged in "*Be-khol derakhekha da'ehu.*" They may be finding the Almighty in the sphere of "*le-ovdah u-leshomrah;*" they may be giving expression to their spiritual selves within the context of what they do. To reiterate, at times it is even possible that a person subjectively may be more *oved Hashem* in an area which is objectively less *avodat Hashem*, if he approaches it in the proper spirit. So a *ben-Torah* should harbor no condescension whatsoever towards those engaged in other spheres of activity.

Surely, there are many who eventually do find that they are in Rabbeinu Tam's world, and one area or another of the general world of *kemach* becomes their *ikkar* in terms of how they spend their day. But what is crucial is their sense of values—that they know that the *ikkar* is *avodat Hashem* in its more narrow definition: Torah, *avoda, gemilut chasadim*, and that they engage in Torah "*kefi kocho.*" To the extent that the opportunity avails itself to bring this factor into play and to choose a new career, to the extent that after choosing a career one can divide his time in one way or another, to the extent that one can apportion priorities within his own being—it is crucial that he act out of a sense of *"Achat sha'alti*, One thing I ask of the Lord." Whatever a person does, he should maintain a sense of longing, of striving to be close to God, to be an *oved Hashem* in the direct and immediate sense.

Ultimately, both approaches are true. On the one hand, *"Be-khol derakhekha da'ehu"*—no area of life, no area of endeavor should be divorced from *avodat Hashem*. There is nothing neutral. Whatever a person does, wherever he is, he can strive to structure his life so that it is ultimately geared to being an *oved Hashem* (though he may not be totally conscious of this at every point).

At the same time, within his total existence, his goal should be to increase that part of his life which is geared to *avodat Hashem* in the more direct and narrow sense. Although we believe that "In all your ways, you can know Him," there are still some "ways" that are more direct than others. To the extent possible, we should build ourselves and our communities so that those elements more directly related to our religious lives become more prominent, with less time devoted to all the ancillary factors which service these central goals. This is the direction which is desirable and worthy of pursuit.

Notes

1   This question is addressed below in Chapter Five.
2   *Shemona Perakim*, Chapter Eight; see also his "Epistle to Rabbi Ovadia the Proselyte," *Iggerot Ha-Rambam*, ed. Shailat, vol. 1, p. 236 (=*Teshuvot Ha-Rambam*, ed. Blau, #436).
3   This broad conception of *devar mitzva* requires considerable study because it appears in many contexts and it is differently defined in them.
4   *Tosafot Rabbi Yehuda He-chasid, Berakhot* 35b; *Hagahot Maimoniyot, Hilkhot Talmud Torah* 3:2; *Tosafot Yeshanim, Yoma* 85b.

CHAPTER THREE

Mitzva:
A Life of Command

I began this series by exploring our commitment to the universal values of "*le-ovdah u-leshomrah*." Simply because we are human beings, we must pursue a life of work and duty as opposed to one of self-indulgence. In this chapter, I would like to move to the next level of responsibility which binds us: not what is expected of us as humans, but more specifically, what characterizes us as members of *Kenesset Yisrael?*

I do not want to speak about details, but rather about the basic quality of our existence, the central category which defines our lives as Jews. Although some of what I will discuss has universal applicability, it nevertheless has a different quality and a different weight for a Jew. My topic is what lies at the center of Jewish existence. This is succinctly described in the verse following the one I discussed before: "*Va-yetzav Hashem E-lokim al ha-adam,* The Lord God commanded the man" (*Bereishit* 2:16); in a word—mitzva. A Jew's life is defined by being commanded.

SELF-FULFILLMENT

We live in a world wherein the ideal of self-fulfillment is taken for granted. Sometimes this assumes a more obviously negative guise, such as when people espouse an ideal of pleasure-seeking. However, it can also assume a noble, moral tone:

every person has a right and a duty to develop his inherent capa-
bilities. Today, this notion is so deeply rooted that sometimes
people don't realize just how relatively new it is as an ultimate
ideal. This goal was particularly championed by the Romantic
movement, and in this respect the contemporary world is still very
much enchanted with Romanticism.

One area in which the changing ideal appears clearly is the
realm of art. In the classical world, the function and method of an
artist was primarily to express, portray or imitate some kind of
objective reality, whether it be natural, historical, social or psychological. The Romantics, on the other hand, saw the role of art as
being primarily one of self-expression. One had to give vent to
one's own personal feelings and experiences, and to find fulfillment by doing thus. The focus of art shifted from the outside to
the inside. The goal was no longer to give expression to what was
out there, and through that to increase one's sensitivity and sensibility, gaining a deeper insight into the nature of existence. As the
function of art changed, its subject matter also changed. It no
longer concerned the outer, objective order, but rather the inner
order of one's own subjective world.

This change in the perception of art was just one manifestation of what was a much more radical change of sensibility. The
element of subjectivity, and the sense that what one was looking
for in life was self-fulfillment, extended far beyond the world of
art, becoming an ideal even for people who had no inkling whatsoever of what art was all about.

If you ask people today what they're looking for—and I'm
talking about serious people—the most prevalent answers are self-
fulfillment and self-expression. When I taught "Freshman Com-
position" in an American university, this almost invariably came
up in my discussions with students. For them, the central goal of
writing was to express their feelings.

To many, there is perhaps no other way of seeing things, and they would be surprised that this goal is even being questioned. But surely, Judaism perceives human existence differently: "*Va-yetzav Hashem Elokim al ha-adam.*" Our perception is that man or woman is fundamentally a being who is commanded, who is called, upon whom demands are made. And the fulfillment of these demands may or may not be congruent with self-fulfillment.

GREATER IS ONE WHO IS COMMANDED

There is a famous halakhic ruling, which can also be understood as a statement of philosophy, that "*Gadol ha-metzuveh ve-oseh mi-mi she-eino metzuveh ve-oseh*, A person who does something after being commanded is superior to one who does it without being commanded." In the *gemara* (*Bava Kama* 87a), R. Yosef, who was blind, initially states that he would make a party if someone would tell him that the law follows R. Yehuda's opinion that a blind person is exempt from performing *mitzvot*. Why? "Because I am not commanded but I nevertheless perform [*mitzvot*]." In other words, his gut instinct was identical to ours: a volunteer is more admirable than a person who is required to do something. We tend to think that there is a greater measure of identification with a cause if you do something as a volunteer. But after he heard what R. Chanina said, namely, "*Gadol ha-metzuveh ve-oseh*," R. Yosef would now throw a party if someone said the Halakha does not follow R. Yehuda!

Presumably, one who is *eino metzuveh ve-oseh*, who is not commanded but nevertheless performs, acts in accordance with his personal inclination and therefore attains more self-fulfillment than one who is simply commanded, "Do this!" No one asks the commanded individual whether he likes what he is doing. Yet *Chazal* said, "*Gadol ha-metzuveh ve-oseh*," thus placing at the center or even at the apex of our spiritual lives the sense of being called and commanded. This is what religious existence in general is about, and certainly applies to Judaism more than to most other religions.

Of course, this has very widespread implications. For example, does a person look for a career where he will feel fulfilled, doing what he likes to do, or will he choose a career where he is responding to some call, to a sense of duty? A person responsive to the call of duty may sense that the historical moment has thrust upon him the need to follow a particular course, although it may not be that which corresponds most intimately and most fully to his own inner instincts.

THE DUAL MEANING OF MITZVA

Judaism very much considers man a "called" being; if you wanted to single out one concept which is at the heart of Judaism, it is probably the concept of mitzva. This term has several ramifications, which are different but not conflicting.

The concept of mitzva presupposes an encounter between someone who issues a command and someone who receives it. This is one sense of the term mitzva: the act and the experience of God issuing the command and man absorbing it.

Colloquially, it has another meaning: a good deed. In our minds, we equate the two meanings of the term "mitzva": a command and a value. This is, in and of itself, an indication of just how deeply the notion of mitzva is ingrained in our thinking as Jews. Imagine for a moment that a non-Jew would say, "That's a wonderful thing to do. Go do that, it's a big command." It sounds ludicrous. The fact that we talk this way is a reflection of the extent to which in our minds spiritual existence and the sense of responding to a divine demand are intertwined. On the one hand, this means that we assume that something which is commanded is good; on the other hand, we could also reason that the good is commanded.

PICKING AND CHOOSING

Now, to live the existence of a *metzuveh*, of one who is called and commanded, involves to some extent the subjugation of one's inclinations and desires. A *metzuveh* leads a theocentric rather than an anthropocentric life. He is guided by God's will, not by his own likes and preferences. "Nullify your will before [God's] will" (*Avot* 2:4) constitutes a cardinal tenet of Judaism. Even within the realm of *avodat Hashem* proper, one needs to beware of imposing his own inclinations excessively. If you are commanded, you do not pick and choose among commands— that would be living an anthropocentric life, placing yourself in the center and building everything around yourself. "*Va-yetzav Hashem Elokim al ha-adam*" means, first and foremost, that God's will is at the center; your will may be factored in, but only secondarily.

A responsum of the Rambam (#263 in the Blau edition) illustrates this point. He was asked about the custom to stand during the reading of the Ten Commandments in the synagogue, and replied that it is inappropriate to distinguish between them and the rest of the Torah. (Similarly, *Chazal* discontinued the practice of reading the Ten Commandments daily in the Temple [*Berakhot* 12a].) A Jew should feel that even though certain parts of the Torah may address him differently than do others, all are God's words, and that in and of itself assigns them importance.

Another important ramification is in the area of learning. The *gemara* in *Eruvin* (64a) compares a person who says, "I like this *sugya* and I don't like that one; I'll learn this section of the *Gemara* but I won't learn that one," to a person who consorts with prostitutes. Similarly, the *gemara* in *Sanhedrin* (99b) has very sharp words for a person who learns Torah occasionally, and does not set fixed times for study: he is "a heartless adulterer." How can learning Torah be compared to committing adultery or consorting with prostitutes? The essence of fornication is self-fulfillment. A man wants to extract sexual pleasure from a woman and, after he has used her to satisfy himself, he has no responsibility towards her and continues on his way. Tomorrow he'll find another woman. This is exactly what *Chazal* criticized so sharply. A person has to approach Torah and *avodat Hashem* not as an adulterer—someone whose goal is to extract whatever pleasure he can, even spiritual pleasure. A person has to subject himself to Torah and not to subject Torah to himself. He must be willing to commit himself to it unconditionally and accept whatever God imposes upon him.

ALL OR NOTHING

As mentioned above, I want to deal with a concept which, while it has universal elements, is more specifically central to Judaism. When a person wants to make the transition from the universal to the Jewish realm, i.e. to undergo the process of *gerut* (conversion), he must accept the authority of Halakha and be willing to do everything it demands. Conversely, if a non-Jew wishes to perform some *mitzvot* because they appeal to him, but not to perform others because he doesn't like them, the Rambam says that we ought not countenance this behavior:

> The general rule is that we do not permit them to innovate a religion and to perform *mitzvot* for themselves according to their own understanding. Rather, they should either convert and accept all the *mitzvot*, or they should remain within their own religion and not add or detract. (*Hilkhot Melakhim* 10:9)

What is the matter with this? If a gentile feels that the entire Torah is too much to accept, but there are certain *mitzvot* that appeal to him—he thinks eating *matza* is very nice and *shofar* is very elevating—then why not? Why impose upon him this whole system in its totality? Why tell him that it's all or nothing? The answer is that a person cannot come and sit in judgment upon

Torah, and upon the Almighty, and enter the world of Torah and *avodat Hashem* as if he were shopping in a department store. One shops in a department store precisely in response to one's own needs and desires. It is part of self-indulgence and self-fulfillment. But one cannot shop around in God's world. Either one understands what it means to accept the discipline of *avodat Hashem* or one doesn't. Either one is called and commanded—in which case you do not pick and choose among the commands, because if you pick and choose they are no longer commands—or one cannot become a Jew.

Judaism is built on the notion of nullifying your will before God's, of defining your existence as being called and commanded. This can be construed in a narrow sense and in a broader sense. In a narrow sense, we are bound by many specific *mitzvot*. Part of the difference between Judaism and general existence is this range of *mitzvot*, the extent to which the tentacles of commandment enter into the fiber of your being and grip you in every area. Apart from the specific *mitzvot* which one is given, there is also the overarching concept of living a life of command, a sense suffusing one's entire existence of living (in Milton's phrase) "as ever in my great Taskmaster's eye." This is very central to our perception.

Therefore, conversion means accepting a certain system, with the understanding that you do whatever you're told. In the army, it doesn't matter whether you volunteered or were drafted; in either case, you must follow orders. A volunteer cannot say, "Since I wasn't drafted, I'm here only for my own self-fulfillment and will do what I please." Like the draftee, he is now a soldier, and does not have the right to pick and choose which orders he will obey.

ENCOUNTER AND DIRECTIVE

B eing commanded entails both an experience of divine encounter as well as specific mandates one must fulfill. Consequently, a person can adopt one of two extreme positions, both of
which are counter to our view.

There are those who stress the notion of encounter and dialogue between man and God, which can even result in a general
sense of subjugation to God, but not in terms of specific commands. This is the Buberian notion of "I and Thou," and is also
found in many Protestant circles. At the other extreme, sometimes we become very much involved in relating to the commands, but in the process we lose sight of the Commander. (I
believe all of us are guilty of this at some point or another.) Either
way, we miss part of the essence of what mitzva means. To live a
life of Halakha is to try to fuse these elements, to maintain a constant sense of God's presence while striving to fulfill God's will.

Furthermore, we should seek to relate to *mitzvot* as being
intrinsically good; in this sense, we identify with the *mitzvot* on a
personal level. But at the same time, we must not lose sight of the
element of command within them. This can explain why *Chazal*
say, "*Gadol ha-metzuveh ve-oseh mi-mi she-eino metzuveh ve-oseh.*"
If someone is a *metzuveh ve-oseh*, then in addition to doing something which is good, he also acts out of a sense of response to
God's demands. The experience of being commanded is something which he has in addition to the fact that he does something
right and good, and this makes him greater than one who is *eino
metzuveh ve-oseh.*

NEGATING SELFHOOD?

I want to add one important point. Some will probably feel that
I'm being very harsh and very severe, asking a person to stifle
his own being and become a robot who exists just in order to

respond to commands. The notion of self-fulfillment is so deeply ingrained in us that we instinctively reject the notion that our own selves are to be almost decimated, our own desires are to be totally discarded, and we must instead respond to an external command. To be perfectly honest, we know that historically there have been many who have indeed felt that this is what a person is asked to do—more so outside Judaism than within. Many of the mystics of the Eastern world and the Western world speak in these terms. And not only mystics—part of Luther's message, for instance, is the negation of self, of "I"-hood.

I am not arguing for anything that extreme. I do not think that Judaism presents the notion of a lost self-identity as a central ideal; I am not sure that it is a Jewish ideal at all. What Judaism does very much stress is not that a person should have no will of his own, but rather that he should learn to identify with God's will. He must train his own instincts in such a way that he will identify with what God wants.

IDENTIFYING WITH GOD'S WILL

There is an old question, going back to the Greek moralists, which the Rambam discusses in a famous passage in *Shemoneh Perakim* (Chapter Six): Is it better for a person to desire to sin but to overcome this desire, or is it better for him not even to desire to sin? The Rambam distinguishes between more rational *mitzvot*, which you should have no desire to disobey, and non-rational *mitzvot*, regarding which you restrain yourself only because God has commanded you. For instance, you should not feel that you would like to steal, but are restrained by the Torah; rather, you should not even want to steal. On the other hand, you may desire non-kosher food, but you avoid it because God has said to do so.

Does this mean that we should all be burning with a lust for

bacon and ham, but simply be restrained because it says in the
Shulchan Arukh that you shouldn't eat it? Is it really an ideal that
we should always pit ourselves against God and then let God win,
or pit, if you will, the biological part of ourselves against our
moral and spiritual selves? Should we encourage this sort of constant conflict? I find it inconceivable that this is the way we are
supposed to live.

Ultimately, the ideal for a person should be that, if the
Shulchan Arukh says don't eat ham, then I should feel revulsion
for ham. But the question is: What is the basis of that revulsion? If
a person feels revulsion toward shrimp or lobster because of some
aesthetic consideration and therefore he doesn't eat it, then his
not eating it is simply a part of the aesthete in him. However, if a
person feels that on aesthetic grounds he could eat it, but now he
has reached a point where his revulsion is due to the fact that God
has forbidden it—how can I want something that God forbids?—
then he has reached a level for which a person should strive.

If one keeps *mitzvot* because they happen to coincide with his
instincts and intuitions, then it is all part of self-fulfillment and
not part of *avodat Hashem. Avodat Hashem* means to serve God
for His sake. But once you identify with what God wants, you can
then bring your own self-fulfillment to be part of your *avodat
Hashem.* Kant believed that a person must always act against his
inclination, but we do not subscribe to this position. Judaism
does not want a person to feel like a *shmatte* (rag) all his life, constantly fighting himself, as if the whole of spiritual existence is to
be realized through inner tension and struggle.

Certainly, it is both psychologically and religiously beneficial
for a person to find happiness and self-fulfillment in what he does.
But we grant this on one condition: that the content and direction of that which makes you feel fulfilled did not start with you.
It started with God, and through a process which admittedly is
difficult, you have gradually been able to shape your own inner

spiritual being in such a way that now there is consonance between what God wants and what you want.

Robert Frost writes (in his poem "Two Tramps in Mud Time"):

My object in living is to unite
My avocation and my vocation
As my two eyes make one in sight.

I agree that a person should strive for this goal—he should enjoy his work as if it were a hobby. In a parallel sense, a person indeed should enjoy his *avodat Hashem* and feel fulfilled by it—but not because these were initially his own desires and intuitions. These started as being God's will, which you are commanded to fulfill. But you have molded yourself in such a way that you find joy in responding to command; your self-fulfillment comes from living the life of one who is called, rather than the life of one who is guided solely by his own inner feelings.

THE CHALLENGE

Of course, this is not easy. We are born with a great measure of egocentricity, and we initially do not place God at the center. *Chazal* (*Bereishit Rabba* 34:10) say that one's evil impulse has a large head-start on his good impulse—the former is present from birth (or even in utero, according to one view), while the latter appears only when a person is thirteen years old. This means that one encounters the basic instinct for aggressiveness and selfishness even in "innocent" children, but it takes time until one has the ability to conquer these and nullify his own will.

Once a person attains a certain maturity, he or she becomes subject to God's commands, and these obligate one absolutely. They define one's life as a Jew, encompassing every area of his existence. He does not select between *mitzvot*, deeming certain areas to be irrelevant to him. At all times, one should hear God's call, and plan even *divrei reshut* with an eye towards the overarching purpose of *avodat Hashem*. In fulfilling *mitzvot*, one should sense the encounter with God and His will, and sense the goodness of the *mitzvot*. One must nullify his own will and accept God's will as the guiding force in his life. Ultimately, one should strive to reach the level where he can translate God's will into his own. This is a process which takes time, and requires a great deal of effort—but it is central to what it means to be a Jew and a *ben-Torah*.

CHAPTER FOUR

Make Your Torah Permanent: The Centrality of Torah Study

The *mishna* in *Avot* (1:15) states: "Shammai says: Make your Torah *keva*." This saying can take on several meanings, depending on how we understand the term *keva*, and I think that each of these meanings teaches us something important about being a Jew and a *ben-Torah*.

MAKE TORAH A PERMANENT FEATURE

Rashi offers two explanations of Shammai's dictum:

1. You should not set aside times for Torah, but rather you should make it *keva* (permanent) the entire day.

2. Set yourself times to learn four or five chapters every day.

Rashi is not talking about a person who spends his entire day, or even most of it, learning. But in terms of this person's attitude, his desire, what he would do were he divested of other responsibilities—he makes Torah primary. He yearns for Torah; he has never given up on it; he has never set it aside. It is always, somehow, at least subliminally, part of his agenda.

This is the sense of Rashi's first interpretation—do not "set aside" time for Torah, like you set aside time for tennis. Rather, make it a permanent, important factor around which your day revolves. How much you will actually be able to learn depends upon circumstances: where you are, what other responsibilities you have, etc. But in terms of your attitude, your commitment to Torah is rock-solid; it is the framework through which you view your life.

FIX TIMES FOR TORAH

Though a person may thirst for Torah, this longing still needs to be translated into practical terms. If you remain with nothing more than this general thirst, it is entirely conceivable that nothing will come of it—it will remain hazy and fuzzy, but will not translate into actual *talmud Torah*.

This is where the second element in Rashi comes to the fore: "Set aside time to learn four or five chapters a day." While you should set no upper limit to your learning, surely you cannot make do without setting a lower limit, a daily minimum. In order to give firmness to your commitment to Torah, you must set minimal designated times for learning.

Thus, Rashi's two explanations do not contradict each other. The latter gives you a minimal real framework. The former gives you a direction, a thirst, a longing, without setting any kind of upper limit.

PRIORITY IN TERMS OF VALUES

The Rambam offers a similar understanding:

> Make *talmud Torah* primary and all your other activities secondary; if you can engage in [the other activities], fine, and if not, not. (*Commentary on the Mishna, ad loc.*)

Torah is the root and basis of your existence, and all else is built around it. Here the Rambam surely is not talking about the quantitative element. Rather, he is talking about the axiological element, about one's values: What is central and what is peripheral? To the extent that it is possible for you to plan, which element is dominant and which is subservient?

It may be that the axiological centrality of Torah will not necessarily translate into its being quantitatively that to which you devote most of your time. When one plans his personal budget, or when a government plans a national budget, there is little disposable income left after one has factored in the various expenses of the necessities of life. Similarly, after one factors in the time he must devote to fulfilling his responsibilities and obligations, how much "free time" is left? But the test is precisely what a person does with whatever time is left to him. He doesn't have a choice about going to work; he has to make a living. But when he comes home, he *can* decide whether to read the paper and watch television or whether to sit down to learn. Here the question of what is primary and what is secondary comes to the fore.

It is also critical how a person defines his professional and economic goals. If a person says he must work twelve hours a day because he has decided that he absolutely must earn several hundred thousand dollars a year, and then he says, "Whatever is left over will be for Torah"—that decision itself reflects his priorities. But if he sets a reasonable level of need and of necessity, and *that* is legitimately set aside, then the question of what he does with his remaining time comes into play.

There are halakhic implications to this question. The *gemara* (*Bava Batra* 7b) rules that *talmidei chakhamim* (Torah scholars) are exempt from paying municipal taxes. Rosh (1:26) says that a *talmid chakham* is defined as a person whose Torah is his occupation (*torato umanuto*). Today we think of this in terms of someone whose profession it is to learn Torah, someone who does nothing else. But Maharam of Rothenberg (cited in Responsa of the Rosh, 15:8) says that it doesn't mean this at all. *Torato umanuto* applies even if a person spends most of his day at work, but his natural bent is to learn Torah. When he has a free hour, he devotes it to Torah; when he has a vacation, he uses it to learn Torah. That is *torato umanuto*—his natural self realizing itself. When he is at work and cannot learn, he is, in a sense, suppressing his natural bent.

NOT TRANSITORY

Thus far, we have spoken of *"Aseh toratekha keva"* in two senses: 1) making Torah primary in terms of values, and regarding our relation to Torah—and to God via Torah—as all-pervasive in our lives; 2) making it a fixed element of our day, with the attendant commitment and discipline. But there is yet another sense of *keva* which is implied in a *baraita*:

> *"Aseh toratekha keva"*—how so? This teaches that if a person heard something from a sage in the *beit ha-midrash*, he should not regard it as transient but rather as permanent. And what a person has learned, he must do and teach others to do, as it says (*Devarim* 5:1), "You shall learn them and keep them to do them." And so it says of Ezra (7:10), "He prepared his heart to study the Torah of God and to perform it," and afterwards it says, "And to teach statute and justice in Israel." (*Avot de-Rabbi Natan* 13:2)

Here we are not contrasting *keva* with that which is *tafel*, minor and secondary, but rather with that which is *ara'i*, transient or transitory, a passing experience. The *beraita* here speaks of this at two levels.

The latter portion of the *beraita* presents Ezra as an example of someone who made Torah *keva*. What was it that Ezra did? Above all, Ezra ensured the permanence of Torah. During his time, the Jews returning from the Babylonian exile had a very tenuous relationship to Torah. *Chazal* tell us (*Tanna De-bei*

Eliyahu Rabba, Chapter 31) that when the Jews went into exile in Babylonia, they came to the prophet Yechezkel and said, "We are now exempt from Torah and *mitzvot*, because a slave whose master has sold him is no longer obligated to do the master's bidding." The prevalent conception in classical antiquity was that religion was only a function of geography and society: you worship the local gods of the country and society in which you find yourself. All the more so was this the feeling among the Jews in exile, since their entire national fabric had seemed to disintegrate. When they went to Babylonia, they felt that they were finished with *avodat Hashem*. (The Ramban [*Shabbat* 88a] says that the re-acceptance of Torah in Persia about which we read in *Megillat Esther*—"*kiyyemu ve-kibbelu*"—came partly in response to this.)

We read in the books of Ezra and Nechemia that there was a great deal of assimilation and intermarriage among the Jews in Babylonia. Moreover, those who returned to Israel were certainly not of the more established strata, nor members of the intellectual or social elite. Ezra was faced with a tremendous challenge: to ensure that Torah would become permanent within *that* community. He made it clear that Torah is part of the essence of *Klal Yisrael*; it is not dependent upon geography, history or society—it is *keva*, permanent and essential. He did not just explain and extend Torah through rabbinic enactments, but saw to it that the people understood that adherence to Torah was not negotiable; it is part of what being *Klal Yisrael* means.

This is what Ezra did, and this is what each person needs to do within his own environment, as part of his or her historical and social responsibility. If you have learned some Torah, "*ya'aseh vi-yelammed acher*"—observe it and teach it to others. If you are in a community where Torah is in danger of disappearing, see to it that it does not disappear. Make it *kavu'a*. Make it clear that there is no vanishing American, English or French Jew. Judaism is here to stay. It is your responsibility to make it clear to yourself and to others that Torah and *avodat Hashem* are the very backbone of Judaism. Prove that all the sociological projections about the end of the Jewish people are nonsense. We are *keva*.

INTERNALIZING TORAH

However, before we get to this level, the *baraita* speaks of something else:

> If a person heard something from a sage in the *beit ha-midrash*, he should not regard it as transient but rather as permanent.

What does this mean? There are certain facets of our experience that we regard as being peripheral and temporal; we lose no sleep over the fact that they are nothing more than that. They may be pleasant at the time, but you do not expect them to become a permanent aspect of your being. Does a person make any effort to remember what he reads in the newspaper? When you read it, you think it is important to know what is going on in the world. But unless you are a professional historian or an archivist, you do not really care whether you remember what happened ten years ago.

There are other experiences which are somewhat on the borderline between what you want to be permanent and what is ephemeral. Maybe you do not care if you remember what you read in the paper, but if you read a serious magazine, you may want to remember it. There are people who save their copies of *The Atlantic Monthly* or *Commentary* for many years. You would be happy to remember what you read in those magazines, and you would not feel that it is cluttering your mind—but you are not going to make a great effort to remember it. Similarly, a person who goes to see a play will probably regard it differently than he would the evening news, but he will not make the kind of effort to remember that a theater critic would in order to be able to analyze and compare it.

But there are things to which a person is committed to the degree that he wants them to be part of him. When he has that kind of experience, he wants it to be internalized, not to remain ephemeral. This is what the *baraita* tells us with regard to Torah. "*Aseh toratkha keva*"—see to it that it is ingrained and absorbed, that it becomes a part of you. This, of course, has implications for the nature of the experience at the time. A person who hears a symphony and wants it to become part of his musical repertoire will listen to it differently than a person for whom it is only so much background music. It is a different kind of exposure and experience; there is a certain intensity and seriousness. If you want something to remain with you, you must immerse yourself in it.

The *gemara* (*Shabbat* 31a) says that a person after his death is asked by the Heavenly tribunal: "*Kavata ittim la-Torah*, Did you set fixed times for Torah?" Similarly, the Rambam places great emphasis on this:

> Every Israelite man is obligated in Torah study, whether he is poor or rich, healthy or suffering, in the vigor of youth or old and feeble. Even a man so poor that he is maintained by charity and goes begging from door to door, as also a man with a wife and children, is obligated to set aside fixed times to study Torah by day and by night, as it says (*Yehoshua* 1:8), "You shall meditate upon it day and night." (*Hilkhot Talmud Torah* 1:8)

One is not just obligated to study, but to set a fixed time for study. Why is this important? Because when a person is *kove'a ittim la-Torah*, he has indicated that Torah has a permanent place in his life. It is not one of those things which you do only if you have time. A person who enjoys playing basketball will play if he has time, but won't if he doesn't have time. On the other hand, there are certain things that you do regularly because you understand that these are part of your very being. The question is: How is Torah going to fit into a person's life experience? Will it be like reading a fine novel, or will it be part of one's regular daily schedule? Will it be part of the very essence of his being?

"*Kavata ittim la-Torah*" thus suggests *keviut* not only in terms of "making the time for it," but also in terms of what remains with you from your learning. What are you trying to accomplish when you learn? Is it enough to have gone through the motions, like going for a swim or a walk? The *baraita* is talking about *keva* in the sense of making it part of you. If you forget—you forget; you are considered an *anuss* (coerced). But, ideally, you strive to build up an *otzar*, a treasury of Torah, and to have it remain with you forever.

THE LAYMAN'S OBLIGATION

Let us return to the *baraita* in *Avot de-Rabbi Natan*:

"*Aseh toratekha keva*"—how so? This teaches that if a person heard something from a sage in the *beit ha-midrash*, he should not regard it as transient but rather as permanent.

There are several terms employed in this *baraita* which deserve further attention: "If a *person* heard something from a *sage* in the *beit ha-midrash*. . ." The *gemara* (*Shabbat* 31a) which discusses the six questions one is asked by the heavenly tribunal, three of which deal with *talmud Torah*, uses the same phrase: "*Be-sha'a she-makhnisin* adam *la-din*, At the time a *person* is brought to judgment." The *gemara* and the *baraita* are referring to the same *adam*, the same person. The *adam* referred to here is not the professional *lamdan* (scholar), not the *kollel* student, not the *yeshiva* head, but *adam*—a plain Jew, an ordinary layman. What is striking is that this kind of demand is made of a regular person— he should strive to make his Torah *keva*.

In certain respects, this an extraordinary demand, because one might have thought, "You can ask an ordinary person to engage in *talmud Torah* or to be in touch with Torah; but you cannot ask the average person to internalize his learning into something which is permanent." In other areas, we assume that there is a great difference between professional scholars and those who have a dilettantish interest, and maybe even a love, for a certain field—we don't expect of the latter to try to build up a permanent repertoire of knowledge. A professional scholar will read books, take notes, and compare the different works he has studied; a music expert may remember symphonies and conductors, and compare them, examining their respective styles and interpretations. But an ordinary person just wants to enjoy himself when he goes to a concert.

However, regarding *talmud Torah*, the demand on the average person really is to make it a permanent part of himself. He cannot simply attend a *shiur* (class) and think, "Fine, I'll hear the *shiur*—it will be a nice experience, he's a good speaker. I'll enjoy it. I'll be enlightened. And I'll go home." You cannot treat it in the same manner as if you were going to the theater.

PLUMBING THE DEPTHS

This radical demand to make Torah *keva*, which one would not expect of a layman in other areas, represents a different kind of commitment. Of course, it reflects the tremendous importance we assign to Torah within our perception of the ordinary person's spiritual life. This is heightened by the concluding questions in the catalogue of the *gemara* in *Shabbat*. One might have thought that even if a layman is required to learn Torah, it is enough for him to engage in it in a shallow manner—let him learn *bekiut*, maybe some *mishnayot*, etc.; in-depth study is the realm of the *ben-yeshiva* or of the professional *lamdan*. Do we expect of someone who goes to a concert to read up on the literature? Of course not.

But the *gemara* indicates otherwise. A person is asked by the heavenly tribunal not just whether he made time for learning, but what was the quality of that learning: "*Pilpalta be-chokhma? Heivanta davar mi-tokh davar?* Did you debate matters of wisdom? Did you infer one thing from another?" Or did you just run through the material, superficially skimming it? This is far from what is expected precisely because it is superficial. The three questions in the *gemara* are connected: to the extent that a person is not *mefalpel be-chokhma* and does not strive to be *meivin davar mi-tokh davar*, then he has not been *kove'a ittim*—his learning lacks *keva*. In order for it to be *keva*, it must have a certain depth. One has to be engaged both emotionally and intellectually.

Consequently, in order to make your Torah *keva*, it has to be accompanied by a certain grappling and wrestling, trying to plumb the depths of what you are learning. Every day, the ordinary Jew—not just the *rosh yeshiva*—prays, "*Avinu Av harachaman . . . ten be-libenu lehavin u-lehaskil,* Our merciful Father . . . inspire our hearts to understand and to discern." He does not just ask God to give him the desire and ability to learn Torah, but rather *lehavin u-lehaskil*—to penetrate its depths. Of course, not everyone realizes this in great scope; but these are his values. And ultimately a person is judged not so much by his attainments as by his efforts.

I remember some years back talking to a person who was affiliated with a certain socio-religious movement here in Israel. He told me that in their communities, the ideal is that *balebatim* (laymen) should learn *mishnayot*. I said to him, "I can perhaps come to terms with the fact that *balebatim* end up learning *mishnayot*. Maybe that's the level of the people there—they can't get much beyond that. But should it be the limiting case of the ideal!? Is one striving for that?"

The Rambam talks about how to divide one's learning:

The time allotted to study should be divided into three parts.

A third should be devoted to the Written Law; a third to the Oral Law [which basically means *mishnayot*]; and the last third should be spent in reflection, deducing conclusions from premises [the same terms we just saw: *yavin ve-yaskil acharit davar me-reishito*], developing implications of statements, comparing dicta, studying the hermeneutical principles by which the Torah is interpreted, until one knows the essence of these principles, and how to deduce what is permitted and what is forbidden from what one has learned from tradition. This is termed *"gemara."* (*Hilkhot Talmud Torah* 1:11)

Then the Rambam goes on to say (1:12) that this tripartite division applies only when a person starts learning. But when one has become more proficient, he should review the first two categories on set occasions, and devote himself almost solely to the final category:

[He] should devote all his days exclusively to the study of *gemara* according to his breadth of mind and maturity of intellect.

Here *"gemara"* means not necessarily a particular text, but rather an approach to and perspective on learning. It means studying in depth, not just reviewing dicta. Of course, at some point a person must acquire basic knowledge. But in terms of your ideal, where do you want to get to? Do you want to be left with just raw knowledge? That is not a *keviut* of Torah, that is not an internalization of Torah, and that is not a striving for the *"ve-ha'arev na"* that we pray for each morning—a sense of love and pleasure in Torah. The fullness and the richness of *talmud Torah* is the *"pilpalta bi-chochma,"* the *"heivanta davar mi-tokh davar."* If one strives to master the complexity, the depth, the range of Torah, then he attains *keva* in its fullest sense—not just by skimming the surface, but by plumbing the depths.

MOTIVATION TO STUDY

I know many are troubled by the question of how to develop the requisite passion and yearning for Torah. People would like to find some formula which would enable one to attain this automatically. I can't speak of any formula, but I think there are certain directions which can be mentioned.

Perhaps it is most important to stress that this is not a phenomenon we can regard in isolation. The extent to which a person is committed to Torah is very much a function of his commitment to God, and therefore it is related to the place of *avodat Hashem* and *yirat Shamayim* (fear of Heaven) within his life generally. There may be some people who simply have a fancy, as it were, for Torah. But for most people, if the depth of *yirat Shamayim* is lacking, then it is unlikely that, of all the things to which they are exposed, specifically the Talmudic passage of "an ox which gores" is going to interest them most. There is a circular relation between *yirat Shamayim* and cleaving to Torah: the more you have the one, the more you have the other. One needs to develop a certain dialectic dynamic between these two. Inasmuch as a person is involved with Torah because he sees it as divine, as *Torat Hashem*, then the extent to which he relates to God is also going to have a great impact on how he relates to Torah.

Love of Torah is also not to be regarded in isolation in the social sense. The *baraita* (*Avot* 6:5) says that one of the ways in which Torah is acquired is through *dibbuk chaverim* (joining with friends). Apart from its value in sheer intellectual terms—finding people with whom you can talk—*dibbuk chaverim* is also valuable in the sense of being part of a community of Torah, which will reinforce your values.

I think there is also something to be said not only for *dibbuk chaverim* in a social sense but in a historical sense as well. A person should deepen his sense of belonging to a community of

Torah spanning all generations. Although one cannot have direct contact with earlier generations, I think there is importance in getting to know this community. Among other things, this entails becoming familiar with *Gedolei Yisrael*.

A person should also make some effort to relate to this problem directly, by studying the books and statements of *Chazal* which speak of the value of Torah. Not all of these are equally effective for everyone, but surely in some way one should try to encounter them. Some people may find that the Vilna Gaon speaks to them, others may read Rav Kook, and others the Ramban. Some may find that *mussar* study in the classical sense speaks to them, and that is certainly valid.

It would be difficult for me to say that one thing will be effective for everyone, and that one should adopt only one approach to tackling the problem. It is a complex issue, but I think a person surely needs to recognize that we must address ourselves to it. Maybe at one time people lived in a world where all of this occurred through osmosis. However, most of us do not live in a world which breathes Torah all the time. That being the case, a person has to work on this in a way that at one time one didn't need to (and perhaps in certain communities today, one doesn't need to).

A MATTER OF VALUES

In summation, when we speak of Torah as a central value, we are dealing with both a quantitative and a qualitative question. Quantitatively, how much time and effort does a person devote to it? This question applies both in terms of how many years he devotes to it on a full-time basis, and in terms of how much time he devotes to it daily or weekly once he has started working. Although we believe that *"Echad ha-marbeh ve-echad ha-mamit,* Whether one does much or little, what truly matters is that he should direct his heart to Heaven" (*Menachot* 110a)—this does not mean that it is immaterial whether you are *marbeh* or *mam'it*. To the contrary, it is very material, both as a reflection of what your values are, and as something which subsequently molds and shapes those values.

Moving to the qualitative level, a person is asked to make the Torah central to his life, to see that it has a *keviut*, a permanence, and is not just somewhere on the periphery. It should have a *keviut* within his own life, and also a *keviut* within his society, within his historical situation, analogous to Ezra. In practical terms, the element of *keva* means that, minimally, one has certain designated time frames for study, such that his Torah is not simply adventitious, but rather fundamental and inherent to his schedule. Furthermore, *keviut* means making Torah into one's framework and planning everything else around that, rather than planning everything else and sticking in a bit of Torah in the remaining space.

This is, of course, a large demand, and what is significant and striking about it is that this demand is made of each and every Jew. One cannot allow his social setting to determine for him whether or not Torah has a place in his life. It must be clear that, wherever he ends up, Torah is a central value, a framework for his life, something which is inherent in his very being. Like Ezra, he must influence his community—be it a social, economic, professional or academic community—in order to make Torah *kavua* there as well.

For a *ben-Torah*, for a yeshiva student, there is an additional level. The *baraita* above speaks of "a person (*adam*) who hears something from a sage (*chakham*) in the *beit ha-midrash*." This distinguishes between "a person" and "a sage." Of course, a *ben-yeshiva* should strive ultimately to be not just the *adam* who listens to the *chakham*, but to be the *chakham* himself.

CHAPTER FIVE

Determining Objectives in Religious Growth: Spiritual Specialization or Spiritual Breadth?

In charting a course for spiritual growth, a person can choose to follow one of two general paths. On the one hand, a person can assume a more general approach to his or her spiritual existence, trying to encompass the full range of values and to strike some kind of balance between them. Alternatively, one can seek to focus narrowly but intensively upon a particular area.

The question of the extent to which one should follow the former or the latter path is a problem which confronts all of us. Indeed, it is a universal religious issue; nevertheless, given the nature of Halakha and its dual normative and axiological thrusts, this issue has a very specific Jewish dimension. The attempt to develop a variety of approaches with respect to this question (and not necessarily a single, uniform solution) constitutes a challenge both to us as individuals and to our spiritual community as a whole.

Of course, in trying to envision the religious life, the point of departure for a Jew needs to be the framework of Halakha. That framework is one which, on the one hand, is very comprehensive; it runs the gamut of all aspects of human existence, addressing itself in its totality to the whole community. Yet, at the same time, it is a system which does allow, indeed does insist upon, a certain measure of specialization.

DIVISION OF LABOR

There are certain areas of Halakha, certain *mitzvot*, which are assigned to particular groups of people and limited only to them. An outstanding example is the area of *avoda ba-Mikdash* (Temple service). Firstly, there is the familiar distinction between those who are not only permitted, but upon whom it is incumbent to perform the *avoda*, and *zarim* (outsiders), who are absolutely prohibited from engaging in any such activity, upon threat of severe punishment. Within the context of *Mikdash*, we encounter not only the division between *Kohanim*, *Levi'im* and *Yisraelim*, but even beyond that, a certain measure of specialization within those groups themselves, particularly with regard to *Levi'im*. The *gemara* states:

> Rabbi Yehoshua wanted to assist R. Yochanan ben Gudgada in shutting the doors [of the Temple]. And he was told to withdraw: For you are among those engaged in song, and not those to whom the care of the gates is assigned. (*Arakhin* 11a)

This is formulated by the Rambam in more general terms:

> Just as *Levi'im* are proscribed from engaging in the labor of the *Kohanim*, likewise *Kohanim* are proscribed from engaging in the labor of the *Levi'im*, as it is written: "Both you and they" (*Bemidbar* 18:3). Similarly, *Levi'im* proper are forewarned that one should not engage in the labor of his fellow, that the singer should not assist the gatekeeper, nor the gatekeeper the singer, as it is written: "Each person to his work and his labor" (*ibid.* 4:49). If a *Levi* performs the labor of a *Kohen*, or if one *Levi* assists another with regard to work which is not his, they are then liable to death at the hands of the Divine Court. (*Hilkhot Kelei Ha-Mikdash* 3:10-11)

Here we have a very clear example of institutionalized specialization in Halakha.

A PERSON ENGAGED IN ONE MITZVA IS EXEMPT FROM ANOTHER

In other areas, too, we find recognition of division of labor— not within such formal, clearly defined, institutional terms, but within a more pliant context. By this I mean the rule of "*Ha-osek be-mitzva patur min ha-mitzva*:" a person who is engaged in performing one mitzva is then absolved from another. This concept can be interpreted in two ways, one of which is more directly relevant to our immediate topic.

The *Rishonim* dispute how broad the scope of this rule is, focusing particularly upon one specific question. We say that a person who is performing one mitzva need not concern himself concomitantly about another. For instance, a person who is engaged in taking care of an *aveida*, a lost object which he has found, need not give money to a pauper who then knocks upon his door, inasmuch as he is already engaged in some other facet of *avodat Hashem* (divine service) by fulfilling another mitzva. Does this rule apply even in circumstances under which it is possible for a person to perform both *mitzvot* (*efshar lekayyem sheneihem*)? Or is it limited to situations in which a person would have to desist from the first mitzva in order to perform the second?

The *Ba'alei Ha-tosafot* in various places (e.g. *Sukka* 25a s.v. *Shluchei*) are generally of the opinion that the rule of "*Ha-osek be-mitzva patur min ha-mitzva*" applies only if it is impossible to perform both *mitzvot* (*ee efshar lekayyem sheneihem*). If it is possible to perform both, why not? *Tosafot* not only ask this question on the basis of simple logic, but raise a seeming absurdity. If we do not accept this limitation, why should we not then say that a person who is wearing *tzitzit* or *tefillin* or has a *mezuza* on his door is exempt from giving *tzedaka* (charity) in all cases? We have never heard of this being the case.

However, this position is disputed by one of the *Ba'alei Ha-tosafot*, R. Yitzchak of Vienna, in his work *Or Zaru'a* (II:299), and even more emphatically by his son, R. Chayim *Or Zaru'a* (Responsa, #183). The *Or Zaru'a* clearly says that even if it is possible to fulfill both *mitzvot*, nevertheless the principle of "*Ha-osek be-mitzva patur min ha-mitzva*" applies. The Ran (*Sukka*, 11a [Alfasi]) likewise adopts this opinion and, addressing *Tosafot's* question, points out that the *gemara* does not say "*ha*-mekayyem mitzva patur min ha-mitzva*," but rather "*ha*-osek *be-mitzva*"—it does not exempt a person who is passively fulfilling a mitzva (such as *mezuza*, *tzitzit* or *tefillin*), but rather one who is actively engaged in a mitzva. In the latter case, regardless of whether or not that mitzva physically prevents him from fulfilling other *mitzvot*, the *esek* itself—the involvement, engagement and commitment—absolves him from engaging in other *mitzvot*.

THE RATIONALE OF THE DEBATE

Probably the simplest way of understanding this dispute is to assume that the issue at stake is a very basic one of defining the fundamental concept of "*Ha-osek be-mitzva patur min ha-mitzva*." According to *Tosafot*, it may very well be that the term *patur* (exempt) as applied to the *osek* (one engaged in a mitzva) is a misnomer. It is not that he is somehow exempt, but simply that he is told pragmatically: If you are confronted by a choice between two *mitzvot* and have already begun fulfilling one mitzva, then you should not—and, in the opinion of many, may not—leave the first mitzva in order to attend to the second. This is not because you have been personally exempted from the second mitzva; it is simply because, even assuming that the duties of both devolve upon you as an individual, practically speaking you cannot fulfill both. The Halakha has established priorities and has stated that the mitzva which comes first is that which you should fulfill.

Of course, the question may then be asked: If this is all that the Halakha says, then what has it taught us? Why should one have assumed that he should leave the mitzva he has already started and go on to another? There are two possible answers. The Ra'ah (*Sukka* 25a) suggests that even if there is a qualitative difference between the *mitzvot*, namely, the second one which confronts you is somehow qualitatively weightier than the first, nevertheless, you should not move on. Alternatively, perhaps the *chiddush* (novelty) here is that the matter is not left to one's discretion, but rather one is positively told not to leave the first in order to fulfill the second.

Be that as it may, in all likelihood we do not have according to *Tosafot* a kind of personal exemption, whereby a person is told: This mitzva is for you, that mitzva is for others. One is simply afforded some kind of practical guidance as to how to establish priorities when confronted by two conflicting duties.

However, if one accepts the opinion of the Ran and *Or Zaru'a*—that even if it is possible to fulfill both, one does not need to tax himself to the utmost in order to fulfill both *mitzvot*—then clearly we are confronted here by a kind of personal exemption, whereby a person who is doing mitzva A is simply exempt from mitzva B. This opens up the possibility of division of labor with respect to *mitzvot*—not a formal, institutional division, whereby Reuven is told on an ongoing basis, "You are a *Kohen*, you do this," and Shimon is told, "You are a *Levi*, you do that;" but rather, within a more flexible context, a given individual may under certain circumstances be personally exempt from a certain mitzva, that mitzva then to be left as an opportunity for others.

THE SCOPE OF THE EXEMPTION

There is some question as to the scope of this rule. Surely, if we take only the particular example from the *gemara* which was mentioned before—a person who happens to be dealing with a lost object at a particular time—the implications, while conceptually significant, are practically not very meaningful. But it is entirely conceivable that the concept may have a much broader application. The *gemara* in *Sukka* (26a), for instance, quotes a *baraita* in the name of R. Chanina ben Akavia, who says that those who are engaged in writing or selling Torah scrolls, *tefillin* and *mezuzot* are *"patur mi-kol ha-mitzvot she-baTorah"*—a person who owns a *sefarim* store or is a *sofer stam* (scribe) is exempt from all the *mitzvot* in the Torah!

This has a very radical ring to it, and it is quite possible that it is indeed a *da'at yachid* (a unique, individual opinion). The Rambam does not quote this ruling. R. Ya'akov of Karlin (*Mishkenot Ya'akov, siman* 54) suggests that inasmuch as the principle of *"Ha-osek be-mitzva patur min ha-mitzva"* appears in the *gemara* in many contexts, but this particular *baraita* is quoted only once and in the name of an individual, there is a Tannaitic dispute only with regard to this ruling. Other *Tannaim* accepted the general principle of *"Ha-osek be-mitzva patur min ha-mitzva,"* but within a much more limited context, whereas R. Chanina ben Akavia came and said that people who are engaged in a certain field as their general activity are then exempt from the whole range of *mitzvot* generally.

Lest there be any misunderstanding, when I speak of being exempt from *mitzvot*, I mean only *mitzvot aseh* (positive commandments); the question of *issurim* (prohibitions) is a totally separate one. One who is engaged in a mitzva is not permitted to transgress prohibitions; he is merely exempt from actively fulfilling other positive commandments.

If one does accept R. Chanina ben Akavia's formulation, then we can certainly reach a situation within which something quite analogous to the formal, institutional division between *Kohanim* and *Levi'im* can apply to a broader range of people. People who devote themselves to a particular mitzva—which then becomes the focus of their spiritual and religious existence, the vehicle through which they relate to God as normative beings and the field through which they can experience their sense of calling— consequently become exempt from all other *mitzvot* in the Torah, from the realization of other values and the performance of other norms.

"EACH ENGAGES IN HIS OWN LABOR"

We find elsewhere a simile which Rav Paltoi Gaon quotes in the name of *Chazal*. I neither know where this saying appears in the writings of *Chazal*, nor have I been able to find someone who did know. But Rav Paltoi quotes it, and he is a reliable witness. The problem he dealt with is a very narrow one, but the simile, I think, is very significant. The question arises: If a person is in the middle of praying and, for one reason or another, hears someone saying *Kedusha* or *Kaddish*, does he in any way have to take note of it? One certainly cannot respond in the middle of *Shemoneh Esrei*; there is a problem of *hefsek* (interruption). But perhaps he should at least listen and fulfill the mitzva of responding via the principle of *shome'a ke-oneh* (one who hears is as one who responds).

The *Ge'onim* generally assumed that one does not need to take note of other prayers being recited. Rav Paltoi explains that, notwithstanding the fact that a person has ignored *Kaddish* and *Kedusha*, nevertheless:

> There is no transgression involved in this. Thus have *Chazal* said: When Rav Dimi came [from *Eretz Yisrael* to Babylonia], he said, "It is as if you had two servants who have been assigned separate tasks by their master—each engages in his own labor and takes no heed of his fellow's labor." (*Otzar Ha-ge'onim, Berakhot* 21a, p. 54)

Here we have the principle of division of spiritual labor or, if you will, spiritual specialization, fully formulated and clearly articulated. It is applied, to be sure, within a narrow context: the question of whether one should pause for ten or twenty seconds during *Shemoneh Esrei* to hear *Kedusha* or *Kaddish*. But the possible implications of the simile can be very wide-ranging.

PERSONAL DUTY AND PUBLIC NEED

So far, I have spoken about possible specialization as not only permitted, but mandated by Halakha, where what is at issue is one's personal duty—the *mitzvot* which are incumbent upon a particular individual. We generally regard *mitzvot* as applying fundamentally to most everyone. Not everyone is in a situation to fulfill all *mitzvot*; for example, a person who has no home is exempt from the *mitzvot* of *mezuza* and *ma'akeh* (fencing one's roof). But were his personal circumstances to change, he would then be obligated in the mitzva—unless he happens to be in a situation where the concept of *osek be-mitzva* comes up.

However, one can deal with the problem of specialization at a second level, where the point of departure is not one's individual duty. At this level, the focus of our attention is not the norm as it applies to the individual, but rather a desired result we wish to attain. This kind of division of labor arises in a celebrated example cited in a *baraita* in *Yevamot*:

> R. Eliezer says: If a person is not engaged in procreation, it is as though he is guilty of murder, for it is written, "A person who spills human blood through the instrumentality of man, he in turn is to be punished by death" (*Bereishit* 9:6), and then it is written, "And you shall be fruitful and multiply" (*ibid.* 9:7).
>
> R. Ya'akov says: It is as if such a person has taken the divine image and diminished it, for it is written, "In the divine image

He created man" (*ibid.* 9:6), and thereafter it is written, "And you shall be fruitful and multiply," [the implication being that procreation is part of enlarging and enhancing that "human face divine"].

Ben Azzai says: It is as if he has committed murder *and* has diminished the divine image. . .

They said to [Ben Azzai]: There are people who can expound well on various issues and also perform well [i.e., they practice what they preach]. Others lack the tools in order to expound properly, but nevertheless succeed in implementing what they believe. But you preach so beautifully, yet do not act in accordance with your own prescriptions!

Ben Azzai replied: What can I do? My soul yearns for Torah, and the world can be sustained through others. (*Yevamot* 63b)

The question which confronts Ben Azzai is a dual one. First, in terms of his normative duty, is not the mitzva of procreation a mitzva like all others, incumbent upon each and every person? How is it that Ben Azzai is not performing this mitzva? The second issue, quite apart from his duty as an individual, is: What are the social and political implications of desisting from the mitzva of procreation?

Indeed, *Chazal* cite two separate texts which deal with this mitzva. One is the verse in *Bereishit* (9:7), "And you shall be fruitful and multiply," which is a mandate imposed upon the individual, and the other is a verse in *Yeshayahu* (45:18): "*Lo tohu bera'ah, lashevet yetzarah*"—The world was not created by God in order to be a vacuous wilderness, but He molded it in order to be inhabited and cultivated. Whereas the first verse speaks of an individual's duty, the second speaks of some desideratum, goal or public need—the shape of society and of the world.

Ben Azzai, being confronted by the question of procreation, needs to deal with the issue on two separate levels. First, what about his personal mitzva—isn't he obligated in procreation, just as in eating matza? Secondly, what about that world which was created in order to be inhabited and developed? In his response, he addresses himself to each issue separately. With regard to the first, he answers, "What can I do? My soul yearns for Torah." For some reason—I do not wish to enter here into halakhic analysis as to whether this can be regarded as ample exemption—this becomes for him a personal exemption. Then the second question is: Fine, you want to learn all the time, you will be innovative in Torah, you will write books, you will teach, but meanwhile the world will become desolate? Here he answers: Do not worry about the world; there are others who will take up the slack. While Ben Azzai is sitting in the *beit midrash* learning Torah, others will see to it that the world does not return to wilderness.

Thus, in confronting the question of specialization, we need to deal with two separate dimensions of the issue: one, in terms of a person's individual duty and religious growth; another, in terms of trying to satisfy certain public, social, national or universal needs. As long as we are dealing with the specifically normative element, the obligation in *mitzvot*, we are, by and large, dealing with the first element, one's individual duty. But to the extent that we move from defined duty to the realization of values, then the question of attaining certain general goals becomes more pressing. At the axiological (as opposed to the normative) level, in terms of values and not just formal duties, the question of specialization becomes much more demanding and complex.

TORAH, AVODA, GEMILUT CHASADIM

What makes this such a serious question is the fact that in the axiological dimension, we encounter some of the central, crucial areas of our religious and spiritual existence. As Jews, we are responsive to a whole range of obligations and prohibitions; at the same time, we are also responsive to more general aims, to the need to realize certain values.

> The world stands on three things: on Torah, on *avoda* (service or worship, narrowly defined as the Temple service, more broadly defined to include prayer) and on *gemilut chasadim* (acts of kindness). (*Avot* 1:2)

The common denominator of these three pillars of human existence is the fact that they are not clearly defined; they have no sharply limited parameters. The parameters exist perhaps at some minimal normative level. There is a certain modicum of *talmud Torah* incumbent upon each person daily, and a minimum of prayer, whether biblically or rabbinically mandated. Surely, the mitzva of *chesed* also must exist within each person's life, whether it derives from, "You shall love your neighbor as yourself," as the Rambam would have it (*Hilkhot Avel* 14:1), or from, "You shall walk in His ways," as the *gemara* in *Sota* (5a) states.

But nowhere do we have any clear definition as to how an individual's spiritual existence is to be divided amongst these. According to the *gemara* (*Menachot* 99a), a person fulfills the mitzva of Torah study even if he only says *Keriat Shema* in the morning and at night. The Vilna Gaon (*Mishnayot Shenot Eliyahu, Pe'a* 1:1) pushes this to its logical extreme and asks: Why specifically *Keriat Shema*? One word of Torah by morning and one word by night would suffice to fulfill the mitzva of *talmud Torah*! On the other hand, we have the directive to study boundlessly—"*Ve-hagita bo yomam va-laila*, You shall meditate upon it day and night" (*Yehoshua* 1:8).

Similarly, with regard to the *avoda* of prayer, the *gemara* (*Berakhot* 34a) records a critique both of those who pray briefly and those who pray at length. The *gemara* then responds: Who is briefer than Moshe? He prayed a five-word prayer for his sister's recovery (*Bemidbar* 12:13). And who is lengthier than Moshe?

He prayed for forty consecutive days for God to forgive the people after the sin of the Golden Calf. Here again, very dramatically portrayed, is the range of *tefilla* (prayer).

The same is true of *gemilut chasadim*. As is self-evident, if one wishes, he can spend virtually all of his time helping the sick, mourners, orphans and widows. Yet perhaps there is a limit to how much time a person should spend visiting the sick and helping others.

We have here, with respect to the very pillars of our spiritual existence, an open-ended area and no clear definition of how extensively or how intensively a person is to engage in them. This opens up the possibility, on the one hand, of trying somehow to touch all bases, or, on the other hand, of dedicating and devoting oneself to one area as the matrix and focus of one's *avodat Hashem*. That being the case, once we have moved beyond that level of *avodat Hashem* which is directly and immediately incumbent upon us, we are then confronted by the question of priorities and objectives, and must decide how to divide our labors and attention.

PUBLIC VS. PRIVATE INTEREST

The question of whether to strive for the achievement of a kind of Renaissance ideal, the "man for all seasons," or to try to master a given area intensively—not only in theory, but in practice—confronts us at both a public and a private level. Perhaps part of what makes the choice sometimes difficult is the fact that the public and the private interests very often diverge.

If you want to regard this issue from a purely personal perspective, whereby the spiritual interest of the individual alone is to be our guide, then I suppose that our intuitive response—at least, my own—is towards the Renaissance ideal, whereby a person is not limited to working in one particular area, but is a complete *oved Hashem* (servant of God)—"In all your ways, know Him." A person is thereby enriched; there is a fructifying reciprocation between various aspects of his spiritual existence. He does not live as a fragmented being. He is not only able, as Matthew Arnold said of Sophocles, "to see life steadily and see it whole," but to live it steadily and live it whole.

On the other hand, if we regard the public interest, then surely there is a great deal to be said for specialization. If a person is very much at home in a given area, then when a problem comes up within his particular area, he is able to cope with it in a way that a person who has a more general perspective and a broader field of vision cannot. The specialist obviously can do much better from a public standpoint than can the generalist. Therefore, we are often confronted by the question of the extent to which we want to emphasize the public or the private element.

This is not to say that the public interest always militates for specialization, and the private one for a broader vision. Surely, on the one hand, the public interest too requires that people who deal with central and basic issues have a somewhat broader horizon and more general perspective. Public issues dealing with our civil existence must not simply be left to technocrats, who narrowly master a small area but lack the ability to relate it properly and sensitively to other areas. This consideration has been at the heart of the British tradition, whereby civil servants have been specialists, but those who make the more general decisions on the cabinet level have had broader training. The familiar comment, "War is too important to be left to generals," is likewise important in many other areas of public life.

On the other hand, from an individual's perspective, some measure of specialization is valuable. There is an interesting responsum of one of the early sages of Provence, R. Avraham ben Yitzchak *Av Beit Din* (the so-called "first Ra'avad" and the father-in-law of the famous Ra'avad), which has survived in the *Orchot Chayim*, one of the later *Rishonim* of Provence:

R. Meshullam ben Ya'akov explained: We have been given 613 *mitzvot* from Sinai, and all of these would be fulfilled to the letter and never transgressed by those who were particularly pious. As we learned in the *gemara* in *Shabbat* (63a): A person who fulfills one mitzva in its totality, with all that attends to it, will never hear ill tidings, as it is written: "A *shomer mitzva* (a person who keeps or guards a mitzva, with emphasis upon the singular—one mitzva) will not know a bad thing" (*Kohelet* 8:5).

We also learned in the *mishna* in *Kiddushin* (1:10, 39b): One who performs a single mitzva is blessed and enjoys long life. The *Yerushalmi* (1:9) explains that this *mishna* applies to a person who has singled out a particular mitzva which he is particularly careful never to transgress, for instance, the mitzva of honoring parents. Therefore, some of the later *Amoraim* would pride themselves on the fact that they were particularly careful about certain *mitzvot*. One would say that he would always be careful about *tzitzit*, *tefillin* or *shalosh se'udot*, and one would ask another: "With regard to what was your father particularly careful?" That is, which mitzva did he never transgress?

It is in this vein that [the *gemara* (*Makkot* 24a) states that 613 *mitzvot* were given to Moshe at Sinai, and then] these were reduced by David to eleven and subsequently to six, to three, and to one. [Generally, we understand this to mean that in terms of details, the *mitzvot* number 613, but the underlying principles, the values from which these branch out, are reduced to a smaller number. He understands differently:] The *gemara* spoke of a specific dedication and commitment to a smaller number of *mitzvot* with an intensity that one does not bring to bear upon the range of *mitzvot* generally. (*Orchot Chayim, Hilkhot Rosh Ha-shana, siman* 25)

No mention is made of a public need to have *tallit* specialists or *tefillin* specialists, in the same way that in the medical area you want to have heart specialists or endocrinologists. Here, he deals specifically with the individual *per se*. Clearly, the thrust of this responsum, and of the range of sayings quoted within it, is that a person stands in danger of achieving a kind of uniform mediocrity throughout the whole field of *avodat Hashem* if he tries to devote himself with equal intensity to each mitzva. Ideally, of course, a person would like to serve God with his whole heart and soul and to bring the full range of his energies, talents and commitment to bear upon every single mitzva. But one is unable to do that. Such an attempt would result in some form of compromise or luke-warm performance, a *pareve* kind of *avodat Hashem*, because one would be spread so very thin and have only so much energy to devote to any given mitzva.

Evidently, these sayings of *Chazal* held that a person needs to address his religious growth from two perspectives. On the one hand, he certainly needs to attain a basic, fundamental level of mitzva observance, and of *zehirut* and *zerizut* (care and alacrity) with regard to all *mitzvot*. At the levels of both concrete obser-vance and realizing values, there is a need for a minimal level of *avodat Hashem* with respect to the whole range of our existence. At the same time, it is important that there be some sort of upward thrust, an aspiration beyond that of ordinary day-to-day *avoda*. At least in one area, we must attain a measure of dedica-tion and intensity which adds a qualitative dimension to our *avo-dat Hashem*. All of this is relevant quite before we reach any kind of public consideration.

A GENERAL EDUCATIONAL DILEMMA

This question is analogous to the problem of a more general vs. a more specialized approach to education. Surely, from a pub-lic standpoint, the more specialized the person to whom you address a particular question, the better off you are. If you happen to have a question which deals specifically with Tibetan history 1500 years ago, you have a Tibetan specialist; if you want to know something about French prosody in the sixteenth century, you have a specialist for that too. However, from the individual's standpoint, this issue assumes a totally different character. As we know all too well, it is a question which has become increasingly pressing as the explosion of information has become an ever more dominant factor, and the attempt to master the full range, at a significant level, becomes increasingly impossible in virtually all areas of knowledge.

Only a century ago, it was deemed possible for a person to be genuinely a master of many sciences. A person would undertake to write, as Richelieu did, the history of France in its entirety, or undertake, as Trevelyan did not so long ago, to write a complete history of England; today, ambitions are more modest. The celebrated remark which Browning inserted into the mouth of his grammarian ("A Grammarian's Funeral"), "Grant I have mastered learning's crabbed text, / Still there's the comment," hangs very heavily on anyone engaged in any area of scholarship.

Inasmuch as the ability to realize the Renaissance ideal becomes more and more a remote and cherished dream, it becomes increasingly difficult in the educational sphere to choose between an encompassing, sweeping knowledge and the intensive mastery of a narrow area—to the point where, in a *reductio ad absurdum*, someone once said, "Specialization is a process whereby people know more and more about less and less, until they know everything about nothing."

A LIBERAL EDUCATION

There is a solution which attempts to cope with this problem, an approach less familiar to those with a European or Israeli education, but more familiar to those of us who have an American education (although, unfortunately, it is also being eroded in America). This is the ideal of the "liberal education," enunciated in its most celebrated and cogent form in Cardinal Newman's *The Idea of a University*, but of course the product of a long history within the Western world. The basic notion attendant upon a liberal education is the sense that there is a certain basic level of familiarity and knowledge a person needs to attain with regard to a wide range of areas and disciplines. Subsequently, however, one moves on to a more specialized approach.

If we want to single out the major components of this approach, I think that there are three elements to keep in mind. The first is the assumption that a person needs to relate to a wide range of disciplines. This is to be distinguished clearly from assuming that one is going to try to encompass the whole of human knowledge; that is an ideal which has long gone by the boards. At the beginning of this century, Thomas Wolfe, ravaged with the hunger for knowledge, entered Harvard's Widener Library, which at that time held only a million volumes, and began to read from the first with the hope that he would finish the whole million. Today, surely, we do not think of anything remotely approaching that kind of aim.

But what we do have in mind is the notion that there should be exposure to a range of disciplines, or—addressing the formulation of this problem in C. P. Snow's celebrated book, *The Two Cultures*—to a range of cultures. Even from the perspective of a person who is committed to the concept of a liberal education, it is not critical whether one has studied both chemistry and physics, or whether one is versed in both French and Russian history. What is important is that a person, at some point and at a meaningful level, should come face to face with a scientific discipline, understand the scientific mentality and approach and, on the other hand, that a person at some point should be exposed to the historical sensibility, the sense of history and historical perspective.

This is the first assumption: that a person should be exposed to the range of cultures at a meaningful level.

The second assumption is that, at some point, a person should then zero in on one area and develop the skills and the passion for dealing with that particular area in greater depth. The third assumption posits that one's area of specialization should be dictated by both individual inclinations and the public interest.

I think that if we want to approach the question of spiritual specialization, of determining objectives in one's religious growth, we need to think in somewhat analogous terms. Judging matters from the perspective of one's individual interest, there is much to be said for a "liberal" approach to *avodat Hashem*, meaning that there should be a significant involvement in and exposure to all major areas—Torah, *avoda* and *gemilut chasadim*; and this quite apart from that with regard to which we do not have very much choice, namely, the specific *mitzvot—matza, tzitzit*, etc.—which we are obligated to perform.

Additionally, as the *Rav Av Beit Din* indicated, we must recognize the need, both from a public and a private standpoint, for some degree of more intensive commitment to a particular area. In determining or finding that area, one should factor in both one's individual inclination and the public need.

THE DANGERS OF SPIRITUAL NARROWNESS

Surely, if one were to adopt a degree of specialization which would preclude other major areas of *avodat Hashem*, focusing intensively and exhaustively upon a single area, this would be false to the cardinal message of Judaism, which addresses itself to the whole person and demands, "In *all* your ways, know Him."

For example, important as Torah is, *Chazal* nevertheless note clearly that it is inconceivable that a person should regard the totality of his *avodat Hashem* as being realized through Torah alone. The *gemara* (*Shabbat* 11a) informs us that Rabbi Shimon bar Yochai and his friends, whose "Torah was their trade," would not interrupt their learning for *tefilla* (i.e. to pray *Shemoneh Esrei*). The *gemara* then asks: I understand why he would not interrupt for *tefilla*, since *tefilla* is only rabbinically mandated; but would he interrupt for *Keriat Shema*, which is a Biblical commandment? The *Yerushalmi* (*Shabbat* 1:2) answers that R. Shimon bar Yochai would not interrupt even for *Keriat Shema*. It then asks in amazement: How is this possible? Does not R. Shimon bar Yochai subscribe to the principle that Torah must be learned *al menat la'asot*, in order to be performed? After all, we have learnt that if a person's involvement in learning is devoid of any normative commitment, but is merely stimulated by intellectual curiosity, then better that he had been stillborn! The *Yerushalmi* offers a technical answer, but the formulation of the question is of interest to us.

There is another very telling *gemara* relating to the link between Torah and *gemilut chasadim*, two of the three pillars mentioned earlier:

R. Elazar ben Parta and R. Chanina ben Teradion were caught [by the Romans. They understood that, if they had been jailed, apparently it was a divine punishment.]

R. Elazar ben Parta said to R. Chanina ben Teradion: Fortunate are you, that you have only one sin and I have five.

R. Chanina responded: You are fortunate, for notwithstanding the fact that you have five transgressions, you shall attain salvation; I have been caught because of only one thing, but I shall not be saved. You have engaged both in Torah and in *chesed*, while I have devoted myself to Torah exclusively. [The *gemara* comments:] As R. Huna said, A person who engages in nothing but Torah, it is as if he has no God; as it is written, "And many days passed for Israel without a true God" (*II Divrei Ha-yamim* 15:3). [Apparently, they believed in God, but not a true God. Their *avodat Hashem* was not true.] This refers to one who engages in nothing but Torah; it is as if he does not have a God. (*Avoda Zara* 17b)

The *gemara* teaches us that where *avodat Hashem* is partial, totally oblivious to whole areas of human existence and whole spheres of Torah values, then it is not only partial—it is false. If you have only half, you do not have even that half.

Likewise, *Chazal* say with regard to a person who engages in *avoda* but is oblivious to Torah, "*Lo am ha-aretz chassid*, An ignoramus cannot be pious" (*Avot* 2:5). With the best of intentions and the purest of hearts, nevertheless, there are certain levels of *avodat Hashem* which simply are not attainable if they are not grounded in commitment to Torah, knowledge of Torah and study of Torah. Similarly, if a person engages in *gemilut chasadim* but is oblivious to Torah and *avoda*, he reaches a kind of secular ethic, at best a kind of moralized religion, devoid not only of a sense of the numinous, transcendental presence of God, but devoid also of a sense of what it means to relate to Him at a profound, passionate, experiential level.

If we are to strive for *avodat Hashem* in its totality, we need to realize that what is demanded of us in determining our objectives is the realization that not only the world at large—the macrocosm—stands on the tripod of Torah, *avoda* and *gemilut chasadim*. We need to realize that individual existence too, in order to be true, genuine *avodat Hashem*, needs to be based on the fusion and the fructifying interaction of Torah, *avoda* and *gemilut chasadim*.

THE VARIETY OF RELIGIOUS APPROACHES

At a second level, there is room, perhaps even need, for some measure of specialization. One's area of specialization can be chosen based on the awareness of public need—obviously, a single community does not need ten endocrinologists while it does not have a single heart specialist—and also, to some extent, with an eye to personal inclinations.

Although the Halakha prescribes a certain regimen, it never-theless leaves enormous range for individual perspectives and pri-orities. Within the same world of mitzva observance according to the *Shulchan Arukh*, there is room for a range of religious pos-tures, such as *Mitnagdut* and *Chassidut*, which differ widely in emphasis, spiritual content and a variety of other issues.

Indeed, we find within *Chazal* themselves differences of spiri-tual perspective. The *gemara* (*Rosh Ha-shana* 18a) recounts that while Rabba dealt in Torah, Abbaye dealt in Torah and *gemilut chasadim*. The *gemara* also tells us:

> Rabbi Yehoshua ben Levi would go to comfort mourners only at the home of a person who had died childless, based on the verse (*Yirmiyahu* 22:10): "Cry for him who goes, for he will no longer return to see the land of his birth." (*Mo'ed Katan* 27b)

Rabbi Yehoshua understood this verse as a reference to one who has left behind no progeny. Another *gemara* records:

> Rava noticed that Rav Hamnuna took a long time in his prayers. [Rava] said: He leaves [Torah, which is] eternal life, and spends his time engaging in temporal life. (*Shabbat* 10a)

Apparently, Rava understood that Rav Hamnuna's prayer was lengthy because of the element of *bakasha*, in which we petition God for our mundane needs. Rava was critical of this; he believed one should pray more briefly and get on with the business of *tal-mud Torah*. The *gemara* continues,

> But Rav Hamnuna felt that Torah has its time, and prayer has its time.

Clearly, Rava and Rav Hamnuna present two different perspec-tives with respect to the optimal division between Torah and *tefilla*.

Two Caveats

While allowing for a certain division of labor, there are several elements we need to bear in mind. Firstly, if a person accepts the notion of division and decides to focus upon a particular area, this must not be done out of a sense that other areas of *avodat Hashem* are insignificant. Nor must it give rise to the notion that those who devote themselves to other areas are second-class *ovdei Hashem*. Rather, one's decision to specialize in a particular area must proceed from a recognition that all areas are important, but since I cannot practically devote myself to all of them in equal proportions, I therefore choose to focus upon only some. This is not to say that there cannot be a hierarchy within the world of *avodat Hashem*. However, a hierarchy need not deny the significance of other areas within which one is unable or unwilling to specialize.

Secondly, a person must understand that even if he specializes in a given area, nevertheless, the sense of a liberal *avodat Hashem*, whereby there is some involvement at a significant level in other areas, is central to the religious life as Judaism has understood it.

Regarding R. Chanina ben Teradion, the above-quoted *gemara* continues:

What do you mean? Did R. Chanina ben Teradion indeed divest himself completely of any interest in *gemilut chasadim*? But we learned: R. Eliezer ben Ya'akov says that a person should not give money to charity unless he knows that the trustee is as honest as R. Chanina ben Teradion. [Thus, we see that he was a trustee of public property. Then the *gemara* suggests:] Perhaps he was a trustee but was not actively engaged. [The *gemara* answers: No,] we learned that R. Chanina ben Teradion said that one time he had money designated for the Purim feast, and he inadvertently gave it to the poor to be used for other purposes. [The *gemara* answers:] Of course he was actively engaged in *gemilut chasadim*, but not at the level which was requisite for a person of his stature (*ke-de-ba'i lei lo avad*). (*Avoda Zara* 17b)

If one thinks of the range of *avodat Hashem*—running the gamut of Torah, *avoda* and *gemilut chasadim*—then one is to think not of a rudimentary level of engagement, but rather of a significant involvement, "as is requisite."

DIFFERENT STAGES OF LIFE

Now, of course, that multiple involvement can for practical purposes change from one period to another. A person cannot devote himself to all aspects of *avodat Hashem*, simultaneously, with equal vigor. Sometimes it is entirely conceivable that whole periods of his life may be devoted primarily to one aspect, to the neglect of others.

In the previously-mentioned responsum of R. Chayim *Or Zaru'a* (#183), he makes a fairly radical statement. In general, there is a question as to whether the concept of "*Ha-osek be-mitzva patur min ha-mitzva*" applies to the study of Torah. Assuming that it does, he cites the *gemara* (*Sukka* 26a) that says that when R. Chisda and Rabba bar R. Hunna were en route to learn Torah from their teacher, they regarded themselves as being exempt from the mitzva of *sukka*. Even though it may have taken them several weeks to get there, they nevertheless applied the principle of "*Ha-osek be-mitzva patur min ha-mitzva*." Similarly, R. Chayim *Or Zaru'a* says, students are exempt from *mitzvot* the entire period they are "in their teacher's house." To translate this into contemporary terms: During the entire period of a student's sojourn in *yeshiva* or *kollel*, he is exempt from all other *mitzvot*!

Surely, this is a radical statement; but putting aside its practical implications, it should not be regarded as being at loggerheads with the position I suggested before. When they are "in their teacher's house," the students should indeed devote themselves—in the radical sense of R. Chayim *Or Zaru'a*—exclusively to Torah, to the point that they are exempt from other *mitzvot*. If we wish to moderate this position, we nevertheless may say that during a certain period of their lives, they need to concentrate upon *talmud Torah*, possibly to the neglect of certain other areas, such as *gemilut chasadim*.

However, from an educational and ultimately from a moral and spiritual point of view, it is critical that the focus upon the particular area of Torah be done not out of the sense that other areas are unimportant. Rather, it must proceed from a sense that during a particular phase of life, a person needs to focus upon one thing, and other equally important elements need to wait their turn. However, within the total configuration of one's spiritual universe, and therefore within the range of one's spiritual activity as viewed across the space of a lifetime, one must realize the need for the integration and fusion of various elements.

No Single Solution

B en Azzai, who never married due to his intense commitment to Torah, is a radical example, and an example singled out as being feasible or desirable only for a very few. But the ability to postpone marriage in order to learn Torah appears in the Rambam as the accepted ruling (*Hilkhot Talmud Torah* 1:5). Of course, this kind of approach is merely that—an approach. It does not enable us to do that which, in my experience, students so desire, namely, to formulate in clearly defined terms exactly what and how much to do in this area or that.

There is a very telling remark in the Rosh with regard to the ruling that a person may postpone marriage in order to learn (*Kiddushin* 29b). The Rosh says (*Kiddushin* 1:42): "It is not defined how long [a person may postpone marriage], and I do not know." Obviously, it cannot be postponed over the span of a lifetime—that is only for a rare individual such as Ben Azzai. So for how long? Should one wait the way the Mirrer *yeshiva bachurim* used to, until they were close to forty? Or until the *mishna*'s recommended age of eighteen? Or somewhere in the middle? This kind of dilemma—which is, as the Rosh says, undefined—confronts us as individuals and as a community.

I do not believe we should be looking for a single, clear solution, which can be applied uniformly across the board. Uniformity in this case is neither attainable nor desirable. The mix of Torah, *avoda* and *gemilut chasadim* is one which is to be individually conceived and perceived, in one proportion for one individual and in a different proportion for another.

There is a marvelous essay in F. H. Bradley's *Ethical Studies* entitled, "My Station and Its Duties." Bradley speaks there of the fact that a person's historical situation is one which has a direct bearing upon his ethical duty. One cannot speak of ethical duty simply in terms of abstractions, certainly not if one is dealing with the question of priorities or the relationship between different values. There are times when one need is urgent and another less pressing, and situations when the reverse is true.

In summary, I do not think we should be looking for a single solution, but I feel we do need to adopt an approach which maintains an awareness of the need for the richness of a full spiritual life, while also being aware of the need for intensity in some aspect of *avodat Hashem*. Then we must grapple as best as we can with the question of how to determine—with an eye toward both our own needs and general needs—the proper mixture between the various components within a given situation.

Within the context of his spiritual existence, a person faces fundamentally two tasks. One is to mold himself as an individual, to "prepare himself within the anteroom, so that he can then enter the inner chamber" (*Avot* 4:17). Second, a person is given the task of trying, to some extent and within the limits of his ability, to move, to prod, to change the historical scene within which he finds himself. He should try to see to it that the world he leaves behind be a little bit better, just a bit closer to the fulfillment of the great spiritual and historical vision of the messianic era than it was when he entered it.

In trying to determine the course of one's spiritual growth, a person needs to bear in mind the objectives relevant to it, with an eye to the fusion of those two elements: to grow personally, while contributing generally. In that way, he or she must strive for the interaction of Torah, *avoda* and *gemilut chasadim*, while trying at the same time to grow and contribute on a personal level.

CHAPTER SIX

Being *Frum* and Being Good: On the Relationship Between Religion and Morality

PART 1:
God's Will and the Good

How are we to understand the relationship between being *frum* and being good? The answer depends, of course, on how we understand these two terms.

Popularly or sociologically defined, *frumkeit* (loosely, "religiosity") and goodness are neither quite the same nor opposed. We all know people who are absolute *apikorsim* (disbelievers) and whom we would nevertheless define as being "good" by virtue of their high moral standards. Conversely, we also unfortunately know others whom we would surely designate as *frum* (observant)—they keep *Shabbat* and are scrupulous in their *kashrut*—but who are nevertheless ruthless or dishonest in personal and commercial relations. That, of course, hardly fits our conception of goodness. So, although popularly defined, these two terms are simply independent of one another, we are concerned with philosophical rather than sociological definitions, and on that level the relation between these two terms is less certain.

DEFINING GOODNESS

Let us begin therefore with definition. Both our referents, *frumkeit* and goodness, have historically been exhaustively analyzed. In the twentieth century in particular, a whole litera-ture—largely fathered by G.E. Moore's *Principia Ethica* at the turn of the century and subsequently stimulated by the school of linguistic analysis—has sought to explore and define what is "the good." For our purposes, we need not enter into the minutiae of this discussion, other than to stress a cardinal, albeit possibly obvi-ous point: the term "good" has both a functional, pragmatic sense and a moral, axiological sense. On the one hand, it relates to the effectiveness of an object or a person; on the other hand, to its value. We may, for instance, speak of a "good" pistol which can shoot to kill efficiently, and therefore can be employed very effec-tively for implementing evil purposes. And straddling both spheres, the functional and the moral, there is also an aesthetic sense.

Thus, to look back at *Parashat Bereishit* (2:9), we hear first of a fruit which is *tov le-ma'akhal*, good for eating in a pragmatic sense; surely there is no moral attribute attached to that. Subsequently, we hear of *etz ha-da'at tov va-ra*, the tree of knowl-edge of good and evil, where the moral sense is intended. In cer-tain verses, the meaning may be ambiguous or multiple—for instance, "*Lo tov heyot ha-adam levado*, It is not good for man to be alone" (*ibid.* 2:18). My understanding of the intent of this verse is that it is neither good psychologically nor good morally.

In our context, while being mindful of the various senses of the word, we shall be focusing primarily and directly upon the moral sense. That is, we shall try to define what we understand by a "good" person and how we relate to him or her (not in the functional sense of a "good" parent or a "good" citizen). We understand goodness to be that which is intrinsically morally good; not something which factually is desired, but something inherently valuable and desirable.

Defining *Frumkeit*

Likewise, the term "*frumkeit*" or "religion" has to be thoroughly analyzed. Here, too, for our purposes I will content myself with a general concept. But even in dealing with very general terms, we surely need to differentiate between several strands. The term signifies first an existential and experiential connection to God—*emuna* (faith), and beyond that, *yira, ahava, deveikut* (fear, love, cleaving). Second, and this is particularly true within a Jewish and halakhic context, that relation to God needs to translate into an obedient and obeisant response to His normative demands. The interrelation between these two elements as being part of a single concept is made very clear in the verse in *Ekev*:

> And now, O Israel, what does the Lord your God demand of you? Only this: to fear the Lord your God, to walk in all His paths, to love Him, and to serve the Lord your God with all your heart and soul; to keep the Lord's commandments and laws, which I enjoin upon you today, for your good. (*Devarim* 10:12)

The *gemara* understands from this verse that God has one fundamental demand of us: *yirat Shamayim* (fear of Heaven).

> Rav Yochanan said in the name of Rabbi Elazar: God has in this world fear of Heaven alone, as it says, "And now, O Israel, what does the Lord your God demand of you? Only this: to fear the Lord your God, etc." It is further written (*Iyyov* 28:28), "Indeed (*hen*), fear of God is wisdom," and in Greek "*hen*" means "one." (*Shabbat* 31b)

Although the *gemara* says we are dealing with a single entity, the verse seems to specify a whole list of demands: fear of God, walking in His paths, love, service, keeping His commandments. The reason for this is that fundamentally we can speak of one category, but one which then has several components. These components break down into the two elements that I mentioned earlier:

the existential, experiential relationship to God (love and fear), and the response to God's commands (keeping His *mitzvot*). The latter takes place both in broader terms ("walking in all His paths and serving Him") and in the specific details of Halakha ("to keep the Lord's commandments and laws, which I enjoin upon you today").

For us, it is the combination of these two elements which constitutes *frumkeit*. In the famous penultimate verse in *Kohelet*, we again find a single focus on the conjunction of these two elements:

> The sum of the matter, when all is said and done: Fear God and observe all His commandments, for this is the whole of man. (*Kohelet* 12:13)

Both the inner and outer responses to God's normative demands, their acceptance and implementation, are central. "Nullify your will before His will" (*Avot* 2:4), both inwardly and in terms of practice. The move from an anthropocentric to a theocentric existence is the essence of halakhic living. As the Torah, particularly in *Sefer Devarim*, repeatedly emphasizes, the central category of Judaism is mitzva. As we discussed in an earlier chapter, religious human existence, not to mention Jewish existence, begins with the verse (*Bereishit* 2:16): "*Va-yetzav Hashem E-lokim al ha-adam*, And the Lord God commanded the man." *Frumkeit* for us surely does not exhaust itself in an emotional experience, but also responds to a divine call and transcendental demands.

THE CENTRALITY OF COMMANDMENT

Moreover, for us, God's normative commandment frames the totality of our existence, even with respect to presumably "neutral" areas. I think that it is in this vein that the first commandment to Adam is to be understood. There is something strange about the formulation,

Of every tree of the garden you are free to eat; but as for the tree of the knowledge of good and evil, you must not eat of it. . . (*Bereishit* 2:16-17)

We might have expected the verse to impose certain limitations upon man, to command him merely not to eat of the tree of knowledge. He had been told a long time ago that he could eat from the rest of the trees. So why repeat this permission here—is there a mitzva to eat from the other trees?

I think that the point here is very clear. The Torah is telling us that the moment that the category of commandment appears as an essential component of human existence and experience, this fact has implications not only for *devar ha-mitzva* (obligatory actions or prohibitions), but also for *devar ha-reshut* (non-obligatory actions). So long as man does not live under the impact of "*va-yetzav*," all his actions are the product of absolute freedom (understood as taking what one likes). But the moment the category of "*va-yetzav*" presents itself, it then defines man's existence not only within the parameters of a particular commandment, but within the totality of his existence. Once there is a "*va-yetzav*," then when one imbibes of the *devar reshut*, that too becomes an act of moral choice. One now needs to ask himself: Is this particular action a *devar reshut* or does it fall under the *tzav*; is it subject to individual choice or to a divine command?

In other words, the "*va-yetzav*" addresses itself not only to the tree of knowledge, but rather to all the trees of the garden. The fact that we live, in Milton's phrase, "as ever in my great Taskmaster's eye," constantly under *tzav*, is to us the central, cardinal fact of our existence as a whole. This is what we are to understand by *frumkeit* specifically: "*Be-khol derakhekha da'e-hu*"—Know God in *all* your actions.

SOCRATES' QUESTION

However, to understand *frumkeit* in these terms, as a single concept with two components, as the abnegation of our will in response to our acceptance of God's normative will—this only begs the question. At the heart of the problem of the relationship between *frumkeit* and goodness, or, if you will, between religion and morality, lies the question which Socrates poses to Euthyphro. In trying to define piety, Euthyphro explains that piety is that which the gods want us to do. Socrates then asks him whether the gods love piety because it is pious, or is it pious because they love it? We can reframe the question with God, *le-havdil*, in the singular.

Are we to understand the content, value and significance of mitzva, of "the good," as simply deriving from the fact that God wants it? He may wish it for purely arbitrary reasons guided by no criteria, bound by no standards, impelled by no reasons. Or do we believe that there is some antecedent reason inherent in a particular phenomenon which "leads" or "impels" God to decide upon it? Are we to understand that, at the Divine level, there is a kind of moral relativism where everything is equally good or bad and God has chosen between them arbitrarily? Or do we believe that His will is not purely arbitrary, but rather guided by certain standards, and God has commanded us based on these criteria?

This question has been the subject of protracted and at times intensive controversy throughout the history of Western thought. In medieval times, William of Ockham championed the voluntarist position, namely, that God's will is indeed boundless and limitless, and that nothing is either good or bad but God's wishing makes it so. In contrast, Aquinas contended that there are inherent truths and values which are to be found in certain phenomena and that these are the subject of God's choice, not by accident but by dint of their very being.

Similar controversies are to be found subsequently in the seventeenth century, not only at the moral level but at the level of fact. Descartes, for instance, contended that had God so desired, two times two would not have equaled four. What we have here essentially is a conflict between two fundamental tendencies which, to a great extent, are rooted in different conceptions of God.

THE POWER AND THE BEAUTY: TWO CONCEPTIONS OF GOD

The verse says (*Tehillim* 29:4), "*Kol Hashem ba-ko'ach; kol Hashem be-hadar*—The voice of God is power; the voice of God is splendor." We perceive God in one sense as boundless, unbridled power. In another sense, we perceive Him in terms of values, of truth and goodness. To the extent that our perception of God and our relation to Him is primarily in terms of power, then surely we will regard as anathema the notion that somehow His will is guided or impelled. The sense of power is most keenly felt precisely when it is arbitrarily exercised, when one need not answer to any kind of standard, when nothing but sheer will is being expressed.

On the other hand, one thinks in terms of "*Kol Hashem be-hadar.*" *Hadar* is presumably some kind of objective beauty, a moral beauty, a beauty of truth. If so, then one is appalled at the thought God could have commanded to kill as easily as He commanded not to kill.

Those who indeed relate to God primarily out of a sense of His awesome power and their own weakness and impotence, are perhaps likely to move in the direction of the voluntarist position. On the other hand, those who take a more rational and moral position contend that rationality and goodness are part of God's very essence. It is true, therefore, that certain things are simply inconceivable for Him; but this is not an external constraint, and therefore we need not be shaken by the thought that somehow His power is not boundless.

GOD'S MORAL ESSENCE

If the issues, as I have said, have been subject to protracted controversy—one writer once described the answer as being the line which divides Eastern from Western religious thought—I think that the Jewish position is absolutely unequivocal. We indeed hold that God's will, His Being, is moral and rational; that He does act, and will, in accordance with certain standards. By virtue of His very essence, certain things not only shall not but cannot be willed by Him. God and moral evil are simply and purely incompatible.

Chabakuk (1:13) describes God as, "You whose eyes are too pure to look upon evil, who cannot countenance wrongdoing." But why wait until Chabakuk? The Torah itself states (*Devarim* 32:4): "A faithful God, never false, true and upright is He." Indeed, this position had already been assumed by Avraham. One of the seventeenth-century Cambridge Platonists, Benjamin Whichcote, pointed out that when Avraham questioned God (in his pleading against the destruction of Sodom), "Shall not the Judge of all the earth deal justly?" (*Bereishit* 18:25), this implied that there is a standard of justice to which God, *ki-veyakhol,* can be held accountable. One can ask: Is God's plan regarding Sodom compatible with justice? This position is likewise implicit in the recurrent formulations of the problem of *tzaddik ve-ra lo, rasha ve-tov lo,* the suffering of the righteous and prosperity of the wicked.

If we move from morality to the related sphere of rationality, these limits (so to speak) upon God's will are the basis of the persistent quest for *ta'amei ha-mitzvot* (reasons for the commandments) chronicled in Yitzchak Heinemann's book, *Ta'amei Ha-mitzvot Be-sifrut Yisrael.* The controversy over *ta'amei ha-mitzvot* has centered upon the legitimacy and advisability of our seeking and suggesting reasons, and not upon their very existence. The *Gemara* (*Sanhedrin* 21b) asks: Why were the reasons for the Torah not revealed? Because once they are revealed, there is a risk that someone will think he can transgress the commandment without violating the reason behind it. The Ramban was very emphatic with regard to this point:

> The intention of the Rabbis [in defining *chukkim* as divine decrees for which there is no reason] was not that these are decrees of the King of Kings for which there are no reasons whatever, "for every word of God is pure" (*Mishlei* 30:5). [Rather, they meant] only that *chukkim* are like the enactments which a king promulgates for his kingdom without revealing their benefits to the people, and the people, not sensing these reasons, entertain questions about them in their hearts but they accept them nonetheless out of fear of the government. Similarly, the *chukkim* of the Holy One, blessed be He, are His secrets in the Torah, which the people by means of their thinking do not grasp as they do in the case of *mishpatim* (laws whose rationale is more apparent). Yet they all have a proper reason and perfect benefit. (Commentary on the Torah, *Vayikra* 19:19)

THE VALUE OF OBEDIENCE

To be sure, if we are dealing with *ta'amei ha-mitzvot*, it is conceivable that another factor comes into play. Perhaps the rationality of the commandment need not relate to the inherent value and significance of a particular *tzav*. The *midrash* relates:

> What does it matter to the Holy One, blessed be He, whether we slaughter an animal from the front of the neck or its back? Rather, the *mitzvot* were given in order to purify mankind. (*Bereishit Rabba* 44:1)

The Rambam (*Guide of the Perplexed* III:26) takes this to mean that we cannot understand the reasons for the *details* of the commandments, and perhaps there are no reasons for these. Why is *shechita* (slaughtering) from the front of the neck, and *melika* (a method of killing birds for sacrifices) from the back? As opposed to the kabbalists, the Rambam takes the position that the details of *mitzvot* perhaps have no inherent significance. It could have been just the reverse. (See Ramban, *Devarim* 22:6, for an opposing view.) But even for the Rambam, this does not mean that the concept of *shechita* per se or *melika* per se has no reason.

One might go beyond this and assume that inherently a particular mitzva does not have a reason, but it is still meaningful. Let me quote you a passage from a very fine little book by C.S. Lewis, *The Problem of Pain*:

> It has sometimes been asked whether God commands certain things because they are right, or whether certain things are right because God commands them. With Hooker [a late sixteenth-century Anglican theologian], and against Dr. Johnson, I emphatically embrace the first alternative. The second might lead to the abominable conclusion (reached, I think, by Paley [late eighteenth-century]) that charity is good only because God arbitrarily commanded it—that He might equally well have commanded us to hate Him and one another and that hatred would then have been right. I believe, on the contrary, that [quoting Hooker], "they err who think that of the will of God to do this or that there is no reason besides His will." God's will is determined by His wisdom which always perceives, and His goodness which always embraces, the intrinsically good. But when we have said that God commands things only because they are good, we must add that one of the things intrinsically good is that rational creatures should freely surrender themselves to their Creator in obedience. The content of our obedience—the thing we are com-

manded to do—will always be something intrinsically good, something we ought to do even if (by an impossible supposition) God had not commanded it. But in addition to the content, the mere obeying is also intrinsically good, for, in obeying, a rational creature consciously enacts its creaturely role, reverses the act by which we fell, treads Adam's dance backward, and returns. (p.100)

I think one can go beyond Lewis and suggest that since, as he correctly points out, one of the things which is intrinsically good is that a person accustom himself to obeying God, perhaps certain things might have been commanded simply in order to drill the habit into us. In fact, perhaps things were commanded precisely because there is no apparent reason for them, and therefore the habit of obedience is ingrained all the more deeply, to the extent that no reason is perceived. To what can this be compared? A sergeant in the army sometimes puts his soldiers through certain drills precisely to ingrain in them the habit of obeying a commander. He orders them to do things for which there is no apparent reason, and for which indeed there is no reason other than the fact that they develop a habit. This is not equivalent to adopting the voluntarist position. It is simply an expansion of the notion of what we are to understand by that which is intrinsically valuable and desirable.

Now, if we understand that God's will and His *mitzvot* are grounded in goodness, rationality and morality, then if we also submit that *frumkeit* means doing God's will, and that goodness is an integral component of that will—then of course ideal and comprehensive *frumkeit* includes goodness. It is not synonymous with goodness; it includes it, it comprehends it. To us, certainly, this is a *davar pashut*, a simple, obvious matter.

PART 2:
Frumkeit Devoid of Goodness

Although this may be true theoretically, *frumkeit* is, of course, never ideal or comprehensive. We still need to ask ourselves, both philosophically and educationally: How do we regard a *frumkeit* devoid of goodness? Does it exist? Does it have merit?

TZADDIK RA, RASHA TOV

Presumably, the humanist or moralist in us is inclined to hasten to reply, "*Frumkeit* without goodness is worthless! Can someone see himself as relating only to one area of *avodat Hashem* (divine service)? He follows the dictates only of *bein adam la-Makom* (*mitzvot* between man and God) but not *bein adam le-chavero* (interpersonal *mitzvot*)? What kind of *frumkeit* is that!?"

But before we hasten to let the moralist and the humanist in us answer, as *benei Torah* we need to confront the following *gemara*:

> Said Rava: Rav Idi explained this verse to me, "Say of the righteous, when he is good, that they shall eat the fruit of their doings" (*Yeshayahu* 3:10). Is there then a righteous man who is good and a righteous man who is not good? Rather [explain thus:] He who is good to Heaven and good to man, he is a righteous man who is good; good to Heaven but not good to man, he is a righteous man who is not good. Similarly we read, "Woe unto the wicked [man who is] evil; for the reward of his hands will be given unto him" (*ibid.* 3:11): Is there then a wicked man who is evil and a wicked man who is not evil? Rather [explain thus:] He who is evil to Heaven and evil to man, he is a wicked man who is evil; he who is evil to Heaven but not evil to man, he is a wicked man who is not evil. (*Kiddushin* 40a)

The *gemara* here apparently understands that the terms *tzaddik* and *rasha* (righteous and wicked) are defined by a person's conduct with respect to the area *bein adam la-Makom*. Whether he is *tov* or *ra* (good or evil) is a function of his conduct in the area of *bein adam le-chavero*. One can therefore be a *tzaddik ra* and a *rasha tov*.

"THOUGH YOU PRAY AT LENGTH, I WILL NOT LISTEN"

Nevertheless, I do not think that our instincts are all that wrong. Moreover, they are not just our instincts. It is not just the humanist in us which somehow rises against the possibility of *frumkeit* which is antithetical to and devoid of goodness. From where did Western culture absorb the cardinal truth that *frumkeit* without goodness is meaningless and at times worse, if not from Judaism? We all know the famous words of the prophet Yeshayahu:

> What need have I of all your sacrifices? says the Lord. I am sated with burnt offerings of rams, and suet of fatlings, and blood of bulls; and I have no delight in lambs and he-goats. When you come to appear before Me—who asked this of you, to trample My courts? Cease bringing futile oblations; your incense is offensive to Me. New moon and Sabbath, proclaiming of solemnities, assemblies with iniquity, I cannot abide. Your new moons and fixed seasons fill Me with loathing; they have become a burden to Me, I cannot endure them. And when you lift up your hands, I will turn My eyes away from you; though you pray at length, I will not listen, for your hands are stained with blood. Wash yourselves clean; put your evil things away from My sight! Cease to do evil; learn to do good. Devote yourselves to justice; aid the wronged. Uphold the rights of the orphan; defend the cause of the widow! (*Yeshayahu* 1:11-17)

This is the prophet's message. To be sure, these verses focus primarily upon *avoda*: sacrifices, prayer, the Temple service. When these are attempted by a person devoid of goodness, they are particularly problematic, inasmuch as they entail an audacious advance towards God, an attempt at a rendezvous with Him. Here the governing principle is, "One may not approach the king's gate in sackcloth" (*Esther* 4:2), actual or figurative. To the extent that one penetrates (so to speak) God's domain, one must be not only physically but also morally pure: "Prepare for your God, Israel" (*Amos* 4:12)—not only in terms of clothing and physical purification, but in terms of one's inner being. Hence, we encounter in a particularly sharp form the revulsion against *avoda* which is unaccompanied by inner purity: "The offering of evildoers is an abomination" (*Mishlei* 21:27). With regard also to prayer, there is a concept of *to'eva* (abomination), a term which is not equally applicable to other *mitzvot*.

Nevertheless, the conjunction of *frumkeit* and goodness, the sense that goodness is both a component and a condition of *frumkeit*, does surely apply to other *mitzvot* as well. There is another chapter in Yeshayahu, which we read on Yom Kippur:

> Is such the fast I desire, a day for men to starve their bodies? Is it bowing the head like a bulrush and lying in sackcloth and ashes? Do you call that a fast, a day when the Lord is favorable? No, this is the fast I desire: to unlock the shackles of wickedness and untie the cords of the yoke, to let the oppressed go free and to break off every yoke. It is to share your bread with the hungry, and to take the wretched poor into your home; when you see the naked, to clothe him, and not to ignore your own kin. (*Yeshayahu* 58:5-7)

"His *Mitzvot* are Thrown Back in his Face"

The Rambam develops the notion that when a person lacks moral consistency, then beyond a certain point one cannot see him simply as observing half of Torah but missing the other half (i.e. being *frum* but having no goodness), but in fact the absence of one component totally invalidates his performance of the other component:

> How exalted is the level of repentance! Only yesterday, this [sinner] was divided from God, the Lord of Israel, as it is written (*Yeshayahu* 59:2), "Your sins were dividing between you and your God." He would call out [to God] without being answered, as it says (*ibid.* 1:15), "Though you pray at length, I will not listen." He would perform *mitzvot*, only to have them thrown back in his face, as it says (*ibid.* 1:12), "Who asked this of you, to trample My courts?" and it says (*Malakhi* 1:10), "O that there were one among you who would shut the doors [that you might not kindle fire on My altar for no reason! I have no pleasure in you, says the Lord of Hosts, nor will I accept an offering from your hand]." Today, [after having repented,] he clings to the Divine Presence, as it is written (*Devarim* 4:4), "And you who cling to the Lord, your God." He calls out [to God] and is answered immediately, etc. (*Hilkhot Teshuva* 7:7)

There is a certain situation wherein a person performs *mitzvot* and they are thrown back in his face. How are we to regard the person who relates solely to the area of *bein adam la-Makom* and is totally oblivious to the area of *bein adam le-chavero*? Is he not separated from God, the Lord of Israel?

I do not want to get involved in the question, which we ought certainly to avoid, of the respective importance of *bein adam la-Makom* versus *bein adam le-chavero*. (Although if we got involved in that issue, we might look at the Rosh in the beginning of *Pe'a* who says that *bein adam le-chavero* is more important.) Regardless of that question, it seems inconceivable that a person who is lacking a whole area of *mitzvot* would not be regarded as being separated from God. But the question persists. How do we resolve the inherent contradiction between the *gemara* in *Kiddushin*, on the one hand, and the verses in *Yeshayahu* and the evident extension of them by the Rambam, on the other?

ACTIVE EVIL AND OBLIVIOUSNESS

I think that we have to distinguish between two kinds of obliviousness or insensitivity to the area of *bein adam le-chavero*. I find it inconceivable from a Jewish perspective to refer to a person as a *tzaddik*, albeit a *tzaddik ra*, if he is *mehader* (excessive) in the area of *bein adam la-Makom*—he has *Rabbeinu Tam tefillin, kaful shemoneh tzitzit* (ritual objects conforming to stringent opinions) and eats only hand-baked matza and *glatt* meat—but within the area of *bein adam le-chavero* he tramples everything underfoot. Is it really possible that a person who is a thief, murderer, liar and cheat can be described as a *tzaddik* (but a *tzaddik ra*) all because he has fancy *tefillin*?

I think the *gemara* in *Kiddushin* is referring to something else: not a person who tramples underfoot the whole area of *bein adam le-chavero*, but a person who is simply oblivious to it. He pours his energies into and concentrates upon the area of *bein adam la-Makom* to such an extent that he has neither the energy, resources, nor motivation to work within the area of *bein adam le-chavero* as well. It is in this sense that he is *ra la-beriyot* (evil to mankind). He does nothing for them. He has no social conscience and is insensitive to the needs of others. He is totally concerned with the area of being *tov la-Shamayim* (good to Heaven).

This person represents a partial and limited *frumkeit*, but a legitimate *frumkeit*. This is not to say that it is in any sense ideal, nor is it recommended. After all, we need to strive not only to be *tzaddikim* but *tzaddikim tovim*. But, insofar as it goes, it is legitimate and real. Were a person, however, to be evil in an active sense—he wrongs others, injures them knowingly, willfully, viciously—then he surely could not be defined as a *tzaddik* in any sense, and of him it is said that his *mitzvot* "are thrown back in his face." He buys *Rabbeinu Tam tefillin* and he has *kaful shemoneh tzitzit*, "and they are thrown back in his face."

I believe that one point should be added. I have distinguished here between a kind of *aseh ra* (actively doing evil) and an insensitivity to the area of good and evil. I believe that there is a level of insensitivity, of egocentric religiosity, of concern and involvement solely with oneself and with what one understands to be one's relationship to God, at which the obliviousness to others becomes so complete that passive insensitivity translates into a kind of active evil. There are areas in Halakha where a specific demand is made to do something, and where passively not doing anything is conceived as being a positive evil: "Do not stand by your brother's blood" (*Vayikra* 19:16); "You may not ignore it" (with regard to returning lost objects—*Devarim* 22:3). The rabbis extended this concept to other areas. To take one radical example, Ben Azzai says (*Yevamot* 63b) that whoever can have children and does not—he is like one who sheds blood, a murderer. He could have built, and he didn't. So there is, I believe, a level of inactivity and insensitivity at which one's mere passive absence is in itself a positive evil. I do not want now to offer any suggestions regarding where that line is to be drawn. I do believe, however, that in principle this is the case.

INTERIM SUMMARY

Thus, we need to strive first for *frumkeit* in its totality, and that of course means *frumkeit* including goodness—a goodness which, I repeat, is not synonymous with *frumkeit* but included within it. We need to strive for both components of that *frumkeit*, "Fear God and keep His commandments," but of course by way of understanding its scope. Our aim, both for ourselves and for our children and students, is to be formulated in terms of the *gemara* in *Shabbat* (31b): the central, overriding aim is *yirat Shamayim*, and all other values are constituent elements within it. There is educational merit in understanding that indeed there is an *unum necessarium*, one thing necessary, and this is *yirat Shamayim*. But we must simultaneously recognize that inasmuch as moral goodness is part of God's will, and inasmuch as *yirat Shamayim* means accepting and responding to His will, then moral goodness is part of what we understand by *yirat Shamayim* and part of what we strive for when we talk about *frumkeit*.

Nevertheless, while this aim can be easily stated, (a) its implementation is very difficult, and (b) there are a number of educational and philosophic problems which arise. Therefore, I now want to focus on those problems which I believe have specific and immediate educational ramifications.

PART 3:
Goodness Devoid of *Frumkeit*

"WITHOUT GOD, EVERYTHING IS LAWFUL"

We spoke previously of the problem of *frumkeit* devoid of goodness. Now I would like to address the reverse phenomenon: How do we relate—personally, philosophically, professionally—to goodness devoid of *frumkeit*, to a secular moral idealism?

Of course, some people question whether such a phenomenon can even exist. They argue that morality without religion is simply inconceivable, a position succinctly summarized by Ivan Karamazov (in Dostoyevsky's novel): "Without God, everything is lawful." This claim is made on a philosophical plane. Others, however, argue from a practical standpoint: even if, conceptually, goodness can exist independently of a religious outlook, on a practical level a person or a society can arrive at morality only through religion.

Regarding the philosophical argument, it is perhaps true that a strong case can be made for the notion that without God everything is lawful. First, one could argue that the substance of morality derives only from God's will; but we have already discussed this position and have established that Judaism rejects it. Alternatively, one could contend that objective goodness can exist only within a universe where one postulates the existence of God and the existence of man as a spiritual being. If one were to think only in secular terms, regarding man as nothing more than "a kind of combination of carbon and water" (in Bertrand Russell's phrase), then in such a universe there cannot be any good or bad because there is no ultimate end or purpose for man.

But even if one were to concur with this philosophical argument, can we factually deny that there exist people who are totally removed from religion yet nonetheless act in accordance with high moral standards? Perhaps they are logically inconsistent; perhaps if they were deeper philosophers, they would be worse people. Yet they regard themselves, and we would regard them too, as moral individuals. We cannot be oblivious to the existence of this phenomenon. How, then, do we relate to it?

IMMORAL REJOICING

Before answering this question, I would like to address the above-mentioned claim that religion is necessary in order to arrive at morality. This argument has been advanced frequently in the modern period. It is a reflection of the secularization of modern culture that religion needs to be sold to masses on the basis of its contribution to morality. In eighteenth-century England, the novelist Henry Fielding advanced this claim; in the nineteenth century, Cardinal Newman rejected it precisely because he said it was a debasement of religion: you are basing religion's legitimacy purely upon its moral significance.

Nonetheless, I encounter this argument all the time in Israel among religious educators. In order to impress upon everyone the importance of religious education, they enumerate its benefits to society. "Do you want people to be loyal citizens? Make them religious. Do you want them to be honest? Make them religious. Do you want them to have a sense of purpose in life? Make them religious." Whenever new statistics are published about the degree of sexual licentiousness or drug addiction or some other kind of delinquency within the secular schools, even within the elite schools, there is jubilation among these educators. (This is akin to the rejoicing you encounter among certain staunch advocates of *aliya* every time they read about a murder in Brooklyn or Long Beach; they make sure to republish it in their newspaper in large type.) Brandishing these statistics, they argue: "Do you see what happens in your secular education? You get drug addicts; you get thieves; you get young people stabbing each other. If you want the stabbing and the drug addiction to stop—send the kids to us and we will make *menschen* out of them."

Let me make it clear that we must categorically reject this attitude. Is this what we want? Should we be happy every time a higher degree of corruption and greater depths of delinquency are discovered in some secular school!? Who are those delinquents? Our brothers! In order to score points and to increase registration at our religious schools, are we to gloat that the system of secular education is presumably crumbling? That it no longer turns out idealists? That it only produces pragmatists? We should weep!

Thus, returning to our original question, we surely should not dismiss nor denigrate moral idealism simply because it springs (in certain cases) from secular sources. Certainly, we believe deeply that a moral idealist would be at a much higher level were his morality rooted in *yirat Shamayim*, were it grounded in a perception of his relation to God and of the nature of a man as a respondent and obedient being. But that surely is not to say that we therefore ought to dismiss totally the possibility or the reality of secular morality. First, we should not do this because it is simply untrue— there are genuinely moral people within the secular community. Second, we ought not do this because, after all, the results are not what we should be seeking. Whether we score points here or there is not crucial. In the process of "scoring points," we increase *sinat achim* (fraternal hatred), we sharpen divisions, we heighten tensions; and that is, in and of itself, a moral and ethical problem.

PART 4:
Conflicts Between Religion and Morality

"THE DUNGHILL OF MORALITY"

Having addressed the phenomena of *frumkeit* devoid of goodness and of goodness devoid of *frumkeit*, I would like to move on to the next issue. I emphasized before that *frumkeit* and goodness are not synonymous; rather, goodness is ideally to be included within *frumkeit*. But if they are not to be regarded as synonymous, is there a possibility that *frumkeit* and goodness can sometimes be antonymous?

There is such a possibility, and we should confront it. At one level, there is a question as to whether the quest for morality somehow conflicts with one's religious commitment. Some would claim that the focus on developing one's character undercuts the central experience of one's religious being, namely, relating directly and submitting to God. This point of view was expressed in early Christianity, and it reared its head again during the sixteenth and early seventeenth centuries within the Protestant world. In the controversy regarding salvation through faith or through works (i.e. deeds), those works which were rejected most sharply were the moral works. In this perspective, morality is regarded as an audacious human undertaking, a challenge to God, where one stakes out an independent moral area instead of gearing one's entire spiritual being to submitting to God. Puritan preachers used to describe works as "the dunghill of morality" and regarded them simply as a spiritual abomination. For them, being good was indeed antonymous to being *frum*, because via "morality" you set yourself up as an alternative to the *eved Hashem* (servant of God) in you.

This notion has a history in Christianity, but it surely has no place within our *beit midrash*. Our conception of religious life highlights man's free will and emphasizes our efforts to build ourselves spiritually. As I mentioned before, these certainly include an emphasis upon morality. Therefore, this kind of tension between morality and religion is not a significant factor for us.

THE *AKEIDA*

However, there is a second kind of conflict, a different sort of tension. I mentioned before that the quest for goodness is an integral component of *frumkeit*. Generally speaking, this is true. But regarding certain particular *tzivuyyim* (divine commands), surely we find instances in which obedient response to God's normative demands stands in apparent opposition to what we conceive to be good and, if you will, to what we understand that God conceives to be good. Here, a problem arises: How do we relate to this?

What makes this problem more acute is the fact that it arises particularly in individuals who are morally and spiritually sensitive. Those who are relatively coarse are not concerned with these issues. Who is troubled by the command to wipe out Amalek? Those people who have succeeded in developing the kind of moral sensitivity that is important to us.

When there is a conflict between the *tzav* and the moral order, what do we do about it? For us, the answer is perhaps practically difficult, but surely it is conceptually clear and unequivocal. This, after all, is what the *akeida* (sacrifice of Yitzchak—*Bereishit* 22) is all about. Kierkegaard emphasized that the *akeida* represents a conflict between Avraham's moral sense and the divine command; as far as understanding the problem, he was unquestionably correct. On the one hand, Avraham is commanded to offer his son to God (which, at this point, he understands to mean "Slaughter him," not "Offer him"). On the other hand, he knows that murder is forbidden. The message of the *akeida* is clear: God's command takes precedence, in every respect, over our moral sensibility and our conscientious objections.

This is not to say that in such a context there is no room for moral sensibility. Surely, in relating to Halakha, including those areas which one may find morally difficult, there is some role for conscience, some role for the goodness in us, particularly in an interpretive capacity. Conscience does and legitimately can have a role in helping us to understand the content and substance of the *tzav*. In the *Midrash*, *Chazal* depict Avraham's thoughts during his three-day journey to the *akeida*. He tried to understand God's command: perhaps God meant something else. Surely, one can, and presumably should, walk the last mile in order to try in every way to avoid a conflict. But even when one has walked the last mile, at times the conflict may remain, and—as in the *akeida*—the decisive element is clear. It was only a *tzav* of God, or of the angel sent by God, which was able to countermand the command to sacrifice Yitzchak.

The task before us is multifaceted. As those who educate towards *yirat Shamayim*, we must communicate the message of the *akeida*—boldly, loudly and clearly. On the other hand, as those who do seek to ingrain moral sensitivity in ourselves and in our children, we need not dismiss the ambivalences, the difficulties and contradictions (at the initial level, surely). We need not wish away Avraham's three days of spiritual groping. We need not dismiss the wrestling and grappling as being a reflection of poor *yirat Shamayim*, of spiritual shallowness, or of a lack of *frumkeit*. Inasmuch as goodness itself is an inherent component of *frumkeit*, the goodness which is at the root of the problems, struggles and tensions is itself part of *yirat Shamayim*—and a legitimate part. If the sense of moral goodness is legitimate, then the questing and the grappling are also legitimate.

But, of course, the resolution must be clear, and the grappling must all be done within the parameters of the understanding that, however much I wrestle, I do not for a moment question the authenticity or the authority of the *tzav*. I do not judge God. I assume, a priori, that "His deeds are perfect, for all His ways are just; a faithful God, without iniquity, righteous and upright is He" (*Devarim* 32:4). If He commands, "Take your son and offer him as a sacrifice," then it must be good (in a sense which perhaps, at the moment, I do not understand). But within the context of my a priori obedient submission, I may try to understand. I may grope, I may ask, and I may ultimately seek resolution.

PART 5:
Risks and Priorities

INNER CONSTRAINT

I spoke before of the importance of morality and the need to emphasize it. There are, to be sure, certain risks involved. First, there is indeed a risk that if you sensitize people morally and ethically, they will then have difficulty with certain areas of Halakha. Presumably, if Elisha ben Avuya had been less sensitive to the problem of God's justice and consistency, then he would not have become an apostate. If Voltaire had believed from the outset in a Calvinist God, rather than in one who is just and decent, the Lisbon earthquake might not have unsettled him. We must be conscious of this risk.

Second, when emphasizing the relationship of goodness to *frumkeit*, we may also face the opposite kind of risk: that one will then think that the only significance of the moral element is that it is part of the divine command. At the end of the war in Lebanon, some cast doubt on the halakhic severity of the prohibition of killing non-Jews. My colleague Rav Yehuda Amital spoke out very forcefully on this issue,[1] and among other things, he quoted the opinion of the Ra'avan (*Bava Kama* 113a) that this is an *issur de-oraita* (biblical prohibition). I recall that someone was critical of this, and he said, "What kind of education is this? It teaches the student that whether or not he's going to kill a gentile should be dependent upon a Ra'avan in *Bava Kama*!"

There is a point to this. Emphasizing the integration of *frumkeit* and goodness harbors the risk that the inherent significance of goodness somehow will get lost. The Rambam in *Shemoneh Perakim* (Chapter Six) certainly does not favor that. He asks whether a person ideally should constrain himself from transgressing a Torah law only because of the *tzav*, the divine command, or whether he should feel that even had there been no *tzav*, he would not transgress it simply because it is bad. The Rambam answers that with regard to *mishpatim*, or areas *bein adam le-chavero* (between man and his fellow), certainly a person should not feel constrained solely by the *tzav*, but rather should feel an inner constraint because of the moral element *per se*. The conjunction of *frumkeit* and goodness can undercut this sense.

AN EDUCATIONAL DIFFERENCE?

There is a third risk as well. I spoke before of accepting the problem of the *akeida*, of recognizing a certain conflict here between morality and mitzva, and of granting legitimacy to one's grappling with this issue. This too can present an educational problem. Let me illustrate with an incident which occurred to me during the Lebanon War.

After the massacre at Sabra and Shatila, I published an open letter to the Prime Minister.[2] Among other things, this letter dealt with the use of force and the motivation behind it. I asked: Why was it that King Shaul was punished for not killing Agag, King of Amalek? Was it simply for not having killed the last remaining Amalekite? I suggested that he was punished not just for sparing Agag, but because the fact that he refused to kill Agag placed in a totally different light his killing of all the other Amalekites beforehand.

Shaul had been commanded to take a whole people and kill them—and this is, morally, a frightful thing. The only justification lies in it being a response to an unequivocal divine command. Therefore, if Shaul had been motivated in his actions purely by fear of God, by obedience to the *tzav*, then he should have followed the command to the letter. God didn't say, "Kill Amalek but spare Agag." Now, if he didn't kill Agag but killed everybody else, what does that indicate? It indicates that what motivated him in killing the others was not the *tzav* of God, but rather some baser impulse, some instinctive violence. And the proof is that he killed everyone, but spared his peer, his royal comrade. If that is the case, then Shaul was not punished for sparing Agag: rather, he had to be punished because of the Amalekites he did kill! Why? Because he killed them not purely due to a divine command (which is the only thing that can overcome the moral consideration), but rather out of military, diplomatic or political considerations.

Subsequently, I heard that a leading Religious Zionist rabbi in a prominent yeshiva had taken thirty minutes out of his *Gemara shiur* in order to attack what I had said. I called and asked him, "What did I say that merits this great wrath?" He replied, "I think it is a terrible thing to speak in this way, describing the divine command to destroy Amalek as asking a person to do something which ordinarily is not moral. This poses an ethical problem."

I said to him, "Wiping out Amalek does not conform to what we would normally expect a person to do. Normally, you should not be killing 'from child to suckling babe.' But I'm not saying, God forbid, that it is immoral in our case, where God has specifically commanded the destruction of Amalek—'A faithful God, without iniquity, righteous and upright is He' (*Devarim* 32:4). Although generally such an act would be considered immoral, it assumes a different character when God, from His perception and perspective, commands it. The same holds true of the *akeida*—it demanded that Avraham do something which normally is immoral. But in the context of the divine command, surely it partakes of the goodness and morality of God. We must admit, though, that there is a conflict in this case between the usual moral norm and the immediate *tzav* given here."

He said, "Yes, but you shouldn't describe it as being something which is not moral in a sense." So I asked him, "Do you agree that the *tzav* given here is something which we would not normally encourage people to do, something that we would normally consider to be immoral?" He said, "Yes, but it should not be described that way." And he added, "*Yesh kan hevdel chinukhi*—there is an educational difference."

I admit, there is something to this. The moment one speaks of a kind of clash between the demands of *yirat Shamayim* and the demands of morality—even given the qualifications which I mentioned—there is some kind of problem. There are risks in this approach.

LOVE NOT MORALITY LESS, BUT PIETY MORE

Nevertheless, I believe there is little choice. I think that the importance of moral sensibility as the grounds for moral action in our lives is of such scope, depth and magnitude that we need willingly to accept certain risks. To be sure, we should try to minimize them, but I don't think we can avoid them. We avoid them only by, in effect, almost totally neutralizing the moral element in our educational endeavors. What we need to do is not to instill morality less, but *yirat Shamayim* more.

I recall in my late adolescence there were certain problems which perturbed me, the way they perturb many others. At the time, I resolved them all in one fell swoop. I had just read Rav Zevin's book, *Ishim Ve-shitot*. In his essay on Rav Chayim Soloveitchik, he deals not only with his methodological development, but also with his personality and *gemilut chasadim* (acts of kindness). He recounted that Reb Chayim used to check every morning if some unfortunate woman had placed an infant waif on his doorstep during the course of the night. (In Brisk, it used to happen at times that a woman would give birth illegitimately and leave her infant in the hands of Reb Chayim.) As I read the stories about Reb Chayim's extraordinary kindness, I said to myself: Do I approach this level of *gemilut chasadim*? I don't even dream of it! In terms of moral sensibility, concern for human beings and sensitivity to human suffering, I am nothing compared to Reb Chayim. Yet despite his moral sensitivity, he managed to live, and live deeply, with the totality of Halakha—including the commands to destroy the Seven Nations, Amalek and all the other things which bother me. How? The answer, I thought, was obvious. It is not that his moral sensitivity was less, but his *yirat Shamayim*, his *emuna*, was so much more. The thing to do, then, is not to try to neutralize or de-emphasize the moral element, but rather to deepen and increase the element of *yirat Shamayim*, of *emuna*, *deveikut* and *bittachon*.

I have subsequently thought of that experience on many occasions. I recall once hearing someone, regarded as a philosopher of sorts, raise moral criticisms of various halakhic practices. When asked about these criticisms, I said, "I know that particular person. He doesn't look for a foundling on his doorstep every morning."

So what we need to do, I think, is not to weaken our moral sense or that of our children and students. Rather, we need to deepen and to intensify our commitment, our faith, our sense of obedience, our *yirat Shamayim*. We need to deepen our sense that God has nothing in this world besides *yirat Shamayim*, and that our moral conscience needs to develop within its context.

DIVISION OF RESOURCES

There is, finally, another problem—one which affects us within the Centrist Orthodox community more than others. Let me illustrate. I remember some years back, when I was still living in America, a man who had given a lot of money to the Skverer chassidic community invited my wife and myself to see their institutions. When we came to the elementary school, we saw the walls plastered with signs dealing with the *mitzvot* of *hashavat aveida* (returning lost objects), *bikkur cholim* (visiting the sick), *gemilut chasadim*, etc. I was struck by the fact that all the posters dealt with the area of *bein adam le-chavero*—not a single mention of Shabbat, *tefillin* or *tzitzit*! In any Centrist Orthodox school, you would have seen posters only on the latter subjects (to the extent that there would be posters dealing with *mitzvot* at all).

I immediately realized the reason for this difference. In the Skverer community, you had children growing up in an environment where their teachers could take Shabbat, *tefillin* and *tzitzit* absolutely for granted. That was the given; the possibility that a person would reject these never occurred to them. Therefore, they were able to focus all their energies upon those areas within

which even people who are practically and philosophically committed to Shabbat and *kashrut* may nevertheless fail. This is something which we, unfortunately, cannot do. Within both our educational and political systems, we find ourselves driven repeatedly
to safeguard the ritual area, which we feel is uniquely ours. We
channel so much of our energies and resources into these particular elements both because they are distinctive to us, and because
we feel that unless we emphasize it massively, the kids will not get
it at all.

This judgment may well be correct. In part, we feel comfort-
able focusing on the ritual because we assume that the students
can learn morality elsewhere. It is *efshar la'asot al yedei acherim*
(capable of being done by others)—they can read Camus or
something similar. But we pay a great price for this. First of all, it
is not always *efshar la'asot al yedei acherim*—perhaps instead of
reading Camus they will read Ayn Rand. Even if they don't, the
danger exists that there will be a bifurcation between *frumkeit*
and goodness within their minds and personalities. They might
regard these areas as being not only distinct but disjunct. This
could lead them to identify the world of Torah with only *Yoreh
De'a, Even Ha-ezer* and *Orach Chayim* (the largely ritual areas of
Halakha), while ignoring all the rest. Unfortunately, this danger is
sometimes reinforced by the fact that, at times, there are indeed
communities within which this impression seems to be the correct
one. Certainly, we need and want to avoid this.

So, quite apart from the problems I mentioned before, for us
specifically, within our community, the question of division of
energy, time and resources becomes a problem in its own right. It
is exacerbated by the fact that, in a certain sense, the whole concern with the moral realm is more directly related to our community's philosophy than it is to the philosophy of those on the
right. I say this for two reasons. First, we are, generally speaking,
more involved with the total, universal community. We feel closer

to universal human values than do those on the right. Second, we tend to be more sensitive—and rightly so—to that area in our life within which the ethical is more directly significant, namely, the area of *devar ha-reshut* (where specific commands do not apply). We have a greater awareness of the significance of this area. Defining something as *devar reshut*, of course, does not mean that this is an area which is neutral and therefore it is immaterial what you do. According to many *Rishonim*, whether a person injures himself is defined as *devar reshut*. That hardly means that a person can wantonly and willfully cut off a limb.

These factors sharpen the problem of how we are to divide our resources. On the one hand, we appreciate more fully and encounter more immediately the area of *devar reshut*, where moral factors often come into play. On the other hand, our need to focus on the area of *yirat Shamayim*, narrowly defined, is also greater. The question of division of resources thus becomes for us that much more acute.

"ONE THING GOD HAS SPOKEN, TWO THINGS I HAVE HEARD"

We have a problem that needs to be resolved differently in different contexts, as, in general, the problem of priorities and budgeting cannot be resolved from on high by some kind of universal fiat. What is important for us, though, is that we learn to avoid the implications of the question I mentioned at the outset. First, we must avoid the notion that—broadly and generally speaking (whatever may be true of a particular instance)—there can be any kind of antithesis between *frumkeit* and goodness. On the other hand, we must learn to avoid the notion that the two are simply synonymous. They are not; one is included within the other. Likewise, we must avoid the sense that we need to bifurcate these areas and therefore to grade them: this is more important and this is less. We need to have and to impart a very profound sense not only of the centrality but of the unity of Torah. "One thing God has spoken; two things I have heard" (*Tehillim* 62:12). There are many components, but one overriding message, and for us one overriding duty—to emphasize the interconnection between these two components, in the spirit of the *gemara* in *Kiddushin*:

> Ulla Rabba expounded at the entrance to the Nasi's house: What is meant by the verse (*Tehillim* 138:4), "All the kings of the earth will acknowledge you, O Lord, for they have heard the statements of Your mouth?" It does not say, "the *statement* of Your mouth," but rather, "the *statements* of Your mouth." [This indicates that] when the Holy One, blessed be He, proclaimed, "I am the Lord your God" and "You shall have no other gods before Me," the nations of the world said, "He is saying this merely for His own honor." But as soon as He declared, "Honor your father and your mother," they recanted and acknowledged the first two statements.
>
> Rava said: [This may also be derived] from the following verse (*Tehillim* 119:160): "The beginning of Your utterance is true"—the *beginning* of Your utterance but not the *end* of Your utterance? Rather, from the end of Your utterance (i.e. "Honor your father and your mother") it is evident that the beginning of Your utterance (i.e. "I am the Lord" and "You shall have no other gods") is true. (*Kiddushin* 31a)

Our sense of the truth and vitality of Torah is sharpened and deepened through our recognition of its total unity. This means conceiving of the areas of *bein adam la-Makom* and *bein adam le-chavero* not as different or conflicting elements, but rather as one central unity, albeit subdivided into various components. "The beginning of Your utterance is true," and "From the end of Your utterance, it is evident that the beginning of Your utterance is true."

NOTES:

1   See his articles in Yeshivat Har Etzion's Torah journal, *Alon Shevut* #100 (Kislev 5743).
2   *Ha-tzofeh*, 10/15/82, p. 5.

CHAPTER SEVEN

Bittachon: Trust in God

Before addressing the broad issue of *bittachon* (trust in God), let us begin with one pivotal question: Must a person rely solely on God, or is one permitted to rely upon his or her own abilities?

MEDICAL INTERVENTION

The best-known application of this question pertains to medical intervention. The Christian Science movement, for example, forbids its members from taking any initiative whatsoever in the case of illness. This is for two reasons. Firstly, such an action is understood to be in conflict with the will of God, who providentially decreed that illness visit a particular individual. Secondly, this movement regards medical intervention as a form of hubris, in which mortal man attempts to utilize his powers to alleviate sickness, in spite of the biblical verse which loudly proclaims: "Thus says the Lord: Cursed be the person who trusts in man, and places his strength in flesh, removing his heart from God" (*Yirmiyahu* 17:5).

We generally tend to dismiss this approach, regarding it as a particular strain of Christian theology lying beyond the pale of Jewish thought. However, to be honest, it seems that this view can indeed be found within our tradition. Although it is perhaps not the mainstream approach, I would not characterize it as being completely alien to Judaism. For example, the Talmud quotes R. Acha:

> One who is about to undergo bloodletting says: "May it be Your will, *Hashem* my God, that this procedure will bring benefit to me and will heal me, for You are a trustworthy healer, and Your healing is genuine. It is not the manner of human beings to heal, but this is the customary convention." (*Berakhot* 60a)

Rashi explains:

> That is to say, they should not have occupied themselves with medicine, but rather should have entreated God's mercy. (*ad loc.*)

The talmudic passage, however, continues:

> Abbaye says: A person should not recite this prayer, for in the academy of Rabbi Yishmael it was explained: The verse, "And he shall surely be healed" (*Shemot* 21:19), refers to the granting of permission for the physician to heal.

Although a simple reading indicates that Abbaye is in fundamental disagreement with R. Acha, it is possible to understand Abbaye's objection as does the Taz (*Yoreh De'a* 336:1). He explains that even Abbaye believes that Rabbi Acha's opinion is fundamentally correct. However, since not all people have the merit to "be saved through the mercies of Heaven," it is appropriate and permissible for a physician to heal.

An additional source, quoted by the *gemara* (*Pesachim* 56a) from the *Tosefta*, relates that Chizkiyahu, King of Judea, hid away the "Book of Medical Remedies" and, in so doing, won the support of the Sages. Rashi explains the reason:

> For until that time, people would not be humbled by illness, but would instead effect immediate healing. (*ad loc.*)

This approach is most forcefully expressed by the Ramban in his commentary on *parashat Bechukotai*. In speaking of the blessings promised to the Jewish people, the Ramban explains that these are national in scope, and applicable when "the entire nation is righteous." Under at least those circumstances, the Ramban relates,

> When the entire people of Israel is perfect in their conduct, their matters do not function according to the laws of nature at all, neither with respect to their bodies nor their land, neither in general nor in particular. Rather, God will "bless their bread and water" and "remove all manner of sickness" from among them. Thus, they will have no need of a physician's services nor of medical science, as the verse states that "I, God, am your healer" (*Shemot* 15:26). The righteous people who lived at the time of the prophets would conduct themselves this way, for even if they would fall ill as a result of transgression, they would not consult the doctors but rather the prophets, as, for example, Asa and Chizkiyahu. . . One who seeks God through the prophets does not consult the physicians. What role does the physician have for those who follow God's will, since He has promised them that He will . . . "remove all manner of sickness" from their midst? (Ramban, *Vayikra* 26:11)

The Ramban's conclusion is forceful and unmistakable:

> When God is pleased with a person's conduct, he has no need of physicians.

The Ramban's approach so disturbed Rav Chayim Soloveitchik that he was inclined to believe that the offending words were not the work of the Ramban at all, but rather an interpolation by a later copyist! Rav Chayim's far-reaching claim lacks a textual and historic basis, and I personally cannot accept it. Clearly, however, the tradition that informs Rav Chayim's words is the central one in Judaism. In contrast to the Ramban, the mainstream approach is activist and interventionist, an outlook which appeals to modern man.

We tend to identify more strongly with the Rambam's interpretation of the *tosefta* presented earlier, which stands in stark contrast to that of Rashi. The Rambam, who in his *Commentary on the Mishna* generally concentrates on the *Mishna* itself and ignores the parallel *Tosefta* sources, here goes out of his way to explain the matter in order to preclude erroneous conclusions. He writes:

I have explained this matter at length because of the other explanations that I have heard. Others have explained that Shlomo authored a book of medical remedies so that an individual who fell ill could consult his work and, by following his medical advice, become well. When Chizkiyahu saw that people forsook trust in God and instead followed the prescriptions in the book, he removed it from circulation.

How nonsensical is this explanation of the matter, and how mistaken! It ascribes a degree of foolishness to Chizkiyahu (and to the Sages who supported his efforts) that we would not impute even to the basest rabble! According to this absurd reasoning, if a hungry man assuages his hunger with bread and thus overcomes the "sickness of hunger," shall we say of him that he has thereby forsaken his trust and belief in God?

Rather, just as we thank God at the time of eating for having provided sustenance and allowed us to overcome our hunger and to survive, so do we thank Him for having provided the medical remedy that heals us. I would not even have bothered addressing this issue if not for the fact that so many people are mistaken about its interpretation. (*Commentary on the Mishna, Pesachim* 4:10)

THE HALAKHIC EMPHASIS ON HUMAN EFFORT

It seems to me that the approach that demands passivity and complete dependence on God's intervention does make an occasional appearance in our tradition. Clearly, however, the Rambam's approach is the dominant one, and it is the most relevant for our generation.

This activist approach regarding medicine parallels the activist Jewish approach with respect to spiritual endeavors. In Christian theology there is a time-honored tradition—rooted in the words of Paul and transmitted by Augustine, Luther and others—that sees human redemption as being dictated solely from Above. In Luther's formulation, any human attempt to achieve spiritual or ethical perfection is a grave error, for it bespeaks arrogance. Man, in his view, is a despicable creature who cannot achieve redemption except through Divine intervention. Rather, a person can only wait passively for grace, just as a woman (according to his metaphor) waits for conception to occur after the seed has been implanted in her.

The Halakha, in glaring contrast, is founded on the touchstone of free will, on the principle that human effort constitutes the essential component of spirituality. The *gemara* (*Berakhot* 33b) tells us, "Everything is in the hands of Heaven except for the fear of Heaven." This being the case, it follows that a human being has a central role to play in regulating the events of his or her personal life, as well as in affecting the direction of history in general. This is particularly so in light of the Rambam's declaration that, since all of a person's activities express whether he is Godfearing or not, all human activities are included within the phrase "fear of Heaven" in the *gemara* just cited (*Shemona Perakim*, Chapter Eight; *Teshuvot Ha-Rambam*, ed. Blau, #436; *Iggerot Ha-Rambam*, ed. Shailat, p. 236).

As the Rambam implies in his *Commentary on the Mishna*, the activist posture applies not only to medicine, but to the war against hunger and poverty as well. In fact, it would include any attempts to influence historical processes through the application of human efforts. In his formulation, the verse "Blessed be the man who relies on God" (*Yirmiyahu* 17:7) applies to every area of life, but this in no way precludes human effort and initiative.

"WE DO NOT RELY ON A MIRACLE"

In truth, however, the quandary is not simply whether a person ought to be totally passive or rather should act. The matter is much more complex, for one must consider the degree to which Heavenly intervention should be taken into account as a determining factor *within* the context of human initiative. When faced with fateful decisions, should the situation be evaluated from a purely rational and analytical standpoint, or, since in the end we must rely upon God's help anyway, should one factor that intervention into the decision-making process?

Clearly, when I mention the possibility of factoring in divine assistance, I am not referring to specific Divine assurances addressing defined situations, or to detailed inquiries addressed to the *Urim Ve-tumim*. Rather, I am considering the role of general Divine pronouncements which, of course, are reliable on the grand historical scale, but typically do not have a direct connection to a particular problem that arises at a given time. This leaves the matter undefined and shrouded in obscurity.

For example, *Chazal* declare in a number of places, "Those engaged in a mitzva-related mission do not come to harm" (*Yoma* 11a, *Kiddushin* 39b, *Chullin* 142a). On the other hand, the *gemara* concludes, "This principle is inoperative where danger is to be expected" (*Pesachim* 8b; see also the above sources, where the formulation is slightly different). To complicate matters further, another passage declares that it is forbidden to rely upon a miracle (*Pesachim* 64b).

Obviously, since it is almost impossible to define precisely terms such as "danger" or "miracle," these general statements in the end do not yield practical guidelines for action. When addressing fundamental political issues—for example, whether we should retain Judea and Samaria and rely on God's protection, or whether we should cede these lands in recognition of internal and external pressures—we are likely to discover that sincere and profound disagreements exist even among believing Jews. It is not my desire, nor is it within my ability, to decide such matters either way. I must, however, emphasize one point: Let us not fall prey to overzealousness in the realm of *bittachon*. We would be erring grievously to believe that an approach that seemingly champions excessive trust in Divine intervention is, in fact, imbued with a greater amount of fear of Heaven than a view which adopts a more rational and pragmatic methodology.

In certain instances, to be sure, adopting an adamant or compromising approach indeed results from too much or too little fear of Heaven. But this is not necessarily the case. It is possible for one to be intransigent, spouting slogans of faith, yet motivated in truth by irresponsibility. It is also possible to be pliant and yielding, yet possessed of an abiding trust accompanied by great caution. Certainly, differences of opinion will exist with respect to evaluating the chances of success of a particular diplomatic or military initiative, as well as with respect to the degree of statistical probability necessary to remove an endeavor from the category of "relying on a miracle." In any case, for God's sake, let us not allow a discussion about fateful national issues degenerate into a "competition" over which position expresses greater fear of Heaven.

Two Approaches to *Bittachon*

O ur approach to humanity's role in shaping history thus combines two factors: bold and responsible action accompanied
by a deep and daring *bittachon*. What, however, is the nature of
this *bittachon*? It seems to me that we must distinguish between
two fundamental approaches.

According to the first approach, trust is expressed by the certainty that God stands at your side and will assist you. This is a
variation of the words of the *mishna* (*Rosh Ha-shana* 3:8, 29a):
"As long as the Jewish people looked Heavenwards and humbled
their hearts to their Father in Heaven, they prevailed [in their war
against Amalek]." This approach is fundamentally optimistic, sat-
urated with faith and with hopeful expectation for the future. On
the field of battle, the warrior who can adopt this trust feels that
he is on the threshold of victory; in moments of crisis, one feels
that salvation is on the way; during a night of terrors, this type of
trust heralds the break of dawn. In short, this approach is
expressed in the familiar formula, "With God's help, everything
will be all right."

The Chazon Ish, in his book *Ha-emuna Ve-ha-bittachon*, categorically rejects this approach, complaining that:

> . . . an old error has become rooted in the hearts of many
> concerning the concept of trust. Trust . . . has come to mean
> that a person is obligated to believe that whenever he is pre-
> sented with two possible outcomes, one good and one not,
> then certainly it will turn out for the good. And if he has
> doubts and fears the worst, that constitutes a lack of trust.
> (*Ha-emuna Ve-ha-bittachon*, beginning of chapter 2)

The Chazon Ish continues by criticizing this approach:

> This view of trust is incorrect, for as long as the future out-
> come has not been clarified through prophecy, that outcome

has not been decided, for who can truly know God's judgments and providence? Rather, trust means realizing that there are no coincidences in the world, and that whatever happens under the sun is a function of God's decree.

Unlike the Chazon Ish, I would not go so far as to consider this view as being beyond the pale. It seems to me that many *Rishonim* adopted an approach akin to the one which the Chazon Ish rejects. For example, Rabbeinu Bachya ben Asher (a disciple of the Rashba) writes in his work *Kad Ha-kemach*:

> The matter of trust in God was explained by the saintly Rabbeinu Yona [Gerondi] to mean that a person ought to accept wholeheartedly that everything is within the power of Heaven. God can transcend the laws of nature and change a person's fortune, and though a situation may appear to be hopeless, Divine intervention can change that reality in an instant. God's salvation is close at hand, for He is omnipotent. Even if a sword rests on a person's neck, he should not imagine that salvation is impossible. . . Thus said Chizkiya to Yeshayahu the prophet: "I have received a tradition from my grandfather's house, that even though a sharp sword rests on a person's neck, he should not withhold himself from supplication to God." (*Bittachon, s.v. inyan*)

This theme also characterizes the words of Rabbeinu Bachya ibn Pakuda in his *Chovot Ha-levavot*. There he defines the "essence of trust" as:

> the peace of mind of the one who trusts, that the one upon whom he relies [whether God or man] will do the best and the most appropriate for him in the matter. . . The main definition of trust is that one's heart should believe that the one relied upon will fulfill what he has promised and do good on his behalf, not out of obligation but out of kindness and mercy. (*Sha'ar Ha-bittachon*, chap. 1)

Clearly, this is a description of popular, simple faith, the belief that "it will work out fine," rather than a belief in an all-encompassing Providence. The fact that at this point Rabbeinu Bachya does not distinguish between trust in God and trust in man proves the point. Thus, I would not characterize this first approach as "an old error," nor would I deny its relevance to the issue of trust.

There is, however, a second approach to *bittachon*. The *Kad Ha-kemach* continues,

> Also included in the matter of trust is that a person must surrender his soul to God, and should constantly occupy his thoughts with this matter: If brigands should come to kill him or to force him to abrogate the Torah, he should prefer to give up his life rather than go against the Torah. Concerning this, David said, "To You, God, I shall offer up my soul" (*Tehillim* 25:1), and it further states, "My God, in You I have trusted, let me not be disgraced" (*ibid.* 2). One who gives up his life under such circumstances has performed an act of *bittachon*.

Obviously, this approach has a completely different meaning. It does not attempt to scatter the clouds of misfortune, try to raise expectations, or strive to whitewash a dark future. It does not claim that "It will all work out for the best," either individually or nationally. On the contrary, it expresses a steadfast commitment—even if the outcome will be bad, we will remain reliant on and connected to God. We will remain faithful until the end and shall not exchange our trust in God for dependence on man. This approach does not claim that God will remain at our side; rather, it asks us to remain at His side.

Naturally, this approach is much less popular than its counterpart. A demand is always less marketable than a promise. For one who makes an honest assessment, though, this approach also functions as a source of solace and strength. In truth, this approach presents not just a demand but also a message. Being disconnected from God constitutes the greatest tragedy that can befall a person. When the Torah states, "To Him you shall cleave" (*Devarim* 13:5), it simultaneously expresses a demand as well as an opportunity. Similarly, the psalmist's call, "Israel, trust in God" (*Tehillim* 115:9), constitutes both a demand as well as an opportunity.

FAITH AND LOVE

These two approaches stem from different halakhic obligations. The first is, practically speaking, an aspect of the mitzva of *emuna* (faith). This mitzva has a purely cognitive aspect, which asks of a Jew to recognize certain metaphysical or historical facts. Beyond the conceptual component, this mitzva also has an experiential facet. It is important for us to distinguish between these two facets of faith.

When the Torah tells us that Avraham "had faith in God" (*Bereishit* 15:6), this indicates not only his intellectual belief but also his general state of mind—he feels absolutely dependent upon and connected to God. Following God's wondrous promise, "Lift up your eyes to the Heavens and count the stars if you can, for your descendents will be as numerous" (*ibid.* 15:5), Avraham pins all his hopes upon God and is completely convinced, experientially and existentially (not only intellectually), that those promises will be fulfilled. At this time he perceives God to be "a shield to all who trust in Him," and he relies on God to fulfill this great and awesome vision. Thus, the first aspect of trust is obligated by the mitzva of belief.

Concerning the second type of trust, the *mishna* in *Sota* provides insight:

> On that very day, Rabbi Yehoshua ben Hyrcanus taught: Iyyov served God only out of love, as the verse states: "Though He may slay me, still I will trust in Him (*lo aya-*

chel)" (*Iyyov* 13:15). The matter remains unresolved: Shall I rely [on Him] or shall I not? [Which is to say, shall we follow the written text that spells *"lo"* with an *aleph* and should therefore be rendered as "I will *not* trust in Him"? Or shall we follow the directive for reading, which renders *"lo"* with a *vav* and concludes that "I *will* trust in Him"?] The verses therefore continue, "Until I die I shall not surrender my innocence" (27:5), indicating that he acted out of love.

Said Rabbi Yehoshua: Who shall remove the dust from your eyes, Rabban Yochanan ben Zakkai? All of your days you maintained that Iyyov served God only out of fear, as the verse states: "He was a man whole and upright, who feared God and avoided evil" (1:1). Behold, Yehoshua, the student of your student, teaches that he served God out of love! (*Sota* 5:5, 27b)

The proclamation, "Though He may slay me, still I will trust in *Him*," expresses a trust in God Himself, not as a function of what I can *receive from* Him, but rather as trust *in* Him. This trust is unconnected with what one may get out of the relationship, but simply describes a connection to God. The desire to come close to Him, to serve Him, to rely upon Him, to take hold of the Foundation of all else and the Source of existence, is predicated, according to this *mishna*, on love. The second aspect of *bittachon*, then, can be said to flow from the mitzva, "You shall love the Lord your God" (*Devarim* 6:5).

It is true that the Ramban explains the phrase "I will trust in Him" in the above-cited verse in *Iyyov* to mean, "I know that He will reward my righteousness in the Afterlife." This is trust based on the expectation of future reward. A similar sentiment is expressed by the *gemara*:

It was stated: Rabbi Yochanan and Rabbi Eliezer both say that even if a sharp sword rests upon a person's neck, he should not withhold himself from supplication to God, as the verse

states, "Though He may slay me, still I will trust in Him."
(*Berakhot* 10a)

This approach, grounded in a hope for positive results, is based
upon the teaching of Rabban Yochanan ben Zakkai—that Iyyov
served out of fear. In contrast, Rabbi Yehoshua's view in the *mishna* seems to be predicated on service out of love exclusively. The
baraita quoted later in the *gemara* adds a comparison to Avraham
Avinu, the paradigm of love of God:

> It was taught: Rabbi Meir says, Fear of God is stated concern-
> ing Iyyov, and fear of God is stated concerning Avraham. Just
> as Avraham's fear of God was predicated on love, so too
> Iyyov's fear of God was predicated on love. (*Sota* 31a)

The nature of *avodat Hashem* motivated by love was described
by *Chazal* in unequivocal terms. Commenting on the verse "to
love the Lord your God" (*Devarim* 11:13), the *Sifrei* states:

> Lest a person say, "I will learn Torah in order to be consid-
> ered a sage, in order to attend a yeshiva, in order to merit
> length of days in the World-to-Come," the verse therefore
> states, "to love the Lord your God," meaning: Learn in any
> case, and honor will follow in the end.

The Rambam expands this principle from the study of Torah
to the service of God in general. In the concluding chapter of
Hilkhot Teshuva, he writes:

> One who serves God out of love will study Torah, perform
> *mitzvot* and follow the path of wisdom for no ulterior motive—
> not because of fear of punishment nor because of promise of
> reward. Rather, he does what is true because it is true, and in
> the end, good will follow. . . Our early Sages explained: Lest
> one say, "I will learn Torah in order to become wealthy, in
> order to be called Rabbi, in order to receive reward in the
> World-to-Come," therefore it says, "to love God," meaning:
> Whatever you do, do it out of love. (*Hilkhot Teshuva* 10:2)

Rabbeinu Bachya understood this to be the manner in which Iyyov served God. If one loves God properly, then he feels that no matter what, he will not abandon Him:

Such a soul can only love Him more, desiring His favor and trusting in Him. So it is related concerning one of the pious ones, who would arise in the middle of the night and declare: "My God, You have starved me, left me naked, and caused me to dwell in the darkness of night; but I swear by Your strength and might that even if You burn me with fire, I will only love You and delight in You more." Similarly, it was stated concerning Iyyov: "Though He may slay me, still I will trust in Him." (*Chovot Ha-levavot*, section 10)

In this formulation, the quality of trust does not fully encompass the mitzva of love. Trust in God does not imply the readiness to sacrifice oneself on His behalf. It does, however, imply the ambition to attain a constant connection to Him, through fire and water. Therefore, when it is necessary to pass through fire, there is the possibility of cleaving to Him in self-sacrifice as well.

In summary, then, Judaism recognizes both the hopeful and expectant trust based on faith, and the steadfast and yearning trust based on love.

THE DUALITY OF *BITTACHON* IN *TEHILLIM*

The dual nature of trust in God receives strong expression in the *Shir Ha-ma'alot* chapters in *Tehillim*. On the one hand, we have *mizmor* 121:

A song of Ascents. I will lift up my eyes to the mountains, from whence shall my help come? My help is from God, Maker of heaven and earth. He will not allow your feet to slip; your Guardian will not slumber. Behold, the Guardian of Israel neither sleeps nor slumbers. God will protect you; God will shelter you by your right side. The sun will not strike you during the day, nor the moon by night. God will protect you from all evil and will guard your soul. God will protect your going out and coming in from now until eternity.

This *mizmor* provides a classic illustration of hopeful, faithful trust, one that is certain of a positive outcome. *Mizmor* 131, on the other hand, portrays a completely different mood:

A Song of Ascents, for David. O Lord, my heart has not been proud, nor have my eyes been haughty. I did not tread in areas too great or wondrous for me. Did I not wait and did my soul not silently hope, like a suckling infant longs for his mother? Like a suckling, so too my soul. Israel will trust in God from now and forever.

What does the suckling infant think while in his mother's embrace? Does he regard her as the one who will save him from crisis? Perhaps instinctually, this indeed may be the case, but practical expectations are in fact not the main thing on the infant's mind. First of all, he turns to his mother because he wants to be close to her. At that moment, he is not preoccupied with future plans, nor is he anticipating the fulfillment of visions or promises. He knows only one thing: the world is a cold, frightening place, but here with his mother there is warmth and security! The mother, in turn, caresses him and comforts him. Over and above any response on her part, simply being in her presence gives him life and strength. Therefore, the suckling cleaves to her under all circumstances. This is not out of readiness to sacrifice himself for her, but rather because nothing in the world can separate him from her. Wherever she turns, he is at her side, tightly clutching her skirt with his small fingers.

Here, love is characterized by the image: "like a suckling longs for his mother. . . Israel will trust in God now and always." The love is expressed by the kind of trust which led the Jews to "follow Me into the wilderness, through a land not sown" (*Yirmiyahu* 2:2). Again, this does not necessarily imply preparedness to surrender one's soul, but simply the inability to be distant from God. The comparison to an infant's longing for his mother implies an attachment that is experiential and existential, over and above pragmatic considerations of benefit or harm.

HISTORICAL DEVELOPMENT OF THE TWO TYPES OF *BITTACHON*

Just as these two chapters of *Tehillim* are paradigmatic of the two approaches to trust, one can also trace the historical development of these two approaches over time. Of course, the Jewish people have adopted both approaches from their earliest beginnings, with our forefather Avraham being a classic example of both. Nevertheless, it is possible to suggest that the destruction of the First Temple and the consequent exile brought about a fundamental shift in attitude. Although historians have often exaggerated the effects of this turning point, it is nevertheless a fact that our own Sages also viewed this era as pivotal.

> Rav said: The Jewish people offered a clinching argument in response to the words of the prophet. The prophet had said: "Return to God, for your ancestors who transgressed are no more!" The people responded: "And the prophets who did not transgress, where are they?"—as the verse states (*Zekharia* 1:5), "Where are your fathers? And will the prophets live forever?" . . .

> Shemuel explained [that the people had a different retort]: Ten people came before the prophet and sat before him. He said to them, "Return to God." They said to him, "A slave who has been sold by his master or a woman who has been divorced by her husband, can there be any claim between them?" [In other words, by destroying our Temple and exiling us, has God not in effect divorced us or released us from His service?] Said God to the prophet, "Go and tell them

(*Yeshayahu* 50:1): 'Where then is the bill of divorce of your mother whom you say I sent away, and to which of my creditors have I sold you? You have been sold on account of your transgressions, and your mother was sent away because of your misdeeds.'" (*Sanhedrin* 105a)

During the period of the Temple, when the people of Israel dwelt in their own land, it was possible for them to draw strength from *bittachon* born of faith. Of course, even at that time there were crises and difficult moments, but as long as the national and religious frameworks remained in place, it was possible to rely on the fundamental relationship between God and His people. The darkness of night was bearable because one could believe that the dawn would follow. With the Destruction, however, the foundations of that trust crumbled. At that time, the frightening query recorded in *mizmor* 22 (which our Sages attributed to Esther) was first raised:

My God, my God, why have You abandoned me, far from saving me and unheeding of my outcry? My God, I cry out to You by day—but You do not respond; and by night—but You are silent. You, Holy One, are enthroned by the praises of Israel. In You our ancestors trusted, and You saved them; they cried out to You and escaped; they trusted in You and were not disgraced.

But in the aftermath of the Destruction, when Mount Zion was desolate and foxes prowled its ruins, when the Jewish people was shamed and humiliated, how was it possible to trust in God that things would work out for the best? This was neither possible nor necessary, for "a servant whose master has sold him and a woman whose husband has divorced her" bear no responsibility towards their former relationship.

Concerning this, there was a dual response. God offered the awesome and striking rejoinder that we have not been absolved and that the initial obligation remains in place:

That which you are thinking shall never be, that you say, "We shall be like the other nations who serve gods of wood and stone." As I live, says the Lord God, I shall rule over you with a strong hand, with an outstretched arm and with awesome wrath! (*Yechezkel* 20:32-33)

The Jewish people, for their part, discovered a treasure-trove of trust that was new to them, but ancient in origin. They remembered that they were not simply heirs to the *Berit Bein Habetarim* (Covenant between the Pieces, *Bereishit* 15) but also the "descendents of My beloved Avraham" (*Yeshayahu* 41:8). They came to the realization that it is possible to say "the Great, Mighty and Awesome God" even as the enemy forces destroyed His sanctuary and enslaved His people (*Yoma* 69b). It was possible to have a deep and abiding faith even "by the rivers of Babylon."

The Jewish people emerged from the state of exile strengthened and fortified, with a faith that was more profound than before. They learned to appreciate that their connection to God, their reliance on Him and trust in Him, were independent of external, objective factors. This is the meaning of *Chazal*'s statement that the people re-accepted the Torah in the days of Achashverosh. The Ramban, after citing the people's argument that they were like a slave whose master had sold him, comments:

> Therefore when the people returned a second time to the Land of Israel in the days of Ezra, they accepted the Torah of their own accord, without objections or complaints. This refers to the days of Achashverosh, when the people emerged from death to life, and it was more precious in their eyes than the Exodus from Egypt. (Ramban, *Shabbat* 88a)

The Jewish people learned that, even when re-establishing a state, the undertaking is accomplished "not with might nor with power, but through My spirit" (*Zekharia* 4:6). Since that time, these very lessons have remained with us and have strengthened us in difficult hours. The destruction of the Second Temple and the Second Commonwealth did not undermine our national faith and trust as did the destruction of the First Temple. For close to two thousand years, although we underwent great trials and tribulations, we remained attached to God, trusting in Him, yearning for Him, and sustained by Him as a result.

BITTACHON TODAY

While we should generally try to maintain a balance between the optimistic *bittachon* of faith and the steadfast *bittachon* of love, there are historical periods when it seems that the latter type of *bittachon* is on the verge of disappearing completely, and therefore needs special reinforcement. Although it may sound paradoxical, I think that our own period, which has witnessed the rebirth of the State of Israel, is one of those times. All of the religious and national hopes and aspirations that arose with the dawn of the state tended to draw us completely towards "faithful trust," while the second approach of "loving trust" was pushed aside.

Perhaps this is due to the fact that under favorable conditions, it is more difficult to demand religious self-sacrifice. As the Catholic historian Christopher Dawson pointed out, it is much easier to dismiss this world and to adopt an otherworldly stance when there is not much to lose in this life. In contrast, for a person burdened with many possessions, disdain for the material realm is much more difficult. It is also possible that our almost exclusive embrace of the first aspect of trust is engendered by our continuous accomplishments, which raise expectations even further. Perhaps the popularity of the teachings of Rav Kook, suffused as they are with national and cosmic optimism, is also partially responsible.

Whatever the cause, the phenomenon is clear: the equilibrium between the two aspects of trust has been lost by the Religious

Zionist community in Israel. This fact was and is reflected in our educational system. We inculcated the ideas of faithful trust, redemption, hope and expectation very well, but neglected to teach the values of loving trust, of cleaving to God without hesitation under all circumstances. We did not fortify our children or ourselves concerning the possibility of crises, conveying that the song to God must be sung even on the rivers of Babylon. We did not allow ourselves to wrestle with the possibility of national setbacks.

We taught our students about the "human comedy" but never about the "human tragedy," on either the individual or the collective plane. We did succeed in nurturing the younger generation to be ready and willing to make personal sacrifices for the sake of the nation and the land. All of this was accomplished, however, while riding a wave of optimism, that all would work out because the process of redemption was unfolding. The engine of this process was faithful trust, and it found expression on the individual as well as on the national level.

I fear, however, that today we are beginning to pay the price for this skewing of values, and now is the time to rectify the error. Our obligation is to redirect our focus to embrace loving trust, to acknowledge that we are ready to hold tight to God because He is our steadfast Rock, and let the chips fall where they may. We must deal with the tragic dimension of trust, to renew the spirit of "Though He may slay me, still I will trust in Him." This expresses the essence of Jewish trust in the face of tragic situations.

I hope that my words are not misconstrued to mean that we must abandon faithful trust. Personally, I am brimming with the belief that God will not abandon His people and that our national existence in this Holy Land is secure. I do my utmost to pass on this belief to my children and students. At the same time, I feel that I must simultaneously instill in them loving trust, not as a spiritual insurance policy in case of crisis, but rather because sacrifice and connectedness to God are essential in their own right, even under the most favorable circumstances. The ability to trust during suffering is important for a person, even when he thinks that difficulties do not lie on the horizon.

I also hope that my words are not taken to imply a devaluation of suffering or a negation of the pain of tribulation. In his essay, "Beyond Tragedy," Reinhold Niebuhr writes, "Christianity is a religion above and beyond tragedy. Tears as well as death are swallowed up in triumph." This is because, for Christianity, suffering is transformed by becoming the foundation for personal redemption. Let it be stated explicitly that Judaism is not "beyond tragedy," nor does it "swallow up" suffering. Jewish tradition educates the person to accept suffering, but also to bemoan it. Grieving—not philosophical detachment, stoic fortitude or open-armed joy—is the response which Halakha mandates when a person is faced by a loved one's death. As the Ramban writes in the introduction to his work on the laws of mourning, *Torat Ha-adam*, "Strength of heart in this matter is of the path of rebelliousness, and softness of heart is of the path of confession and repentance." Jewish tradition teaches the person to respond to suffering and to be educated through his or her experience of it, but certainly not to downplay or negate it. Let us recognize the magnitude of pain and suffering, but let us also continue to trust in and cleave to God.

The attribute of trust is thus antinomic, i.e., it contains conflicting aspects. On the one hand, trust demands that a person be convinced that God will assist him; on the other hand, it demands that a person be prepared for a time when, God forbid, help will not be forthcoming. That it is antinomic makes it more difficult to teach, but the model nonetheless exists.

Let us recall that our tradition preserves the account of a towering and heroic figure—Rabbi Akiva. He was full of faithful trust and optimism, convinced that the Jewish people would be restored to sovereignty and spiritual greatness in their land. In the sound of Bar Kokhba's advancing footsteps, he heard the approaching herald of messianic redemption. On the other hand, his life was a paradigm of loving trust, for he literally fulfilled the verse in *Iyyov*, "Though He may slay me, still I will trust in Him."

Rabbi Akiva hoped; he anticipated the best and believed that it would transpire. Yet when this did not come to pass, when faced with a cruel and painful death—in this last, most bitter hour, he smiled. As he explained to Turnus Rufus, the wicked Roman governor, his smile was not an indication of "belittling of suffering," but rather a sign of great *bittachon* (*Yerushalmi Berakhot* 9:5).

Do we succeed in following Rabbi Akiva's example? I suspect that the movement that bears his name, a movement I admire, tends to emphasize the first aspect of Rabbi Akiva's faith more than the second. This, in turn, is a reflection of our spiritual and educational state in general.

THE EDUCATIONAL IMPERATIVE

Practically speaking, I think that we must concentrate on one point: Trust is not an independent topic, but rather is associated with both faith and love. The ability to nurture the quality of trust depends upon one's internalization of a general fear of Heaven, which is related to the quest for closeness to God as well as to the centrality of religious values in a person's life. The attribute of trust, especially with respect to its second aspect of love, is not independent of other qualities, and it certainly cannot simply be activated, like a proverbial faucet, during an hour of need. Rather, *bittachon* is a function of a person's general relationship to God, and depends upon his service of the heart, practical mitzva observance, devotion to study of Torah, and sensitivity to God's constant overarching presence, in the sense of the verse (*Tehillim* 16:8), "I have placed God before me always."

This approach is, of course, long and arduous. It offers no shortcuts and eschews facile slogans. Nevertheless, it seems to me that it is, in the final analysis, a "long path which is short;" and I am not aware of any other. This approach is not presumptuous enough to suppose that it can answer all of our questions, but it does remove some of the sting from the questions. It is not the question of suffering *per se* that should trouble us. Our illustrious forebears have already posed the question of why the righteous suffer: David asked, Chabakuk inquired, and Moshe himself requested of God, "Please inform me of Your ways" (*Shemot* 33:13). The issue is rather the background and tone of the question. When one asks why people suffer, does he preface his question as does Yirmiyahu (12:1): "God, You are righteous, and therefore I will contend with You and question Your justice?" Or does he simply hurl rebellious and angry accusations at God?

It is natural that we have difficulties with these issues. Let us encourage the asking of questions. Our responsibility is to transmit a life of Torah that will ensure that these legitimate questions do not become serious doubts. Cardinal Newman assiduously distinguished between "difficulties" and "doubts." From all of religion's tenets, he related, nothing presented him with as many difficulties as the idea of God's existence—yet of nothing was he more certain.

If we are interested in coping with questions concerning *bittachon*, then we must address the general state of our Torah life. Let us deepen our faith, increase our love, and in so doing, we will attain the necessary *bittachon*. This is a trust that will allow us to hope for the best possible outcome, but will also strengthen us for life's most difficult moments. As "believers and children of believers," we trust that God will do His part.

SOME RESPONSES TO QUESTIONS RAISED AFTER THE LECTURE

Q: Is it really possible to teach values, and if so, how?

A: Plato already addressed this ancient question. It seems to me that we champion an approach that maintains that it *is* possible to educate towards the development of values. To my mind, the most effective means of achieving this goal is to combine values-based instruction with the teaching of other subjects. This must be done in a manner that takes advantage of ongoing opportunities to raise, in the course of instruction, philosophical-existential issues, including those of faith and trust. This type of approach can be effective to the degree that it is part of a broader effort, rather than being pursued as a self-contained lecture on faith and trust.

Q: How are we to educate for values, if you present us with a variety of views?

A: Indeed, I did mention differences of opinion and opposing views with respect to several matters. On many levels, I advocate a somewhat pluralistic approach that is based on the Talmudic dictum, "These and these are the words of the living God" (*Eruvin* 13b). In my opinion, this represents a central foundation of Jewish tradition, and we must reject any attempt to impose a narrow interpretation in areas of Jewish philosophy or thought, as if there were only one view on these issues.

This can be compared to the domain of Halakha, where we encounter a range of opinions and disagreements among the *Tannaim, Amoraim, Rishonim* and *Acharonim*. I do not see why we must think that in the realm of philosophical thought there has been absolute consensus throughout the generations. Moreover, in the realm of Jewish thought, matters frequently remain unresolved, since there exists no mechanism similar to the one of *pesika* (rendering a decision) that guides practical Halakha.

In studying *Tanakh*, for example, we find possibilities of interpreting in different directions, with the various options all falling within the parameters of reverence and tradition. For example, is Eliezer the servant of Avraham a positive figure or a negative one? In another vein, was Avraham three years old when he came to recognize God, as the *Midrash* posits, or was he forty or forty-eight, as the Rambam maintains? Obviously, the path of Avraham's spiritual development is very different depending on which of these views is adopted. There is no *pesak* (conclusive decision) to settle the matter.

We ourselves must develop, and inculcate in our students as well, different approaches within the framework of tradition. Whether or not we decide between them, we must realize that there is more than one view. Sometimes we can allow the students themselves to decide. A student should be presented with the primary sources against the backdrop of different interpretations, even if no single, conclusive view emerges at the end. Such a student will be richer, wiser and more sensitive.

Q: Where should our focus lie in trying to instill in our students a love of God?

A: Educating towards love of God and faith must be anchored in the intellectual realm. At the same time, other significant domains must be included, such as the experiential, the existential—the purity of feeling, if you will—and practical application. It is not realistic to concentrate on one area in the hope that it can achieve everything.

Q: But is it not too difficult to actually inculcate our students with love of God?

A: Although it is difficult to educate one to love, it is nevertheless essential, and we must make valiant efforts in this direction. We, as well as our students, must struggle with the fact that the Torah addresses us with demands rather than entitlements. The

Torah commands, "You shall love the Lord your God," discouraging the fulfillment of *mitzvot* for ulterior motives, such as achieving a place in the World-to-Come. Loving God is a central mitzva, which we dare not neglect.

Q: How do you explain the concept of *yissurin shel ahava* (chastisements of love)?

A: With regard to this concept, the fundamental question is whether it is possible for one to suffer without having transgressed. Our sages disagree on this matter, going back as far as *Chazal* and the *Rishonim*. The Maharal believes that *yissurin shel ahava* are indeed a form of punishment. I tend to understand "chastisements of love" as forms of suffering that come to purify a person. We begin with the assumption that there exist individuals who are purified by suffering, just as there exist those who are broken by suffering. One does not know how he or she will perform until the suffering actually takes place. Nevertheless, the experience of suffering is one which can contain an aspect of human refinement.

For example, what was accomplished at the *akeida* (binding of Yitzchak)? We cannot regard it as an exercise that reveals any facts to God, since He knows all at the outset. Rather, the *akeida* is a creative act that stands by itself. Avraham after the *akeida* is not the same Avraham as before the *akeida*, because the experience of suffering purified him.

Judaism does not demand that its adherents revel in suffering. But when suffering occurs, it is essential to turn it into a force for self-rehabilitation and growth. Then it can be transformed into "chastisements of love," which can creatively build the person's soul and enhance his or her spiritual development.

Q: Is it not more effective educationally to present students with an optimistic approach? And can't we explain the suffering of the righteous simply by pointing out that reward is granted in the World-to-Come?

A: I completely reject the exclusive use of the approach that stresses hope and a positive outcome—the common attitude that "It will be OK." We can certainly stress the positive aspects of a given difficult situation, but only on two conditions: a) we are being honest with ourselves, and b) we do not consequently ignore the second aspect of loving trust. Even if a person finds himself in Paradise, he must be prepared to cleave to God even, Heaven forbid, under hellish circumstances.

It seems to me that it does not suffice to explain to our students that the righteous may suffer in this world, but that in the next world they enjoy goodness. This is just one response to the problem of human suffering, but certainly not the only one.

Q: How are we to educate students to have faith and trust, if the secular environment all around us continually sends the opposite message?

A: Indeed, it is difficult to nurture values of faith and trust in an environment dominated by secularism. Faith and trust are not the most marketable merchandise. We must redouble our efforts in the educational realm, and must provide examples through our personal conduct. I am convinced that our students can easily distinguish between a teacher who is truly devoted to his or her calling, whose soul is bound up with that which he or she teaches, and one who only goes through the motions and regards teaching merely as a livelihood. There are many ways of being dishonest in our instruction. We must build ourselves and then try to develop the spiritual potential of our students. I believe that a person who is open and sensitive will in the end come to encounter God.

Q: What has the experience of the Holocaust taught us about faith and trust?

A: Concerning faith during the Holocaust, we must recognize that the most firmly rooted tree cannot withstand great storm winds. There were many whose spiritual roots were deep and strong, who nevertheless were broken by the experience of the Holocaust. It is not possible for us to judge the religious state of particular individuals, or of a particular generation, by inquiring whether they withstood the test of the Holocaust. Of course, if someone emerged from the Holocaust with his faith intact, we have no greater evidence of devotion than this. By the same token, one who was broken by the experience did not necessarily possess less faith and trust in God at the outset. The test was overwhelming, and it is not possible to derive meaningful proof from it.

Teaching values of faith and trust is a slow and incremental process. It presents us, as well as our students, with lofty goals, with the constant challenge of achieving love of God and accepting suffering predicated on a conviction that "Though He may slay me, still I will trust in Him."

Translated by Michael Hattin with Reuven Ziegler

CHAPTER EIGHT

I Am with Him in Distress:
The Challenges of the Holocaust

The Holocaust raises many intractable questions: What were its historical roots and antecedents? How could such a cultured people commit such a crime? But the question which concerns us principally is the prophetic query echoing throughout the generations, the question of theodicy: Why do the righteous suffer?

A number of possible approaches have been put forth to tackle this problem.

a) Not only is it untrue that God ignored what was transpiring, but, on the contrary, the Holocaust was the fulfillment of His will. We need to recognize this and confess that it occurred "because of our sins." If we view the Holocaust as a punishment, we may answer the question of the suffering of the righteous with another question: Why do we ignore our own behavior preceding the Holocaust? If we are so concerned with the fulfillment of the prophecy of "women consuming their own offspring" (*Eikha* 4:10), why do we not conduct an equal level of soul-searching when faced with the image of "priest and prophet have been slain in God's sanctuary" (*ibid.* 2:20)?

b) The completely opposite approach: God has given man free choice, and He now is—as it were—unable to interfere. "When the powers of destruction are allowed to act, they do not distinguish between the righteous and the wicked" (*Bava Kama* 60a).

c) A combination of these approaches: The Holocaust represents *hester panim*, the hiding of God's face. It is neither a purposeful act on His part, nor is He bound by human freedom of choice, but rather it is a situation whereby God withdrew His hand because of the sins of *Am Yisrael*. We may ask why God hid His face, despite the fact that He could have saved us, and the answer (according to this approach) is that since modern secularism broke off all contact with God, as described in *parashat Vayelekh*, this severance became reciprocal. God hid His face as a natural result of our severance of contact with Him—not as a punishment but as a consequence. The Nazis were then able to give free rein to their satanic desires.

However, it may be preferable to leave the problem unresolved—even if it is multiplied six million times—than to accept any of these answers. Not because there are better ones—there are not, and any of these answers may theoretically be correct. We should not reject outright the answer that maintains that we suffered "because of our sins"—who are we to instruct Divine Providence as to how to punish? However, morally we dare not say this, since adopting this answer requires that we see European Jewry as a terribly wicked community, to the extent that it brought the Holocaust upon itself, or alternatively we must adjust our standards and say that such terrible punishments are the appropriate response to very ordinary sins. Yeshayahu was punished for saying, "I dwell amongst a nation of unclean lips" (6:5). For us to make such a serious accusation against the previous generation is certainly more serious than the accusation made by Yeshayahu; who would dare say that there is even some comparison between the victims and the perpetrators? Among the victims were people of the highest spiritual attainments, saints from birth and childhood. On the other hand, if we change our standards of sin and punishment, then we have to see the God of the Thirteen Attributes of Mercy in a completely different light.

The second answer—maintaining that God's hands were tied, as it were—we must also reject, for this would imply that we deny Him any role in the course of history.

The third answer, that of "hiding His face," leaves us with a question: Why? Was the situation so dire that we really deserved for God to hide His face from us?

For those of us who are believers, it is preferable to live with the question and with the faith surrounding it rather than to try and grasp at explanations of one kind or another. We cannot nor will we ever be able to provide an adequate explanation for what happened. Someone once said, in response to a question as to whether he believed an explanation would ever be found for the Holocaust, "I hope not."

A woman once asked my neighbor Leib Rochman, a Holocaust survivor, "Where was God during the Holocaust?" He replied, "He was with us." That is the only response: "I am with him in distress" (*Tehillim* 91:15). The question remains, but we are unable to supply an explanation for even smaller details of history's course because we cannot see the entire picture; how much greater, then, is our inability to explain an event of this magnitude!

We are not judged by our ability to find or create convoluted explanations. Our test lies in not forgetting and in learning lessons for the future.

Firstly, we are obligated to remember, and the remembrance is twofold. The Talmud speaks of acts we perform *zekher la-Mikdash*, in memory of the Temple, and this involves two dimensions. First, there are *mitzvot* prescribed in order to recall the *Beit Ha-mikdash*: shaking the *lulav* all seven days of *Sukkot* (*Sukka* 41a), counting the *Omer* (*Menachot* 68a), etc. Second, we have to remember not only the glory and the splendor but also the destruction and desolation (*Bava Batra* 60b). In our case, too, we have to remember the glorious Judaism that was—not just as historical knowledge, but as part of a personal relationship, with love. We have to remember the vibrant Jewish life that existed there, the Jews who walked with their heads upright in the squalid ghetto and created a rich world within that most difficult socio-political situation. At the same time, we have to remember the personal tragedies, the fearsome destruction, the chaos which befell the community and the individuals. Although there is generally a limit to mourning, namely, twelve months, we nevertheless recount each year in the *Zikhronot* (Remembrances) of *Rosh Ha-shana* our communal remembrances, and these are never forgotten.

In addition, we have to strive for a higher level of love for our fellow Jews—not just on the basis of the communal fate of the past, but on the basis of our destiny and our common future.

Thirdly, we have to learn from the poverty and suffering of the past how truly fortunate we are here and now, in the sense indicated by the *mishna* in *Avot* (4:1): "Who is wealthy? He who is satisfied with his lot." Every person is capable of seeing himself as discriminated against or as unfortunate in some respect, but when we encounter genuine suffering it is easier to put everything into its proper perspective and regain our sense of priorities. As part of this, perhaps we need to learn to appreciate little things too, even levels of spirituality which are less than lofty.

Moreover, we have to learn humility when it comes to historical commentary. Someone who cannot provide an answer for what took place during the Holocaust should not be overly eager to provide explanations for current events (even though this is sometimes convenient).

Furthermore, one of the messages of the Holocaust—paradoxical as it may seem—is that of faith. If a person experiences a period of intense difficulty and his faith wavers as a result of his troubles, he has to remember those Jews who lived through the inferno and persevered with perfect, pure faith; people who, in the midst of the hideous events which they experienced, continued to believe and persisted in their scrupulous observance of *mitzvot*. A person has to remember that each one of us is capable of being an Avraham *Avinu*—someone who believes, even if he is alone in his belief. Emil Fackenheim once said that to be a believing Jew means to be the last Jew on earth, and still to believe. Dr. Zerach Warhaftig recounted how, when he discovered Rav Yechiel Ya'akov Weinberg (author of *Seridei Eish*) at the end of the war, the latter asked him, "Are there any other Jews left in the world?" He had believed that he was the last, but nevertheless remained a Torah giant, firm in his faith.

Finally, we must be animated by a sense of mission, a feeling of duty towards God as well as towards those who sacrificed their lives. Those of us who remain on the battlefield after the great decimation of God's forces have to gird ourselves, take up their vision and carry it forward. The same responsibility they carried is now the lot of a much smaller community, and we therefore have to make much more of an effort. In the past, a person who built himself up was free to consider only himself and his own personal interests. In our generation, we have to see ourselves as part of *Kenesset Yisrael*, the Congregation of Israel, continuing in the path laid down by our fathers, lifting the baton that was struck from their hands. We are all, in a sense, survivors. We must always keep the interests of the community in mind and do our best to serve it. Moreover, our people's great and inspiring vision has in no way dimmed, and we must rededicate ourselves to pursuing its realization.

A survivor was once asked, "After the Holocaust you're still a Jew?" He immediately replied, "What else? Should I then become a gentile?" Let us not become entangled in meaningless questions of how they allowed themselves to be led like sheep to the slaughter, etc. What supreme heroism was demonstrated there! Jews sang on the way to the crematoria, "Joyful are we; how good is our portion, how pleasing our lot!" And it was not only the pious and righteous who proclaimed this.

In addition to devoting rededicated efforts to *Kenesset Yisrael* and the Torah of Israel, let us also take up the task they never had the opportunity to accomplish: building and developing the Land of Israel. Anyone who emerges from Yad Vashem experiences profound depression—and quite understandably so. But when you emerge and see the hills of Judea and Jerusalem rebuilt, you can take some comfort. We should not attempt to do an "accounting" and say that this is God's compensation to us for the Holocaust. The State of Israel is not the solution to that problem but rather an opportunity for us to fulfill our mission. It is not an answer but rather a challenge and a destiny, and our responsibility is to work towards its realization!

Translated by Kaeren Fish

CHAPTER NINE

If You Remain Silent at this Time: Concern for the Jewish People

WHY IS THE *MEGILLA* NAMED AFTER ESTHER?

On Purim, which is a day of soul-searching and not just festivity, we read the scroll known as *"Megillat Esther."* The title of the *Megilla* reflects more than just the identity of a central character around whom the plot revolves. *Chazal* teach us:

> Rav Shemuel ben Yehuda said: Esther sent [a message] to the Sages, demanding, "Inscribe me (my story) for all generations," or, according to an alternate reading, "Establish me for all generations." (*Megilla* 7a)

Hence, the obligation of recording and reading the *Megilla* would seem to arise from a direct request by Esther that *her* story be set down for all generations: "Inscribe *me*, establish *me*." But the *Megilla* in fact recounts a story which unfolds in the public arena. Is it the story of Esther alone? Surely it is the story of an entire nation, dispersed throughout Achashverosh's one hundred and twenty-seven provinces, faced with the threat of genocide. The story also involves other main characters, such as Mordekhai. Nevertheless, throughout history this book has been known not as *"Megillat Ha-Yehudim,"* nor even *"Megillat Mordekhai,"* but rather as *"Megillat Esther."*

This being the case, an accurate and thorough reading of the *Megilla* requires that we pay special attention not only to the public, national aspect of the story—the threat of destruction and the salvation—but also to Esther's personal story. Reading and understanding the *Megilla* requires that we understand what happened to Esther, and take note of the various stages of her development. What is the actual story of the *Megilla* from this point of view?

ESTHER I: PASSIVE AND GENERIC

I believe that Esther's development finds expression on two interrelated levels: strength of character and moral awareness. The Esther depicted in the closing chapters is entirely different from the Esther of the opening chapters. Let us first study her psychological development and then her moral progress.

Who is the Esther who appears on the scene in the second chapter? A beautiful young woman, but one who is powerless and completely lacking in independence of thought or action. She is under Mordekhai's patronage; he treats her like a daughter. Even if we adopt the opinion that she was his wife, we are clearly dealing with a woman who lives completely under her husband's rule. "And whatever Mordekhai said, Esther would do—just as when she was still in his home" (2:20).

There is also a certain lack of sophistication about her, a simplicity and innocence. This point is emphasized not only in her character but also in her outer appearance. All other maidens come to the royal palace with every type of adornment: "Six months [of anointment] with oil of myrrh and six months with perfumes and women's cosmetics. . ." (2:12). But "when it was the turn of Esther . . . to come to the king, *she asked for nothing*" (2:15). She wears no makeup; she is completely natural, simple, innocent and honest.

At the same time, what is equally apparent is her passivity. She does whatever Mordekhai asks her to, because she lives in his home. And when she moves to the royal palace—no longer under the patronage of Mordekhai but rather under the patronage of the royal entourage—she does only "what she is told by Hegai, the king's officer, appointed over the women." She simply follows orders, completely devoid of individual will.

Aside from her beauty, Esther lacks any distinguishing characteristics. Although there was public significance to her entry into the royal palace, there is really nothing that gives her spiritual or national prominence. The *gemara* comments (*Chullin* 139b), "Where does the Torah hint at Esther? From the words, 'I shall surely hide My face' (*Devarim* 31:18)." (This is a play on the similarity of the words *haster astir* and the name Esther.) At the beginning of the *Megilla,* it is not only the Divine Presence which is hidden; Esther herself is hidden from us. "Esther did not mention her birthplace or her nationality" (2:20). There is no Esther; she is a *tabula rasa*—no national identity, no moral identification, no roots and no background. Rather, she projects the type of generic, cosmopolitan image of one who hails from some unknown part of the hundred and twenty-seven provinces and arrives at the royal palace. No one knows whether she is a Mede or a Persian, from the north or from the south. Only one thing is known: she is beautiful and charming. But what is her identity? What is her character? What philosophy drives her?

ESTHER II: ACTIVE AND PROUDLY JEWISH

Such is the Esther of the opening chapters. A glance further on reveals how this innocent maiden suddenly displays initiative that we never would have expected of her. She takes on Achashverosh and Haman at their own game; she displays cunning, leading both of them by the nose. She leads Haman into a trap, simultaneously arousing the anger and desire of Achashverosh. Together with her personal initiative, her inner, spiritual, national and moral identities also come to full expression.

The anonymous Esther, devoid of roots, hailing from the "one hundred and twenty-seven provinces," reveals herself and is transformed into a specific, singular Esther, belonging to a "special nation." What characterizes her from that point onwards is not shrinking back into obscurity, but on the contrary—an emphasis on her uniqueness, her belonging to a special people, a nation whose "ways are different."

From here onwards, Esther not only displays initiative in the sphere of political manipulation, but, brimming with self-confidence, she faces up to Haman. Here Esther takes her place as a worthy member of the royalty, a leader. Her leadership is so outstanding towards the end of the *Megilla* that to some degree it overshadows that of Mordekhai.

Once upon a time, "whatever Mordekhai said, Esther would do." He was the one pulling the strings. Suddenly, Mordekhai's own achievements come only in the wake of Esther's initiative. How does Mordekhai come to possess Haman's home? Through Esther. Who writes the *Megilla*? While Mordekhai is still equivocating, "Queen Esther, daughter of Avichayil, wrote" (9:29), and only afterwards did Mordekhai join her.

Now it is Esther who is prepared not only to stand before Achashverosh, but also to send a letter to the Sages and demand, "Write me down! Remember me for all generations!" Is this really the same innocent maiden who "did what Mordekhai told her," and "whatever she was told by Hegai, the king's officer, appointed over the women?"

STIRRINGS OF CONSCIENCE

The answer—the difference between the end and the beginning—must be sought elsewhere: in the middle of the story, in particular, in the four verses in which the change occurs. These verses represent the key to the entire *Megilla*.

After the royal decree to exterminate all the Jews is issued in Shushan, messengers are dispatched throughout the kingdom to publicize it. Upon hearing the terrible report from her maidens and eunuchs, Esther begins to awaken somewhat from her passivity. "The queen was greatly distressed" (4:4). Esther, who indeed has the power to avert the evil decree, who lives in the royal palace, who can pull the necessary strings, does nothing. She thinks to herself, "The decree has been issued—what can I do? I'm a young and simple girl; I can't move mountains."

What eventually drives her to act? Mordekhai disturbs her complacency. The entire nation of Israel faces mortal danger, and this she is able to bear. But then she hears that her beloved adoptive father Mordekhai has removed his regular clothing and is wearing sackcloth instead. "And she sent clothing to clothe Mordekhai and to remove the sackcloth from upon him, but he did not accept it" (4:4). Instead of trying to have the royal decree annulled, instead of expressing solidarity with her people, instead of joining Mordekhai in protest and mourning, she begs him to stop this nonsense, to accept the decree as it is, and to put on some decent clothing.

Despite everything, this still represents progress. She no longer is completely inactive. Something has started to move, and once she shows active concern for an individual, Mordekhai, once the mire of passivity has been abandoned, things start to happen.

Mordekhai refuses to accept a change of clothes from Esther, so she sends a messenger to Mordekhai a second time, "to learn what this was and why this was" (4:5). What is his problem? Mordekhai sends back a very clear message: a copy of the royal decree. True, it is not clear from the *Megilla*—and this is a critical question in itself—whether Esther knew of the existence of the decree before Mordekhai sent her a copy. Even if we suppose—as I am inclined to—that she had heard mention of it, there is still a vast difference between vague rumors which reach her by various means and a copy of the actual decree sent to her directly by Mordekhai. Esther starts to respond to his message, but in a limited way.

Mordekhai persists in his appeal to her, telling her, in effect: The entire nation of Israel—young and old—is in danger. Everyone. This is the appointed date. Go and do something, in your position as wife in the royal palace: Shout! Appeal! Beg! Pray!

All around, swords are being sharpened, ammunition is being stockpiled, but Esther remains unmoved. She tells Mordekhai that she cannot approach the king: it is against palace regulations. "All the king's servants and the people of the king's provinces know that if any man or woman comes to the king, to the inner courtyard, without being called, there is a standard penalty—he is put to death!" (4:11). Of course, there are exceptions: "Unless the king holds out to him the golden scepter, then he shall live"—but I? "I have not been called to come to the king for thirty days." For a whole month we have not seen each other, and so approaching him will be a problem.

Such was Esther's response even after "the queen was greatly distressed," even after Mordekhai had sent her a copy of the king's decree. Suddenly, Esther might be exposed to personal danger. The entire nation of Israel stands on one side of the scale, and she stands alone on the other. What decides the issue? Obviously, her own problems. If there is a personal interest and a public interest at stake, which is more likely to prevail?

THE TURNING POINT—"DO NOT IMAGINE THAT YOU WILL ESCAPE"

At this point, Mordekhai sends her a message which, if we read it correctly, is quite terrible. I myself tremble anew each time I reach this verse:

And Mordekhai said in reply to Esther: *Do not imagine that you will escape in the king's palace from [among] all the Jews.* (4:13)

What a biting accusation! It would seem that he should have told her, "You don't want to do anything? Then don't. You're cowardly and lacking in any initiative! You haven't been called to the king in thirty days? So what?" This would have put Esther in a more positive light. It is terrible that you are not prepared to risk yourself, even at the expense of the entire nation, but still—it is a result of your inherent weakness.

However, Mordekhai doesn't attribute her response to weakness. He pushes his assault all the way, appealing to the deepest recesses of the Jewish soul. He accuses Esther of refusing to go to the king not because she lacks courage, not out of weakness, but rather as a calculated choice: "Let the entire Jewish nation be destroyed. Let them all perish—young and old, men and women. I will remain secure in the royal palace." This is how Mordekhai interprets her response, and this is what he addresses: not weakness, not a lack of courage, but rather what he fears may lie behind everything. Behind the apparent timidity lies *apathy*. If you really cared, if you considered your own soul to be at stake, would you be able to say, "For a whole month I have not been called to the king"? Is this how someone talks when she believes that her nation is in danger? Is this the response of someone who cares?

Someone who really cares, someone whose consciousness is deeply rooted in the collective experience of *Am Yisrael*, someone whose destiny is bound up with that of the nation, disregards any consideration of danger or possible anger on the part of the king. In fact, such a person does not even have to suppress these thoughts—they do not even enter her mind. Such considerations arise, whether consciously or subconsciously, out of a perception that everyone else may perish, but I will manage to save my own skin.

This, as we have mentioned, is a most serious accusation. What does Mordekhai want from her? He knows her, after all. She had been in his care for a long time, a young and innocent maiden, passive and naive. Why is he attacking her with this terrible accusation? Why not give her the benefit of the doubt? Why not understand her weakness? How can you expect this unfortunate young woman, an orphan who has spent years in the care of others, to courageously enter the royal courtyard?

But Mordekhai does not compromise. He understands that if one knows the situation, and if one is truly concerned, then no considerations are admissible and no rules are relevant. Rather, one must be prepared for self-sacrifice, taking care that not personal interests but rather national interests will dictate one's plans and actions. "Do not imagine that you will escape in the royal palace from all the Jews!"

"IF YOU REMAIN SILENT"

Mordekhai adds a further note:

> For if you remain silent at this time, relief and deliverance will arise for the Jews from elsewhere, but you and your father's house will perish. Who knows, perhaps for the sake of a time such as this you have come to join the royalty? (4:14)

He tells Esther: Your calculations are mistaken. Not only does your response demonstrate moral debasement, but you are mistaken in a practical sense as well. Do you believe that everyone will perish and you will remain there, in the royal palace, just because you have succeeded in entering the king's bedroom? Is that how you think God runs His world? Someone who avoids any responsibility, who doesn't care, who isn't prepared to risk herself, who sets her personal ambitions over the interests of the nation—is that the person you think will survive? Will she be the one to succeed? Will all values just disappear? "And you and your father's house will perish."

"For if you remain silent at this time, relief and deliverance will arise for the Jews from elsewhere." Salvation will come. I don't know how or from where, but it will come! Those who pay heed to sundry considerations and circumstances, the doubters and cowards of many types, those who put themselves first—all of these will perish! "Who knows, perhaps for the sake of a time such as this you have come to join the royalty?" Now is zero hour. This is the test.

This is also the turning point. Mordekhai directs this terrible accusation at the doubtful, hesitating, fearful Esther, pushing her to the wall and demanding that she stop fabricating excuses and abandon her rationalizations. He demands that she look deep into her soul and see what lies behind her hesitation. She must not try to deceive either Mordekhai, herself, or God. If she undertakes such an unflinching appraisal, she will see that what lies behind all her excuses is *apathy*.

The excuses fall away; Mordekhai rejects, one by one, all of her claims and considerations. Morally laid bare, Esther must make her fateful choice: *Do I care or don't I?*

It is now that the young, passive, powerless Esther faces her moment of truth, and she prevails. She passes the test. It is now that she rises to her full stature and reveals herself—not just in title, but in essence—as a queen.

At this moment Esther realizes that what is at stake is not just a private matter involving Mordekhai. She realizes the dimensions of the threat, the potential tragedy looming over the whole of *Am Yisrael*, including herself. She is no longer the anonymous Esther; she is prepared to reveal herself, to identify herself openly. She is ready to contribute, and to stand together with her nation. This Esther understands that her fate and destiny are not a private, personal matter, but rather bound up with those of the nation as a whole. And when the danger and the mission are public, then the course of action, too, will of necessity be a public one: "Go and gather all the Jews" (4:16).

THE WILL AND THE WAY

Well aware of her true destiny, Esther presents herself before Achashverosh. She renounces personal considerations in favor of communal ones. Only after she has passed the test of identification and concern is she capable of standing before Achashverosh, appearing before the people, leading the camp, initiating action, making demands and even deciding events.

The key to the question of where we find the transition from the retiring Esther of Chapter Two to the regal and commanding Esther of Chapter Nine is to be found in the Esther of Chapter Four. In the zero-hour of Chapter Four, the fateful showdown between Mordekhai and Esther decided the struggle between apathy and empathy, selfishness and selflessness.

As mentioned earlier, the *Megilla* recounts Esther's development on two levels: one in terms of strength of character, initiative and courage, and the other in terms of moral awareness, of reassessing priorities. The two processes go hand in hand: when Esther finds the *will* to achieve an important end, she finds the *ability* to do so as well. This is the essence of Mordekhai's message to her—if there is a will, there is a way. But first, you must truly will it.

This is indeed what happens. Once Esther cares enough, she thinks hard and arrives at a solution. Her two-pronged plan consists of prayer—"Gather all the Jews," a call to the Almighty—and donning her royal garb in order to find favor in the eyes of an all-too-human king. There is fasting, crying and raging at the heavens, together with an easy smile and a move to action. When the will prevails, suddenly it becomes apparent that one possesses the means. Those latent character traits which until now have lain dormant burst to the surface. Deeply hidden resources that have been concealed in the recesses of the soul reveal themselves when the will prevails, and prove themselves capable of overturning worlds, annulling decrees and changing the fate of an entire nation.

DO WE REALLY CARE?

Such was Esther's redemption then. *The same applies to us today.*

We are all, to some degree, Esther. Each of us, for whatever reason, has doubts as to his or her abilities. We, too, are hesitant: "What, I'm going to achieve all that? I'm going to save *Am Yisrael?* I'm going to put a stop to assimilation? I'm just a young-ster; I can achieve only a little: a little bit in my neighborhood, a little bit in a youth group, a little bit in the family. But to start a revolution? To determine the future of a nation? To avert an evil decree? Little me?"

Here comes the demand. I don't want to use Mordekhai's words, but I do want at least to pose the question. How much of our resignation is motivated by supposed "inability" and how much is a result of the fact that our concern simply doesn't run deep enough?

Esther's concern does not run deep enough for two reasons, both extremely serious. On the one hand, perhaps she does not act because of a lack of knowledge. True, she may have heard something about the decree, but she did not pay much attention. What penetrated the depths of her soul was only the family issue, the distress of Mordekhai.

The question is obvious: How can this be? The whole of Shushan is shouting it out, there are posters on every corner, chil-dren in the streets are sharpening swords, everyone knows. Can it be that only Esther, who is right in the middle of it all, in the palace, doesn't see?

Today, too, everyone knows that *Am Yisrael* is in grave danger. There is danger of assimilation, danger of mixed marriages, danger of people losing their way, danger of being cut off from roots and values. Can it be that only you cannot see it? As if this information is hidden somewhere? Is there any difficulty involved in obtaining the statistics on Jewish education in Israel and in the Diaspora? Someone who cares enough can get his hands on the figures: at least sixty percent of Jews in the Diaspora are being lost! And the situation here in Israel is nothing to get excited about either. A person is quite capable of finding out, if he's interested enough, the number of students who "drop out" of the Religious Zionist education system or who discard their *kippa* in the army!

But even more serious are Mordekhai's words to Esther. At a certain stage there is an effort to give her the benefit of the doubt: The whole of Shushan knows, except the queen? Still—maybe they told her it was just a possibility, a thought, and she may have thought that the danger wasn't imminent. But after copies of the decree of annihilation are publicly displayed, and Mordekhai brings them to her attention, can Esther still wonder why Mordekhai is trying to disturb her complacency?

Herein lies the ultimate question. It is directed to each and every one of us. Let each person do as Esther did: stand before himself, stand before God, and once the situation is quite clear to him, ask himself, "Where do I stand, who am I, what comes first, what is vital and what is secondary?" This does not imply that what is secondary is necessarily unimportant: Esther's plans of being queen and ruling over one hundred and twenty-seven provinces certainly represented serious career considerations. The question is not whether one's personal plans are inherently improper. Rather, a person must ask himself not only whether what he is doing is good and worthy, but whether it is the *best and most worthy* thing that he could be doing. He has to keep asking himself: Is this really what the circumstances require? Is this the best that I can do at this time?

Chazal teach that God once criticized the ministering angels themselves (*Yalkut Shimoni, Beshalach,* 333). When God saved the Israelites at the Red Sea by drowning the Egyptians, the angels requested to do what would appear to be their rightful job, to fulfill themselves, to express their innermost souls—they wished to break out into a joyous song of praise to God! God said to them: Indeed, song is beautiful and wonderful; it gives expression to the soul. But there are times when even song itself is not worthy of the ministering angels. "My creatures are drowning in the sea, and yet you sing My praise?!"

The angels' song itself is not necessarily wrong; it is just inappropriate at that given time. The question is one of priorities. It is good and worthy to sing praise to God, but is that all that needs to be done at this particular time?

"My creatures are drowning in the sea"—a sea of assimilation, a sea of ignorance, a sea of alienation from *Kenesset Yisrael.* And you—you who are capable of moving the carriage out of the mud, you who could lend a hand, you who could uplift the nation, you who could be inculcating values—you offer song?!

This is the real question. If you understand the situation—and there is no reason or excuse not to—then you hear the cry that emanates from every part of the country, from every corner of the globe, expressed in the spiritual dangers surrounding and threatening us on every side. Someone who cares knows what is going on, and once he knows he must ask himself: What significance does this knowledge have for me? To what extent does it cause me pain? To what extent do I identify with world Jewry, in fasting and prayer? To what extent is my spiritual world structured such that *Kenesset Yisrael* and its dangers are on one side and I, with my considerations and private plans, am on the other?

Like Esther, we will all have to ask ourselves the question when the time comes: We could have saved; did we? What will be our answer then? More importantly, what is our answer today?

Translated by Kaeren Fish with Reuven Ziegler

CHAPTER TEN

Teshuva: Repentance and Return

TESHUVA AS REPENTANCE FROM SIN

In the caption introducing his *Hilkhot Teshuva* (Laws of Repentance), the Rambam says it contains "One positive commandment, namely, that a person who has sinned should repent from his sin before God and confess." The focus of *teshuva*, as formulated here, is the act, the state, the experience of sin. *Teshuva* thus takes place within a context of sin.

The point of departure for *teshuva*, when seen as a response to sin, is *hakarat ha-chet*, the recognition and acknowledgement of sin, and this in a dual sense. First, it entails a general awareness of the impact, the power, the corrosive and pervasive force of sin—in the celebrated line from Spenser, "Sin . . . close creeping 'twixt the marrow and the skin" (*The Faerie Queene* 1:10). Beyond that, it means acknowledgement of a particular sin: not sin as a universal category, but one's own personal involvement in sin; and not one's own sin generally speaking, but a very specific sin. This, of course, is a prelude to *azivat ha-chet*, leaving sin in the present and becoming totally dissociated from it in the future.

One component of this type of *teshuva* is abandoning the path of evil, as in the verse, "Return, return, from your evil paths" (II *Melakhim* 17:13).[1] But there is also a second component. In addition to *teshuva* **from** something, or a backing-off from sin, there is also a component of returning **to** something, or to Someone, as in the verses, "Return, Israel, to the Lord your God" (*Hoshea* 14:2), and, "Return to Me and I shall return to you" (*Malakhi* 3:7).

As a result of sin, the personal relationship between man and God has been fractured, if not ruptured. It has been fractured because, in sinning, man himself is corrupted, spiritually corroded, and hence less worthy and less capable of having a relationship with God. It has been fractured because the sin itself, apart from the evil inherent within it, is an affront to God. Hence, whatever relationship a person had enjoyed with God is adversely affected by sin. Thus, *teshuva* becomes not only a process whereby a person, recognizing sin and dissociating himself from it, goes on to purify and purge himself of the negative influence of sin, but, beyond that, also a process of reconciliation, of rebuilding bridges to God, of removing barriers which sin has established between the sinner and God.

In the context of his celebrated paean to *teshuva*, the Rambam speaks of the removal of these barriers:

> How exalted is the level of *teshuva*! Only yesterday this sinner was divided from God, as it says: "Your sins were dividing between yourselves and your God" (*Yeshayahu* 59:2). He would call out [to God] without being answered. . . He would perform *mitzvot*, only to have them thrown back in his face. . . Today, [in the wake of *teshuva*,] he clings to the Divine Presence. . . He cries out and is answered immediately. . . He does *mitzvot*, and these are accepted with grace and with joy. . . And not only that, but [there are those whom] God thirsts for their *mitzvot*. . . (*Hilkhot Teshuva* 7:7)

This, then, is one facet of *teshuva*: *teshuva* within a context of sin, attempting to repair the evil itself, to rebuild the spiritual personality which has been impaired by the evil, and to arrive at a process of reconciliation and renewed harmony with God. This is the *teshuva* of repentance, which comes as a response to sin and its effects.

TESHUVA AS RETURN TO GOD

There is, however, an alternative form of *teshuva*, one which is not related directly to sin, not an outgrowth of evil, but rather one which takes place within a religious and spiritual vacuum. It occurs not in the context of one's relation to God, but rather within the context of a *lack* of relation to God. In fact, this type of *teshuva* grows out of one's perception of that lack.

Within this track, a person is neither separated from God by a barrier constructed of sins, nor does he cleave to God. He is simply dissociated. He is not engaged in agonized, interlocking combat with God, nor does he wrestle with his conscience; rather, he is oblivious and insensitive to the presence of God.

That being the case, his *teshuva* bears a very different character. It is not *teshuva* in relation to sin, but *teshuva* in response to a life which is insensitive to sin. God and one's relation to Him are not the focal point of one's life, at the epicenter of his being, but are at most a kind of peripheral presence, a set of parameters defining one's being.

This *teshuva* of return, of coming back by somehow traversing a great distance, of reconstructing or resurrecting a person's relation to God and awareness of Him, bears a distinctive stamp. To the extent that one has an awareness of having sinned, it is not the sin of direct affront or confrontation, but rather the sin of apathy, of indifference, of simply failing to relate, of averting one's gaze from God and focusing instead upon alternative concerns. To the extent that there is sin here, it is the sin of *shikhecha*, forgetting.

Two Levels of the Sin of Forgetting

The sin of *shikhecha* itself is multi-leveled. At the maximal level, there is total obliviousness. A person is simply unaware that he lives in a universe created by God, grounded metaphysically in His being, sustained by His aid and His presence. He imagines that he lives in a Never-Never Land within which he is lord and master, or man collectively is master. The sense of the both immanent and transcendent presence of God is totally beyond him. This, of course, would entail total disregard of the range of *mitzvot*.

There is, however, a second level, one which we might denominate not as *shikhecha*, but as *heise'ach ha-da'at*, a lack of attention. Here we deal not with a total lack of knowledge or recollection, but with an individual or a community in whose memory the relevant information is properly stored. If tested, they could probably respond. But they do not actively focus their attention upon it; their mind is elsewhere, upon other concerns.[2]

The term *heise'ach ha-da'at* is, of course, a familiar category in Halakha. One might cite two well-known but contrasting contexts within which it occurs. First, the law of *heise'ach ha-da'at* in relation to *tefillin*: the Rambam writes,

> One should always feel his *tefillin* whenever they are upon him, so that he shall not remove his attention from them even for a moment. (*Hilkhot Tefillin* 4:14)

Although the prohibition of *heise'ach ha-da'at* and the obligation of guarding *tefillin* properly (deriving from *Shemot* 13:10) are incumbent upon an individual, the sanctity of *tefillin* is unaffected if the *tefillin* are left unguarded.

Not so with regard to *teruma* and *kodashim* (priestly gifts and sacred items), whose sanctity—at least as far as the permissibility of eating them is concerned—is totally lost, according to Reish

Lakish (*Pesachim* 34a), if one does not pay attention to them. While R. Yochanan agrees that one may not eat *teruma* or *kodashim* that were not guarded properly, he says that the reason for this is the possibility that they were defiled by *tum'a* (impurity) when unguarded. But were we to know with certitude that they did not come into contact with *tum'a*, then the *teruma* or *kodashim* could be eaten. Reish Lakish goes beyond this, saying that *heise'ach ha-da'at* is a *pesul ha-guf*, something which disqualifies the item itself. The *teruma* or *kodashim* are defiled by the very fact that they did not receive the kind of attention which their unique status deserves. Even if we were to know for certain that no *tum'a* had touched them, the *heise'ach ha-da'at* itself removes something of their very special character.[3]

If we ask ourselves, what is the effect of a person's *heise'ach ha-da'at* in relation to God, I would submit, daring as it may sound, that there is, *kiveyakhol* (as it were), a certain *pesul ha-guf*. In a certain sense, the fact that God is ignored does not merely affect the relationship of the individual to God, but *kiveyakhol* affects His very presence here. We speak of *chillul Hashem*, desecrating the Name, and the Name means the symbolic presence of God. *Chillul Hashem* presumably means that in some sense the Name is, objectively speaking, impaired. To the extent that *malkhut Shamayim* (Divine kingship) is not fully recognized, *kiveyakhol* the presence of the *Shekhina* is adversely affected.

In a celebrated statement (*Midrash Tanchuma, Ki Tetze* 11), *Chazal* note that in the verse, "With hand upon the throne of the Lord (*kes Y-a*), [God swears that He will have a] war with Amalek from generation to generation" (*Shemot* 17:16), only a shortened form of God's Name is mentioned and not His complete Name. The reason for this is, they explain, that "God's Name and His throne are incomplete as long as the name of Amalek has not been blotted out." As long as Amalek, which totally ignores the existence of God, exists, then somehow God's Name is incomplete.

What is said there with regard to Amalek is universally true. Wherever God's Name is not recognized, then it is in some sense desecrated. *Heise'ach ha-da'at* here has some touch of *pesul ha-guf.*

INSUFFICIENT APPRECIATION AND IMPROPER EVALUATION

We have, then, two aspects of *shikhecha*: total obliviousness and inattention. But there is a third level of *shikhecha* too. Even when one relates to God and is aware of His presence, he may fail to apprehend fully and appreciate the significance of that presence and that relation. Hence, he does not perceive accurately the human situation.

Not to perceive that situation properly is a dual fault. It is in one sense an intellectual, philosophical and theological fault. A person whose perception of reality is one which, while not devoid of God, nevertheless does not position Him at its epicenter and apex, is incorrect in his perception of the nature of reality, the structure of the universe, and the quality of human society and individual existence. But, beyond this intellectual failing, there is a spiritual, if you will, a moral and religious failing, and this too is to be understood in halakhic terms.

R. Moshe of Coucy, in his work enumerating the 613 *mitzvot*, the *Semag* (*Sefer Mitzvot Gadol*), describes a dream-vision he had after completing the book:

> In the vision an apparition spoke to me and said: You have forgotten in your list of *mitzvot* the most important thing! You have counted 365 prohibitions, but you forgot the most important prohibition: "Beware lest you forget God" (*Devarim* 8:11).
>
> I had not intended to include this in the list of prohibitions; after all, the Rambam [whom he follows by and large] had

not included it. Then I reflected upon the matter in the morning and decided that indeed this was a very basic foundation in the fear of God and added it to the list. (*Semag*, end of the introduction to the prohibitions)

Within the text of the book, he explains the normative content of this mitzva:

> This is an admonition that Jews should not be proud when God bestows bounty upon them, and they should not say that it is through their labors that they have attained all of this, and they shall then not be grateful to God as a result of their pride. It is to this that the verses refer. . . This is the admonition that a person should not be proud of that which God has granted him, be it wealth, beauty or wisdom, but he is to be very humble and meek before God and before people and to thank his Creator that He has bestowed upon him this particular advantage. (*Semag*, *lo ta'aseh* 64)

Here we have a specific prohibition of *shikhecha*. The transgressor has not necessarily forgotten about God altogether; he need not even have been *meisiach da'at* from God. Perhaps he thinks of Him regularly. But what does he think when contemplating God? How does he divide the credit between himself and God for his accomplishments, nay, for his very existence? To the extent that the division is incorrect, that he gives himself credit for all that he has achieved—he is a *shokhe'ach*, he does not remember God, because he does not remember Him as the sustainer and provider for all human needs, nor does he remember Him as the ground and ultimate goal of human existence.

FORGETFULNESS AND PRIDE

This is, then, a third kind of *shikhecha*, one which is intertwined with pride in a dual sense. It is, first, the result of pride. A person is flushed with success—"So Yeshurun grew fat and kicked; you grew fat and gross and coarse" (*Devarim* 32:15)—and being flushed with success, he indeed forgets: "You neglected the Rock that begot you, and forgot the God who brought you forth" (*ibid*. 18). This theme runs through *parashat Va'etchanan* and *Ekev*: You will have fancy homes, you will build a highly developed society, with the result that this kind of *shikhecha* will become a clear and present danger.

But the relation to pride exists also at a second level. If, on the one hand, it is pride in one's accomplishments that brings one to forget God, on the other hand, it is forgetting God which enables a person to be proud. In this sense, *shikhecha* is not the result of pride, but results in pride. Where there is *shikhecha*, there are skewed priorities, a lack of perspective and narrowness of vision. These very often enable a person to distort the reality of his existence and the range and scope of his accomplishments.

Generally speaking, a vision of greatness, to one who can appreciate it intelligently and sensitively, is humbling. For one thing, it helps a person establish priorities, to see what ultimately is indeed significant and important. Milton, in a celebrated line in "Lycidas," spoke of fame as "That last infirmity of noble mind." In one of Keats' sonnets ("When I Have Fears That I May Cease to Be"), he writes,

> . . . then on the shore
> Of the wide world I stand alone, and think,
> Till Love and Fame to nothingness do sink.

As long as a person resides in a very narrow world, he imagines that he is successful, that he is eminent. He towers over contemporaries; he surpasses his peers. Indeed, he finds the thirst for fame gratifying, and he imagines that he has attained it. But, given a vision of greatness, one not only reestablishes priorities—just how important that fame is within a wide world—but one also attains a clearer perception of his real stature. So long as a person remains within a fairly narrow context, he imagines that he is a *lamdan*, a scholar—he might have a big *shiur* and people come to listen—but when confronted by the Shakh (Rabbi Shabtai Hakohen Rappaport, a seventeenth-century commentator on the *Shulchan Arukh*), one begins to get a much clearer appraisal of what genuine greatness is and therefore a more accurate appraisal of his own stature.

The vision of greatness is humbling. But, of course, what is most humbling is the vision of the ultimate, singular greatness—a vision of God. The Rambam, in a celebrated passage, speaks of the *mitzvot* of loving and fearing God:

> This great and awesome God—it is a mitzva to love and to be in awe of Him. . . And how is one to attain this?

> When a person contemplates His creations and sees within them infinite worth, scope and wisdom, then immediately he loves, praises and is overcome by great thirst to know the living God. . .

> And when he contemplates these very matters, he immediately recoils, fears and knows that he is a very minute and insignificant creature of small and superficial intellect in comparison with the Omniscient. . . (*Hilkhot Yesodei Ha-Torah* 2:1)

The verse in *Mishlei* (16:18) says, "Pride goeth before a fall," but as Augustine noted, pride is itself a fall. So the relationship of *shikhecha* and pride is dual. Pride leads to averting one's gaze from God, but it is because a person has not fully apprehended or appreciated God that he is able to be proud.

FORGETTING SINAI AND TORAH

In addition to the prohibition of forgetting God, we have a similar prohibition of forgetting that which is related to God:

> Be careful and guard your soul very much, lest you forget the things you have seen and lest these be removed from

your awareness throughout the course of your life.
(*Devarim* 4:9)

The Ramban (*ad loc.*) explains that this is to be understood as a binding halakhic prohibition, that "we should forget nothing of the experience at Sinai, nor remove it from our hearts." In his commentary on Rambam's *Sefer Ha-mitzvot*, the Ramban lists this as one of the *mitzvot* he thinks the Rambam has omitted:

> We shall neither forget *ma'amad Har Sinai*, nor remove it from our thoughts, but our eyes and hearts shall be there perpetually.

This formulation is quite comprehensive, in three respects. First, whereas previously we had known that it is forbidden to forget God, here we have an injunction against forgetting a particular historical (and quasi-metaphysical) event, *ma'amad Har Sinai*. Second, not only are we enjoined, according to the Ramban, from forgetting the event in its totality, but we are commanded to strive to remember every particular detail. It is not enough that a person remembers *ma'amad Har Sinai*, that he knows that one time "God descended on Mount Sinai" (*Shemot* 19:20), and He revealed Himself to *kelal Yisrael*, gave the Torah and then He and they moved on. To remember *ma'amad Har Sinai* is to remember it in vivid detail, to reconstruct the historical situation with all its force, to relive the experience, the awe, the majesty, the grandeur! Third, the Ramban tells us that this remembrance of *ma'amad Har Sinai* in all its vivid detail is to be perpetual.

Not only are we enjoined lest we forget God and *ma'amad Har Sinai*, but also that which was given at *ma'amad Har Sinai*:

> R. Meir says: If a person has forgotten one thing of what he has learned, it is as if he is worthy of being destroyed. . . (*Avot* 3:8)

The *mishna* then goes on to state that this does not refer to the normal processes of forgetting; those affect all of us.[4] Rather, we are talking about the *shikhecha* of "*yesirim mi-libo*"—removing it from his heart. A person thinks: It doesn't really matter, so I won't know it, and he is not perturbed. That kind of active forgetting is included in this prohibition.

In summary, then, there is active forgetting and there is passive forgetting, the result of indifference and insouciance, of apathy and anemia.

PERPETUAL REMEMBRANCE

Thus, in addition to *teshuva* within the context of active engagement in sin, there is also *teshuva* within a context of spiritual apathy, of indifference to God, of distance between the world of Torah and one's own being. Within the latter context, the proper *teshuva* is not so much that of repentance, but the *teshuva* of return, of narrowing the gap, of deepening and widening one's bond to God—a process of *teshuva* wherein a person assigns to Him a central place within his consciousness, sensibility, existence and experience.

The response to *shikhecha* is "*zakhor*," remember. *Zakhor* has a perpetual dimension—for example, "to remember *always* [Amalek's] evil deeds." Likewise, on the verse, "Remember the Shabbat day to keep it holy" (*Shemot* 20:8), Rashi explains: "Set your heart to remember continually the Shabbat day." The Ramban elaborates upon this:

> The mitzva is to remember the Shabbat always, every day, that we never forget it, nor confuse it with other days, for by remembering it perpetually we constantly remember the creation of the world. (*ad loc.*)

That perpetual aspect of *zekhira* (remembering) has both a quantitative and a qualitative dimension: quantitatively, in terms of it being the constant focus of our minds and hearts; qualitatively, in terms of the depth of the engagement, the extent to which our being is indeed intertwined in and committed to contemplating and relating to God.

The Rambam describes the nature of *avoda me-ahava* (service from love):

> What is that proper love [which a person is to love God]? A great, exceedingly intense love, until his soul is bound up with love of God and he finds himself immersed within it, like one who is lovesick, whose mind is never free of the thought of a particular woman, and he thinks of her perpetually— whether sitting, standing, eating or drinking. Greater than this should be the love of God in the hearts of His lovers, pondering upon Him perpetually, as we have been command-ed: "with all your heart and all your soul" (*Devarim* 6:5). It is of this that King Shlomo allegorically has said: "I am lovesick" (*Shir Ha-shirim* 2:5), and indeed all of *Shir Ha-shir-im* is an allegory for this. (*Hilkhot Teshuva* 10:3)

We note that the Rambam here speaks of the quantitative dimension—"perpetually," but the source which he quotes is one which relates to the qualitative aspect—"with all your heart and soul." That commandment of *zakhor*, being involved and engaged with God, has something which quantitatively is all-encompassing time-wise and which qualitatively requires your whole heart and soul.

Clearly, this level of *ahava* is very demanding. The Rambam in that very chapter seems to speak of this both as being attainable to all, and as being reached only by a small elite. On the one hand, he says (10:2), "This level is very great, and not even every sage attains it. This is the level of Avraham *Avinu*," of rare indi-viduals. But, in the same breath, the Rambam—aristocratic and elitist in certain respects though he was—nevertheless makes it clear that, normatively speaking, this is not a demand upon only religious virtuosi, but a demand imposed upon every individual. While the ultimate goal is attained by rare individuals, the direction, the thrust, the momentum as a desideratum in normative terms is the lot of each and every one of us.

"Sin Crouches at the Door"

I have spoken heretofore in general, universal terms or, if you want to narrow it somewhat, in terms which address themselves specifically to *klal Yisrael*. I want to add something with respect to a particular segment of *klal Yisrael*—Centrist Orthodoxy. The verse (*Bereishit* 4:7) says: "Sin crouches at the door." But presumably it is not the same sin at every door. Each door, each domicile, each community has its particular sin, a specific spiritual danger indigenous to it, endemic to that group or that individual. The Chafetz Chayim once commented that different generations have different pitfalls. There are generations that succumb particularly to idolatry, others to desecration of Shabbat, some to sins between man and his Maker, and others to interpersonal sins. Each community and each individual has his own "door" and his own sin to which he is susceptible. What might be regarded as the "sin that crouches at the door" of this community?

In one's relationship to God, there are two preeminent spiritual dangers. First, there is *avoda zara* (foreign worship, or idolatry) and, broadly speaking, whatever relates to it—superstition and misguided conceptions of God. There is also a second danger: *kefira*, atheism—not that a person misconstrues and misconceives God, but that he denies God altogether.

There have been debates as to which should be regarded as being worse. Bacon opens his essay "On Atheism" by quoting Plutarch's remark that superstition is worse than atheism because he would prefer that people say Plutarch had never existed, to stating that he had existed but ate his children. The eighteenth century, more rational in its thinking, by and large accepted Plutarch's and Bacon's judgments. Better to deny the existence of

God, better to be removed from Him, than to be caught up in narrow, ignorant, superstitious worship.

The nineteenth century, by and large, particularly in its Romantic religious thought, disagreed. It felt that the groping for some kind of spiritual reality, giving expression to spirituality in various modes—however primitive, narrow or misguided—was to be preferred to the kind of rarefied religiosity (or non-religiosity) which the eighteenth century left as a legacy to the Romantics. In a celebrated passage about England in the 1840's, Cardinal Newman wrote, "What this country needs is not less superstition, but more superstition"—out of a sense that for all its faults, it nevertheless entails an awareness of spiritual reality and a quest for it.

If pressed to the wall, I would opt for Newman without reservation. But of course we ought not, we cannot, allow ourselves to be pressed to the wall. We need to be sensitive to both dangers. Which is more threatening? To a certain extent, that is a function of a given historical and sociological situation, depending upon the era, depending upon the community.

What is the danger lurking at the door of this community? Of what does it need to be particularly wary because its inclination lies in that direction?

I believe that the sin lurking at the door of the Centrist Orthodox or Religious Zionist community, the danger which confronts us and of which we need to be fully aware, is precisely the danger of *shikhecha*. Unlike other communities, this is a community which is not so susceptible to *avoda zara* in its extension—attitudes the Rambam battled against, such as superstition and gross or primitive conceptions of God—because it is more sophisticated intellectually, religiously and philosophically. Unfortunately, however, it is very, very susceptible to extended *kefira* or *shikhecha*, lacking the immanent sense of God felt so deeply, keenly and pervasively in other parts of the halakhically-committed Jewish world.

CREEPING SECULARISM AND
DAMPENED PASSION

The Centrist Orthodox community is one to which the danger of distance from God—the eighteenth-century danger, the danger of a certain spiritual hollowness, of apathy, of pushing God off into the corners—is indigenous and endemic. In part, this is a result of the link this community has—to some extent ideologically, to some extent existentially—to the broader, general, secular community around it. The secular world is, by definition, not so much the world of sin *per se*, but a world of being distant from God, of simply not recognizing Him, having no links and no relation.

Of course, the secular world as such is one which, philosophically and ideologically, denies God totally. But when I spoke before of *avoda zara* as threatening others, I was not referring *chas ve-shalom* to the possibility that an idol is going to be put up and incense offered before it, but of the broader spiritual ramifications. Here, too, in speaking of the dangers of *kefira* attendant upon being linked to the secular order, one needs to think not merely of a kind of dogmatic rejection, but of experiential distance—"You are near to their mouths, but distant from their innards" (*Yirmiyahu* 12:2).

The demands made by the secular world very often have the effect of chipping away at one's religious existence. The secular world very often likes to speak in the name of neutrality. If they speak, for instance, of education, they say: We are not asking for anti-religious education, but for neutral education; not an education of sin, but an education of distance. But from a religious standpoint, neither philosophically nor existentially can such neutrality be sustained—not over the short term and surely not over the long term. An education from which God is excluded is not a neutral education. That is secular, anti-religious education by its very content and definition.

To take an unfortunate, insidious, recent example: We are told that the Israeli army must be religiously neutral, and therefore missives which are sent out by commanders cannot have God's Name or any reference to it affixed to it; and this in the name of democracy and fair play. What we have here is a kind of secularization which does not say, "Throw out God," but effectively does that.

The link with a social order grounded upon a sense of distance from God—both experiential and ideological—can have an impact, and one needs to guard against that. One needs to know that the link to such an order opens up a door through which sin can enter. In order to ensure that it does not enter, we need to be vigilant, we need to intensify our commitment, and we need to avoid *shikhecha* and *heise'ach ha-da'at* all the more.

Secondly, this kind of sin crouches at our door because, in certain respects, there is a certain shallowness, a certain lack of passion and intensity within our own community. Quite apart from whatever rubs off through contact with others, there is a form of *shikhecha*, a lack of total *zekhira*, a dearth of absolute commitment which runs through much of this community.

We need to be aware of this sin at our door, because only to the extent that we are aware of it will we be able to cope with it. If we are to engage in *teshuva* that is particularly relevant to ourselves, it is, perhaps even more than the *teshuva* of repentance (which is within the context of relationship to God), the *teshuva* of return.

Nearness to God

We might single out a particular sin from the "*Al chet*," the litany of sins we recite, which (at least as some have interpreted) relates to this particular situation: "*Al chet she-chatanu lefanekha bi-veli da'at*, for the sin which we have sinned before

You without knowledge." The *viddui* contains two kinds of confessions. There are those which are themselves sins, and others which are not inherently sins, but are either areas of experience or activity within which the sin takes place, or a kind of quality or mind-set which attends upon the sin. *"Bi-veli da'at"* can be understood in two ways. Some, perhaps most, would be inclined to understand it in the second sense: it is that which enables us to be sinners. We were not sufficiently heedful, and as a result a particular sin ensued.

But some have understood *"bi-veli da'at"* as being itself a sin. A certain mindlessness is a failing inasmuch as we do not then fully realize the *tzelem E-lokim* (image of God) within us—to the extent that one accepts the Rambam's view that *tzelem E-lokim* is *da'at*, knowledge. Even if one does not subscribe to that view, surely *da'at* is one aspect of *tzelem E-lokim*. To the extent, then, that our *da'at* is not maximized, we fail to realize our potential *tzelem E-lokim*. Quite apart from that, inasmuch as the *"beli da'at,"* the lack of focus and concentration, defines our relationship to God, we are not "perpetually dwelling upon God." When some quantitative or qualitative *shikhecha* intrudes, that *"bi-veli da'at"* is a sin in its own right. And, I repeat, this is a particular sin which confronts and afflicts this sector of the religious community.

That being the case, the *teshuva* which is specifically incumbent upon us is the *teshuva* of return, of narrowing the distance, of no longer forgetting, of intensifying our awareness, of bridging the gap. At one level, that entails genuinely sensing and understanding with the totality of our being—not simply in our intellectual formulations, but with the whole fiber of our existence— that indeed obliterating the distance is our ultimate good, our *summum bonum*. We must fully identify with King David when he says (*Tehillim* 73:27): "As for me, nearness to God is good"— *that* is good, and *only* that is good. Secondly, it entails making the effort—both personally and communally—to close that gap, to bring ourselves closer to God and hopefully, therefore, God closer to us.

These are days during which He is close already; *Chazal* say, on the verse in *Yeshayahu* (55:6), "Seek God when He is present, call Him when He is near," that this refers to the ten days from *Rosh Ha-shana* to *Yom Kippur*. These are days in which one hears the message of the prophet calling those from afar and those who are close (*Yeshayahu* 57:19). As *Chazal* say: "'To the near and far'—to the far that he should be near" (*Sanhedrin* 99a). This is a call to one who is not necessarily a sinner in the ordinary sense, but simply distant, his mind engaged in other concerns, with God somewhere on the periphery.

These are days when God, being so near, calls for the determination and resolve that we, on our part, shall go towards Him—as He has extended Himself and His hand to us—transcending the sin that lurks at our door, the sin of *shikhecha*, of distance, of dissociation. These are days during which the effort needs to be made and during which, we hope, when the effort is made, it shall be crowned at a personal and communal level with success: that God should accept our return with love. As we say in the *Zikhronot* prayer of *Rosh Ha-shana*:

Happy is the man who does not forget You, who gains courage in You, for those who seek You shall never stumble, nor shall those who trust in You ever be disgraced.

NOTES:

1   See also *Hilkhot Teshuva* 2:2.

2   *Heise'ach ha-da'at* can also be regarded as a *shikhecha* of sorts. At least so it would appear from the *gemara*, which concludes that failing to focus is also defined as *shikhecha*. Regarding the *mitzva* of remembering Amalek, the *gemara* asks:

How do you know that when we speak of "remember[ing] what Amalek did to you" (*Devarim* 25:17), we are talking about reading a text? Maybe it means ruminating upon this matter, pondering it, contemplating it? No, such a presumption should not cross your mind, for the *baraita* [in *Sifri*] says: Perhaps when it says "Remember" it means you should remember this in your heart? But we know that it is otherwise, because when the verse says, "You shall not forget" (*Devarim* 25:19), it has already addressed itself to the area of forgetting in one's heart. What then is the additional dimension of "Remember?" That you should verbalize it. (*Megilla* 18a)

An obvious question obtrudes here. We are told "*lo tishkach*," you should not forget. We presumably would have understood that your knowledge of the facts should be at a level whereby it is stored in your memory, subject to recall. If you would be tested – who is Amalek? what did he do? – you will know the answer. But whether presently you actively recall it is another matter; that is not included in "*lo tishkach*." We would therefore have said that the command of "*zakhor*" then comes along and teaches: Not only should you not forget, but you must think about it. However, the *gemara* says otherwise. The whole realm of one's inner awareness is covered by "*lo tishkach*." Had the Torah not stated "*zakhor*," we would already have known that one must actively think about it, but we would not have known that one needs to verbalize it.

Clearly then, if a person has stored in his memory this information about Amalek, but does not actively consider the matter, then he is already transgressing the prohibition of "*lo tishkach*." Knowledge is thus fully compatible with *shikhecha*. *Shikhecha* in the context of that *gemara* clearly is not to be understood as total forgetting, but simply *heise'ach ha-da'at*. One knows about Amalek, but it is unpleasant to think about him, and consequently one would prefer to keep the information about Amalek as a kind of historical island in his memory, but go on to other activities. That is precisely the prohibition of "*lo tishkach*." You have to think about it, and you have to surmount this *shikhecha* in part by active narrative and in part by permanent, ongoing reflection.

The Rambam is very clear on this point. When he explains the mitzva of remembering Amalek, he says:

> It is a mitzva to remember *always* his evil deeds and his ambush (according to another reading: his enmity) in order to arouse enmity to him, as it says, "Remember what Amalek did to you." From tradition they learned: "Remember" verbally, and "do not forget" in your heart, i.e. it is forbidden to forget his enmity and hatred. (*Hilkhot Melakhim* 5:5)

While the *gemara* says that "*zakhor*" comes in addition to "*lo tishkach*," the Rambam suggests that the two are complementary. What "*zakhor*" adds to "*lo tishkach*" is the verbalization, the objectification, the expression and, therefore, the degree of force and vivacity which comes through verbalization. On the other hand, verbalization cannot be constant, and the dimension of constancy comes from "*lo tishkach*." Thus, if we speak of *heise'ach ha-da'at*, that too is a category of *shikhecha*.

3   With regard to R. Yochanan's view, it is entirely possible that he rejects the whole notion of *heise'ach ha-da'at* as adversely affecting the sanctity of *teruma* and *kodashim*. But not necessarily so. It is conceivable that R. Yochanan would agree that in some sense there is an adverse effect, but not to the point that one cannot eat them at all.

4   As a matter of fact, *Chazal* in certain places regarded normal processes of forgetting as being beneficial. The *midrash* (*Kohelet Rabba* 1:13) says that God has done us a great kindness by causing us to forget. If a person did not forget, then presumably he would learn Torah once and then assume that since he now knows it, he will move on to other things. He would have the knowledge, but would lack the ongoing existential and experiential relation to Torah.

CHAPTER ELEVEN

A Pure Heart: Refining Character and Balancing Values

REPENTANCE FOR NEGATIVE CHARACTER TRAITS

I would like to focus on a single passage in the Rambam, which offers a fundamental perspective on the spiritual life, as expressed in both moral and religious terms.

> You ought not say that *teshuva* (repentance) applies only to sins which entail action, such as fornication, robbery, and theft. Rather, just as a person needs to repent from these, so too he needs to probe which bad character traits (*de'ot ra'ot*) he may have, and to repent from them: anger, enmity, envy, frivolity, the pursuit of wealth and honor, the pursuit of foods, and the like. From all of this, a person needs to repent. And these sins are more difficult than those which entail an action, for when a person becomes immersed in these, it is very difficult to part from them. And so says the verse (*Yeshayahu* 55:7), "Let the evil person forsake his path, and the iniquitous person his thoughts." (*Hilkhot Teshuva* 7:3)

The Rambam posits two categories: "sins which entail action," with respect to which everyone agrees that *teshuva* is essential, and "bad character traits," with regard to which some people presumably would claim that *teshuva* is irrelevant. What is the distinction between these two categories?

The Rambam does not distinguish here between sins of action and sins of thought. Rather, he broadens the concept of *teshuva* to include repentance not only from clearly defined halakhic sins but also from that which initially one might not regard as a formal sin at all.

There are specifically designated and halakhically formulated sins which relate not to one's deeds but rather to one's mindset, to one's psychological inclinations. For example, if a person entertains thoughts denying God's existence, he has transgressed a prohibition (*Hilkhot Yesodei Ha-Torah* 1:6). If a person is full of hatred for a fellow Jew—a focused hatred, not just some general anger at the world—then he has violated the sin of "hat[ing] your brother in your heart" (*Vayikra* 19:17). The *Chovot Ha-levavot* in particular champions the need for sensitivity to this type of commandment. Nevertheless, in the context of this passage in the Rambam, these constitute "sins that entail action."

In the early chapters of *Hilkhot Teshuva*, the Rambam spoke of the need to repent from those sins that are clearly defined as such—and in this context it is immaterial whether they are what the *Chovot Ha-levavot* would categorize as "duties of the limbs" or "duties of the heart." However, in our passage, the Rambam extends the need for *teshuva* to areas which, in concrete halakhic categories, we would find very difficult to proscribe. Although in a narrow halakhic sense these bad traits are not "sins," the Rambam here uses this term to describe them. This suggests that, while these are not formally classified under a particular transgression, nevertheless, to the extent that they are corrosive to one's optimal spiritual personality, they are sinful.[1]

SPIRITUALLY CORROSIVE, BUT
NOT SPECIFICALLY PROHIBITED

Let us examine the Rambam's examples.

ANGER: The Rambam considered anger an extremely bad trait. When he formulated his golden mean, the median route a person should follow in his character traits, he specifically excluded anger: it is always proscribed (*Hilkhot De'ot* 2:3). As support, he cites the *gemara* (*Shabbat* 105b): "Whoever loses his temper, it is as if he has worshipped idols." Anger is dehumanizing; it expresses a loss of self-control. Instead of a person being the master of his passions, he has become their slave. This is why it is "as if he has worshipped idols:" idolatry means handing over control to something else. However, to my knowledge, there is no verse in the Torah or ruling in the *Shulchan Arukh* that tells us what transgression such a person has committed.

HATRED: There are specific prohibitions against hatred, such as the above-cited verse: "You shall not hate your brother in your heart" (*Vayikra* 19:17). However, I believe the Rambam is not referring to this focused prohibition. Suppose that one hates people who are not included in this prohibition, which speaks very specifically of "your brother," your fellow Jew. If a person has great love for his brethren, but hates everybody else, he still falls under the purview of this passage in the Rambam, for he has a poisoned personality, a personality full of bitterness and enmity, a personality that is rotten to the core. In this passage, the Rambam speaks of the need to uproot hatred from one's heart, not because of its impact upon those who are the objects of his hatred, but rather because hatred is a cancer which consumes one's moral and psychological self.

ENVY: *Chazal* expressed very strong words about envy: "Rabbi Eliezer Ha-kappar said: Envy, lust and honor remove a person from this world" (*Avot* 4:21). This refers to a person who has a passionate, sometimes obsessive, quest for the object of his lust or envy. One might interpret the *mishna* to mean that these remove a person from the World-to-Come. But I think that anyone who knows people who are totally consumed by envy, lust and honor realizes that such people have effectively removed themselves from "this world" as well. Even if there are circumstances where envy is not formally prohibited, it nevertheless is to be avoided since it is a "bad character trait."

FRIVOLITY: The Rambam's term "*hittul*" combines two sins mentioned in the "*Al Chet*" litany recited on Yom Kippur: *latzon* and *kalut rosh*, scoffing and lightheadedness. This term describes a person lacking what Matthew Arnold called "high seriousness." The book of *Mishlei* takes a very low view of *leitzanut*, or mocking frivolity, and likewise *Chazal* declare: "All *leitzanut* is prohibited, unless it is directed against idolatry" (*Megilla* 25b). It is a quality of heart and soul, which certainly does not make for the optimal spiritual life. The first verse in *Tehillim* declares, "Happy is the man ... who does not sit in a gathering of *leitzim*"—we do not want to be seen in their company. But, again, there is no specific prohibition here.

PURSUIT OF WEALTH, HONOR OR FOOD: These categories may impinge on actual prohibitions. For example, we find two problems mentioned in conjunction with the rebellious son: first, "he does not hearken to our voice," showing a lack of honor for his parents, and second, "he is a glutton and a drunkard" (*Devarim* 21:20). While the former violates one of the Ten Commandments, what is the prohibition against the latter? The *Sefer Yere'im* (275) writes that this violates the prohibition of "You shall not walk in their statutes" (*Vayikra* 18:3), while the Ramban (*Devarim* 21:18) suggests that it violates either the injunction to be holy (*Vayikra* 19:2) or to serve God and cleave to Him (*Devarim* 13:5). Nevertheless, it is hard to define gluttony as a prohibition *per se*. Likewise, pursuit of wealth is undesirable, and the prophet Yeshayahu rails against those who "love bribes and are greedy for gifts" (1:23). The problem he denounces is not limited to dishonesty in government, but includes the obsessive passion for the accumulation of wealth. Lastly, while pursuit of honor may seem nobler than the other two pursuits, it still is not the spiritual path a person should follow. Yet, while all three of these pursuits are spiritually corrosive, they are not focused prohibitions.

WHY WOULD ONE PRESUME *TESHUVA* TO BE IRRELEVANT HERE?

As noted, the Rambam believes that many readers might be inclined to regard repentance as confining itself to sin in the strict sense, but not relating to the more general qualities of heart and soul that characterize a person's self and his lifestyle.[2] Why would one imagine that *teshuva* does not relate to these things? There might be two answers, one concerning the difficulty of *teshuva* in these cases, and the other related to its necessity.

One might imagine that a person is not in a position to achieve *teshuva* in a meaningful sense with regard to basic character traits. First, there is no particular action which you can regret and recant. Second, many people are likely to be of a more deterministic cast regarding character traits, assuming that perhaps one can change his habits, but it is beyond a person's reach to change his mindset or psychological constitution.

On the other hand, one might assume that *teshuva* here is possible but that it is unnecessary, and this from several perspectives. Many adhere to the school of thought that one's character traits are essentially neutral matters, morally speaking, as long as you do not hurt anyone. By this I do not mean people who hold

John Stuart Mill's view that government should not interfere except in interpersonal matters; Mill certainly thought that, as far as morality is concerned, it makes a great deal of difference what kind of person you are. But there are people who are far more liberal than Mill, and assume that even your character traits are entirely a matter of choice, as long as you do not bother anyone.

There are some who would go even further and idealize possessing some measure of envy, frivolity or greed, in order to be able to resist them. They understand the dictum, "Who is a hero? He who overcomes his inclination" (*Avot* 4:1), as indicating that you should have an inclination to overcome. The Rambam rejects this and stresses the need to repent from these negative traits, because Halakha poses demands and standards regarding character traits no less than with regard to more defined sins.

"THESE SINS ARE MORE DIFFICULT"

In the continuation of our passage, the Rambam posits that "these sins are more difficult (*kashin*) than those which entail an action." In what sense is this true?

Some *Acharonim* have suggested that this is a paraphrase of the *gemara* (*Yoma* 29a), "Thoughts of sin are more difficult (*kashin*) than sin." Rashi understands the term "thoughts of sin" as being sexual in nature; the *gemara* says that it is more difficult to inhibit forbidden sexual fantasy than it is to refrain from an actual sexual infraction. There is a certain line which needs to be crossed if a person is going to transgress a sexual prohibition, and a person can restrain himself more easily from crossing that line. Firstly, he has a clearer and a sharper sense of the fact that this is indeed wrong. Secondly, it is something which requires initiative on his part, and he can prevent that. However, it is more difficult to restrain fantasies. This explanation of the *gemara* understands *kashin* in the sense of difficulty.

In his *Guide of the Perplexed* (3:8), the Rambam interprets the *gemara* differently: *kashin* does not refer to the difficulty of preventing thoughts of sin, but rather to their severity. In a sense (though not in the strictly halakhic sense), thoughts of sin are worse than the sin itself, for the center of the human personality is the heart or mind, and not the body. If a person has sinned with his hands or feet, he has defiled some peripheral and marginal aspects of his selfhood. But if a person sins with his heart, his passions, his thoughts, he has defiled the epicenter of his spiritual personality, and that is, in a sense, worse. Here we have an indication of the seriousness with which the Rambam took one's inner being.

A DIFFERENT TYPE OF *TESHUVA:* MOLDING OF PERSONALITY

Chapter Seven of *Hilkhot Teshuva* contains some formulations that appear surprising at first. After speaking vigorously in Chapters Five and Six about the power of human freedom, the Rambam at the beginning of our chapter draws an inference from this:

> Since every person is endowed with free will, as we have explained, he should try to perform *teshuva* and confess his sins verbally and renounce them, so that he may die penitent and thus be worthy of the World-to-Come. (7:1)

The Rambam's formulation—"he should try"—is uncharacteristic. Does *Hilkhot Shofar* stipulate that a person should "try" to hear the *shofar*? One is obligated, and there is nothing more to say. We are accustomed to hearing the Rambam speak in normative and imperative terms, presenting a substantive and absolute demand.

Another noteworthy formulation is the duration of this attempt at *teshuva*; apparently, he is talking about a lifelong enterprise.[3]

Clearly, in light of the two chapters on free will, Chapter Seven presents a different modality of *teshuva* than the earlier chapters. Chapters One and Two deal with *teshuva* as a very specific halakhic performance, which has a focused *mechayyev* (obligating factor) and mode of fulfillment. After committing a specific sin, there is a focused response, composed of defined stages: abandoning sin, regret, resolve for the future and confession to God. In Chapters One and Two, the Rambam focuses particularly upon *viddui*, confession.

But, moving to Chapter Seven, if a person is guilty of, for example, frivolity, at what point does he engage in confession? Does he confess a particular incident of frivolity, as he would confess to having eaten ham on a specific occasion? I doubt it. I have no proof that it is not so, but it seems unlikely that there is this focused kind of confession when we speak of a general quest, a personal housecleaning.

Clearly, we have here an extension of *teshuva* in two senses.

First, in terms of the ambience: the first two chapters speak about *teshuva* in a very narrow context—there was a sin and there must be a response of *teshuva*. Here the Rambam speaks of something else entirely, namely, the molding of the human personality, the maximization of one's spiritual self and the realization of his psychological, moral and religious potential. It is to this end that the Rambam offers what seems an exaggerated description of the lack of bounds of human freedom: "Every human being is free to become righteous like Moshe our Teacher or wicked like Yeravam. . ." (*Hilkhot Teshuva* 5:2).

Second, the Rambam extends the scope of *teshuva*, in the manner we mentioned before—one must repent not only from sins, but from all kinds of other flaws as well.

These two extensions are related. A very focused procedure of *teshuva*, as in the first two chapters, needs to have an object to which it relates, and that object must be a particular sin. By contrast, in building a personality, we focus not only on one's literal obedience to the *Shulchan Arukh*, but, in the broader sense, on the extent to which he forms himself in line with what *tzelem E-lokim* (the image of God) should be. That may entail many factors which are of great significance to the religious life, but not necessarily classified, narrowly speaking, in particular halakhic categories.

The interplay between the earlier chapters and Chapter Seven highlights one aspect of the total religious balance we seek. One certainly must relate to every jot and tittle of formal Halakha, and beyond this, also to moral qualities.[4] Today we speak of a person as being a *ba'al teshuva* (penitent) when he first led a life of sin and lacked commitment, and then decided to serve God. In Chapter Seven, the Rambam speaks of people who already serve God, and says that each person must attempt to be a *ba'al teshuva*, in the sense that he endeavors to remove himself from sin and to maximize his potential. This is a process, an effort, a direction: "he should try to perform *teshuva*" (7:1). *Teshuva* is not just a response to particular sins, but a lifelong enterprise of building oneself, and therefore everyone should think of himself as a *ba'al teshuva*.

INWARDNESS IN JUDAISM

The Rambam's move to an area of greater inward or spiritual thrust invites a brief glance at where Judaism stands with regard to the element of inwardness.

Some very central and cardinal *mitzvot* are "duties of the heart:" love and fear of God, *teshuva*, prayer, service of God, etc. Nevertheless, the bulk of *mitzvot* relate to actions, and Judaism takes action very seriously. What of intention that does not come to expression in action? Clearly, a person should try to distance himself emotionally and psychologically from sin. Yet, the *gemara* (*Kiddushin* 40a) tells us that God is very liberal with regard to intention. If a person entertained the thought to perform a mitzva, but failed to do it due to some external reason, it is considered as if he had performed it. However, if a person wanted to commit a sin, but for some reason he did not succeed—his gun misfired or he did not aim properly—it is not considered as if he committed the transgression. In terms of evaluating the person, his murderous inclinations are very negative, but we do not regard him as a murderer in the moral sense. This is opposed to the Kantian conception that defining an action as good or bad depends on one's intention, not on what actually happens.

The element of inwardness relates not just to intention but also to motivation. Are we concerned only with one's actions, or also with his reasons for acting? This has halakhic ramifications when dealing with the question of *mitzvot tzerikhot kavvana*—is it enough technically to perform the mitzva, or must the person be impelled by the intent and desire to fulfill the mitzva? This entails a detailed halakhic discussion, but suffice it to note that there are many statements of *Chazal* which indeed focus on the inner element—for example, "God desires the heart" (*Sanhedrin* 106b).

Unquestionably, we strive to recognize the importance of both elements: external action and inwardness. Not only do we believe that a person's actions influence his inner self,[5] which would suggest that the inner self is our ultimate concern, but we also clearly ascribe importance to one's actions *per se*. In moral terms, our actions impact upon society, and in mystical and metaphysical terms, every mitzva performance illuminates a light on the celestial switchboard, so to speak. Thus, those who engage in the search for *ta'amei ha-mitzvot* (reasons for the commandments) can posit a number of categories: *mitzvot* which aim to attain practical results, *mitzvot* oriented towards inner being, and *mitzvot* with a dual focus. An instance of the last category would be the mitzva of *tzedaka* (charity), which intends both to provide the needs of the poor and to educate the affluent.

In many places, the Rambam too insists upon balancing the external and the internal. Take, for example, his famous conclusion to *Sefer Tahara*. Although, he says, the realm of *tum'a* and *tahara* (impurity and purity) is supra-rational, as is the immersion which absolves a person of *tum'a*—"for *tum'a* is not mud or filth which water can remove, but is a matter of Scriptural decree and dependent on the intention of the heart"—nevertheless, there is an axiological message here as well:

> Just as one who sets his heart on purification becomes pure as soon as he has immersed himself, although nothing has changed physically, so too a person who sets his heart on purifying himself from the impurities that beset people's souls— namely, thoughts of evil and bad character traits [which we encountered earlier in *Hilkhot Teshuva*]—is purified as soon as he decides in his heart to distance himself from these counsels and brings his soul into the waters of pure reason . . . (*Hilkhot Mikvaot* 11:12)

THE NEED FOR BALANCE

To a great extent, in Chapter Seven of *Hilkhot Teshuva* the Rambam is trying to redress an imbalance in the earlier chapters.[6] The earlier chapters indeed gave a narrow picture of *teshuva* and therefore a confined image of spiritual and religious life. It was limited in the sense that it related to very specific and focused events, as opposed to a general continuum encompassing the totality of one's being. And it was narrowly focused inasmuch as it dealt only with strictly defined sins. One's religious life should not be confined to observance in the narrow sense; instead, it must be viewed in broader terms. The Rambam does not want to negate what he said previously, but rather to complement, extend and balance it.

Balance, for the Rambam, is very important. We have already noted that in *Hilkhot De'ot* he idealizes balance as an equipoise between two extremes. Throughout his works, the Rambam stresses its importance in different areas of one's life: action, emotion, thought, one's personal, social, religious and moral self. This follows the comment of *Chazal* (*Mo'ed Katan* 5a) on the verse (*Tehillim* 50:23), "To him that orders his way (*ve-sam derekh*), I will show the salvation of God"—"Do not read *ve-sam*, but rather *ve-sham*," meaning, counting and weighing; a person who considers and balances his path will behold God's salvation.

Some people instinctively react against the notion of balance, regarding it as being tepid, placid and overly rationalistic. They feel that the power, passion and intensity of a more total and unbalanced commitment is preferable in religious life. They idealize a different *midrash* (*Bereishit Rabba* 40:2), on the verse (*Tehillim* 111:5), "He has given food (*teref*) to those who fear Him," reading *teiruf* (madness) instead of *teref*. The idealization of Divine madness, the madness of commitment, sounds much more attractive and powerful—it is not constrained, constricted, limited or defined; it knows no bounds or limits.

I submit that, for the Rambam, there is a need to strike the proper balance between madness and rationality. The Rambam, too, certainly knows of *teiruf*; he speaks of the love of God as "great, exceedingly intense . . . like one who is lovesick" (*Hilkhot Teshuva* 10:3). So the rational Rambam, the Rambam of balance, the Rambam of defining limits and seeking equipoise, is also the Rambam who speaks of an all-consuming love. For the Rambam, more broadly viewed, the element of balance as a condition of one's ideal service of God requires some balance between *teiruf* and *ve-sham derekh* as well.

TAILORING THE MESSAGE TO THE AUDIENCE

Now, if a person advocates a balanced view and tries to maintain equilibrium between various values and goals, he will very often find himself, depending on his historical circumstances or social context, speaking a very different language when addressing varying audiences. If a person finds that his interlocutor is failing with regard to one aspect of the ideal balance, then obviously he must tailor his message to counteract the imbalance.

For example, if one addresses an audience which is very punctilious with regard to the technical, formal aspects of Halakha, but perhaps not so careful about the vices the Rambam discusses here—maybe they are very cautious about *tzitzit* and *tefillin*, but not so cautious about the pursuit of honor—then the message may very well be, without minimizing the importance of *tzitzit* and *tefillin*, that this is not sufficient. It then may seem to someone who later reads his words, without taking into account their intended audience, that this is a person who tries to moralize and ethicize the religious life, playing down its more technical and formal aspects.

If the reverse should be true, and a person finds himself in front of an audience that is very deeply committed morally and ethically but is not so careful about details of Halakha, the tone and the thrust of the message will be different. One will stress that being moral is insufficient; if a Jew wants to serve God, he also has to follow Halakha. In either case, the total message will be balanced, but the way it is presented will be very different.

Thus, if one strives for balance, yet finds himself in a situation (either within his own being or in relation to others) where there is a perceived imbalance, his choice of which elements to stress obviously depends on circumstances and on whom he is addressing.

OUR TASK

This is true of the Rambam, and it should also be true of us. If we try to build a proper *hashkafa* of Torah, Halakha and *emuna*, there is no question but that we need to see the total picture. The grandeur and the majesty of Halakha lie precisely in its comprehensiveness. This total picture must encompass thought, action and emotion; it must be seen from social, historical and personal perspectives and must include all the moral and religious elements one needs in order to maximize his standing as an *oved Hashem* and to be fully responsive to God's call.

However, each of us is capable of going only so far in trying to implement everything. Every person and every period has its own emphases and, therefore, its own deficiencies. Every so often, someone will arise and sound the clarion, challenging not only what is being neglected, but sometimes even what is being done. Imbalance can be sinful—a sacrifice brought by an immoral person is rejected by God: "The offering of evildoers is an abomination" (*Mishlei* 21:27). The same holds true of his prayer: "Though you pray at length, I will not listen" (*Yeshayahu* 1:15).

In other contexts, the rejection may not be as severe, but a critique of imbalance will appear. In their respective introductions, the *Chovot Ha-levavot* and the *Mesillat Yesharim* were critical of those who overemphasized theoretical learning while ignoring the more pietistic aspects of religion; R. Yisrael Salanter critiqued what he felt to be a moral deficiency within his Torah community; the Chassidim critiqued what they felt to be an emotional deficiency in the Torah-observant community.

We are challenged, personally and communally, to strive for balance, comprehensiveness and particularly for the balance between the inner and the outer that is so critical to the character and content of Halakha. We are challenged to be honest with ourselves and to ask not only what particular sins we should repent, but also, looking at the broader picture which the Rambam paints, what is our particular area of need, what needs to be strengthened and emphasized.

Here the answers may differ, depending on the audience. This is not because the total message is different, but because the particular *teshuva* which a person requires is a function of where he is now. Additionally, the ideal balance is not a uniform one; it may differ from one person to another, partly as a function of historical circumstances, and partly as a function of one's personal inclinations.7

A person's spiritual accounting should include a focus both on the overarching challenges of the first two chapters of *Hilkhot Teshuva* and on the more personalized challenge of Chapter Seven. To what extent are we tainted in one respect or another? What kind of balance do we need to strike between Chapter Seven and the first two chapters? This, too, differs from one person to another.

In one respect, *teshuva* is uniform, and in other respects, in terms of substantive content and emphasis, it is diverse. The challenge of *teshuva* is not only to be attentive and responsive to its demand, but also to be honest and sensitive in one's self-evaluation—to try to understand how the mitzva of *teshuva* needs to be tailored for you personally within your particular context. When that effort is made, when *teshuva* is indeed comprehensive and constant, when we strive for the proper balance with an awareness of what, in the totality of religious life, is demanded of us, then we can stand in good conscience before the Almighty and ask and hope for His forgiveness. We have tried to do what we can, and He, for His part, can fulfill the promise:

> For on this day will He forgive you, to purify you, that you may be pure of all your sins before God. (*Vayikra* 16:30)

NOTES:

1   Before we speak of *teshuva* for bad character traits, there is an antecedent premise, namely, that there is something wrong with possessing these traits. This assumption is of relevance not only to *teshuva*, but to other areas as well.

In his commentary *Avodat Ha-melekh* on *Hilkhot De'ot* 6:7, R.

Menachem Krakowski notes a parallel between that passage and the one we are discussing. The former reads:

If a person sees his fellow sinning or pursuing a path which is not good, it is a mitzva to bring him back to the right path and to inform him that he is sinning with regard to himself by his wrong deeds, as it says, "You should reproach your fellow" (*Vayikra* 19:17).

One of the Rambam's sources for this ruling (*Berakhot* 31b) derives the law that "a person who sees his fellow doing something improper must reproach him" from Eli's reproach to Chana when he thought that she was intoxicated (*I Shemuel* 1:14). Tosafot (*ad loc.*, s.v. *davar*) comment that this *gemara* refers to one who is doing something "improper," but which is not prohibited, strictly speaking. If the act were truly prohibited, the requirement to rebuke would fall under the rubric of "You should reproach your fellow," and we would not have to derive it from a verse in *Shemuel*.

The Rambam clearly thinks otherwise. The Rambam's formulation, "pursuing a path which is not good," is a paraphrase of the *gemara*'s term, "doing something improper." (Perhaps the latter refers more to a specific and focused incident, while the former refers to a general lifestyle or orientation, but in terms of halakhic status they are very similar.) Nevertheless, the Rambam says that the obligation to critique such conduct falls under the biblical commandment of reproof, and is not to be derived from the verse in *Shemuel*. Having distinguished conceptually between "sin" and "pursuing a path which is not good," the Rambam finds it necessary to establish in *Hilkhot De'ot* that *tokhecha*, reproof, applies even to the latter.

The *Avodat Ha-melekh* thus points to a parallel in *Hilkhot Teshuva* 7:3, where the Rambam extends the need for repentance (not reproof) to that which is improper but not strictly a sin. Both of these passages assume that there is something wrong with "improper behavior" or "bad traits," even if they are not subsumed under formally defined categories of sin. Since these are spiritually corrosive, they too are to be regarded as sins.

Note that in *Hilkhot De'ot* the Rambam suggests that the approach to be taken with one who acts "improperly" is not to tell him that he is sinning against God and the Torah, but rather that he is sinning against himself, or undercutting his own spiritual being. However, in *Hilkhot Teshuva* the Rambam does not restrain himself and says that these bad traits are actually sins. The reason for this could be pragmatic: in *Hilkhot De'ot* the Rambam is concerned with finding an effective form of reproof, while in

Hilkhot Teshuva he is trying to sensitize the reader to the scope of repentance and the severity of bad character traits.

2   It would seem that the Rambam's concern is well founded. For example, how many people today would view gluttony as one of the seven cardinal sins, as it was regarded in medieval Christian thought? Nevertheless, gluttony should be a major concern for us. The *gemara* (*Megilla* 12a) asks why the Jews of Shushan initially had been doomed to perdition. It answers, "Because they partook of the feast of that wicked man [Achashverosh]." What was the problem with this? Was the food not kosher? The straightforward understanding of this *gemara* is that, even if the food was strictly kosher, there is moral rot and corruption involved in taking part in a party lasting one hundred and eighty days. The border between a passion for consumption and responsibility for production, between hedonistic exploitation of the world and useful employment, is a very significant one. [This theme is elaborated in Chapter One above.]

3   In light of this, we can understand the problematic clause, "so that he may . . . be worthy of the World-to-Come." The Rambam was a great champion of *avoda li-shmah*, service for its own sake. If a person serves God in order to attain reward, this is categorized as "service not for its own sake," as he makes clear in Chapter Ten of *Hilkhot Teshuva*. How, then, can he advocate such service here? Since the Rambam is talking about a lifelong effort at *teshuva*, his mention of the penitent's worthiness of reward refers to the result of the *teshuva*, not its motivation.

4   This parallels the Ramban's comments (*Vayikra* 19:2) on a *naval bi-reshut ha-Torah*, a scoundrel with Torah license.

5   See, e.g., *Sefer Ha-chinukh*, 16:

Know that a person is influenced in accordance with his actions. His heart and all his thoughts are always [drawn] after his deeds in which he is occupied, whether [they are] good or bad. Thus, even a person who is thoroughly wicked in his heart . . . — if he will arouse his spirit and set his striving and his occupation, with constancy, in the Torah and the *mitzvot*, even if not for the sake of Heaven, he will veer at once toward the good, and with the power of his good deeds he will deaden his evil impulse. For one's heart is drawn after his actions. And even if a man should be thoroughly righteous . . . but he engages constantly in impure matters . . . then at some point in time he will turn from the righteousness of his heart to become completely wicked. For it is a known and true matter that every man is influenced in accordance with his actions, as we have stated.

6   This is why the Rambam finds it necessary to dispute an imaginary

adversary in *Hilkhot Teshuva* 7:3 ("You ought not say that *teshuva* applies only to sins which entail action..."). Usually, he is not concerned with what you might think, but rather tells you what to think. In our passage, what forces him to relate to possible misconceptions? Beyond sociological considerations, the reason is that the Rambam himself has paved the way for this misconception by focusing on specifically designated sins until this point in *Hilkhot Teshuva*. For example, the caption to *Hilkhot Teshuva* reads: "A person who has sinned should repent from his sin before God and confess"—from a particular sin, one which can be the object of confession. In the opening *halakha*, he writes that *teshuva* is necessitated by transgression of "any commandment of the Torah," but what about things that are not "commandments of the Torah," such as anger, enmity, envy, frivolity, etc.? One might conclude that those are not included. The detailed discussion in the first two chapters about that which obligates *teshuva* and about the techniques of *teshuva* all revolve around this opening. The Rambam himself has, in effect, left us with the clear impression that indeed *teshuva* relates only to specifically defined sins.

7   See Chapter Five of this book for more on this consideration.

CHAPTER TWELVE

Centrist Orthodoxy: A Spiritual Accounting

THE SHIFT TO THE RIGHT

Centrist Orthodoxy finds itself increasingly under attack. While the possibility of attack from both right and left is endemic to centrism by virtue of its dual exposure, the nature and extent of criticism varies. At present, I believe, particularly insofar as the Right is concerned, it is perceived by attackers and defenders alike as being particularly intensive, broad in scope, covering a wide range of thought and activity, and penetrating in depth. It consists not just of carping criticism, sniping with regard to one feature or another, but rather of a radical critique, questioning the fundamental legitimacy and validity of the basic Centrist position.

This phenomenon, the so-called "shift to the right," is, in certain respects, general. The crisis of faith and experience engendered by the spiritual vacuity of modernism has resulted in the polarization of the Western world, and has ushered in the growth of hedonistic individualism, on the one hand, and largely authoritarian spiritualism, on the other. Within the religious world, again broadly speaking, this development has been accompanied by the quest for the rock-ribbed certainty of purism and a concomitant rejection of what many perceive to be the middling and muddling compromises of centrism.

The popularity and bellicosity of Christian fundamentalist political organizations, for instance, would have been unthinkable a generation ago. Islamic fundamentalism, to take another example, has spread like wildfire in countries once deemed by largely secular historians to be inexorably on the road to religious modernization. At another level, as many Jews in the United States particularly and lamentably have learned, cults have become the craze of many who have found no other egress from this spiritual desert.

Nevertheless, we are and should be inclined to treat the specific Jewish, or, if you will, American Jewish situation in its own terms. We are "believers and children of believers," and as such are guided by *Chazal*'s dictum, "*Ein mazal le-Yisrael*" (*Shabbat* 156a-b, *Nedarim* 32a): the Jewish experience is not determined and therefore cannot be fully understood by reference to astrological forces, or, to take the modern counterpart, by historical causation or sociological categories. We are guided by the declaration, both command and promise, enunciated in *parashat Lekh Lekha* (*Bereishit* 17:1): "I am *E-l Shad-dai*; walk before Me and be perfect." The Ramban (*ad loc.*) cites Ibn Ezra's and Rav Shemuel Ha-naggid's interpretation of the name *Shad-dai*: "This is from the root *sh.d.d.*, meaning Victor and Prevailer over the hosts of heaven." The Ramban then comments:

> Therefore, He now told Avraham that He is the Powerful One, the Victor who will prevail over [Avraham's] constellation of birth so that he will have a son, and thus there will be a covenant between Him and his seed forever, meaning that "God's portion is His people" (*Devarim* 32:9), and that He will lead them at His own will, as they will not be under the rule of a star or constellation.

Hence, we strive to interpret events affecting *Kenesset Yisrael* with an eye to their specific elements.

Moreover, we are not just dispassionate observers trying to understand the passing scene. We are measurably affected by the flow of events, either being directly under siege, or, on another level, the potential victims of the erosion of the *terra firma* upon which we presumably stand. Consequently, we are pressed not only to understand, but to respond—and responses vary.

The process of the shift to the right, especially with respect to the younger generation, is for many fraught with pain and a sense of almost bitter irony. Parents who sacrificed so much in order to maintain Shabbat observance or to establish and support day schools at a time when none of these were in vogue, suddenly find that their homes are not kosher enough or their *Kiddush* cups not large enough. Analogously, at the professional level, educators who pioneered in the Five Towns or Johannesburg when these were, from a Torah standpoint, literally deserts, are chagrined to discover that their very students now regard them with a jaundiced and condescending eye.

In some, the pain is assuaged by acceptance, their response being that of the Titans who were superseded by the Olympians in Keats' "Hyperion:" "The first in beauty should be first in might." To most, however, the pain leads to understandable if, in many respects, pitiable anger.

The Need for Soul-Searching

But beyond the psychological reactions, there is a moral response. The challenge posed by the Right confronts us with the need to engage in *cheshbon ha-nefesh*, soul-searching, a spiritual accounting—to examine not only who is "first in beauty," but whether, in the light of basic sources, historical precedent and spiritual sensitivity, Centrism is beautiful at all.

Whatever the origin of this process, I, for one, feel that such an opportunity should be welcomed. I must confess that I am not quite up to the level of self-examination of a colleague *rosh yeshiva*, who once told me that, just as R. Yisrael Salanter had submitted that he would not continue the *Mussar* movement for a single day, were he not convinced that it needed to be founded on that very day, so too this *rosh yeshiva* would not maintain the framework of *Hesder* at all, if he had not been ready to innovate it had it not existed. My own feeling is that at certain points one needs to establish the parameters and direction of his spiritual identity and proceed from there, without bringing basic premises into perpetual question. Nevertheless, I do agree that periodic reassessment is fully warranted.

The Rambam (*Hilkhot Teshuva* 2:6) says that although there is a mitzva of *teshuva* (repentance) year round, during the Ten Days of Repentance there is a special obligation to repent. Many have asked what is the difference between these two obligations, the general mitzva of *teshuva* and the specific mitzva during the Ten Days of Repentance? I once suggested that, while generally one relates to specific sins within the context of his spiritual existence, between *Rosh Ha-shana* and *Yom Kippur* the obligation is to examine that existence proper.

I am afraid it has been far too long since we last collectively effected such a re-evaluation. And I believe we are still paying the price for the moral smugness and ideological complacency which gripped us during the period, relatively speaking, of our hegemony. If we are now pressed to reassess our position, we should not hesitate to pick up the gauntlet. An honest and courageous *cheshbon ha-nefesh* can only help us in every way.

That *cheshbon ha-nefesh* should clearly have two components. Let me cite briefly from a volume to which I shall have occasion to refer later as well. Near the beginning of the chapter "Hebraism and Hellenism" in his book *Culture and Anarchy*, Matthew Arnold quotes a maxim of his contemporary, Bishop Wilson: "First, never go against the best light you have; second, take care that your light be not darkness." *Cheshbon ha-nefesh* does indeed entail an examination of the light by which we walk, and, concomitantly, an analysis of just how well, just how persistently, we do indeed walk by the light which we profess to be guiding us.

COMMONALITIES AND DIFFERENCES WITH THE RIGHT

Let us begin with the examination of the light. What are the hallmarks of so-called Centrist Orthodoxy, and in what respect does it differ from its Rightist critics?

Broadly speaking, of course, our common purpose is identical: universally—"*le-takken olam be-malkhut Shad-dai*, to mend the world under divine sovereignty;" nationally—to realize our destiny as a "*mamlekhet kohanim ve-goi kadosh*, kingdom of priests and a holy nation;" personally—to prepare for the tripartite examination described in the *gemara* (*Shabbat* 31a): "Did you deal faithfully? Did you set fixed times for Torah study? Did you anticipate redemption?" It is important that we bear this community of purpose very much in mind.

When all is said and done, we should recognize and realize that what we share with the Rightist community far, far outweighs whatever divides us—although, in the nature of things, the focus within the community is upon the divisive element. I sometimes have the feeling that, with regard to perceiving that community, we are often somewhat remiss.

Ernst Simon, a professor of education at the Hebrew University, once remarked with reference to the dilemma of a religious professor in Jerusalem (remember, this was years ago), that "The people you can talk to, you can't *daven* with, and the people with whom you can *daven*, you can't talk." For *benei Torah*, of course, the shared universe of Talmudic discourse, of *havayot de-Abbaye ve-Rava*, serves as a great cementing force. But even amongst *benei Torah*, many in our camp no doubt find it easier to talk, perhaps even to work, with an intelligent secular colleague than with a Karliner chassid, forgetting that the pleasantries attendant upon passing the time of day cannot compare with a shared vision of eternity. Surely we need to recognize, and the point can hardly be overemphasized, that our basic affinity is with those—past, present or future—to whom *tzelem E-lokim*, *malkhut Shamayim* and *avodat Hashem* (the divine image, divine sovereignty, and the service of God) are the basic categories of human existence.

Nevertheless, important differences clearly do exist, and these relate to substance as well as to style, to strategy no less than to tactics. While an abstract eschatological vision may be common, its specific content may vary, and quite significantly so. While the ideal of "a holy nation" animates us all, its definition is far from agreed. And if we all labor with an eye to certain ultimate questions, we may—and do—differ greatly with regard to the respective weight to be assigned to them.

If pressed to define the primary area of difference between the various Torah communities, I presume we would get different replies depending upon whether the question were posed in the Diaspora or in *Eretz Yisrael*. In *Galut*, the litmus test probably still is the attitude to secular culture; in *Eretz Yisrael*, the attitude towards the state. Both are, however, clearly major issues in both places, and I would like to deal *seriatim* with each and then to analyze their common denominator.

SHAKING OUR CONFIDENCE IN GENERAL CULTURE

Starting with the question of general culture, I wrote a brief essay in the 1960's setting forth my position with respect to the validity and value of such culture and its relation to the dual problems of *bittul Torah* (taking time from Torah study) and potentially pernicious influences.[1] In certain respects, the piece is unquestionably and clearly dated. I stated as a fact, for instance, that the problem is generally perceived as concerning boys but not girls, because, after all, *gedolei Yisrael* did not hesitate to send their daughters to college. Indeed, looking back to that time, one recalls that, quite apart from the obvious instance of *mori ve-rabbi* R. Soloveitchik, the daughter of *mori ve-rabbi* R. Hutner received a doctorate, as did the daughter of R. Aharon Kotler. At least one of R. Moshe Feinstein's daughters went to college and, if R. Ruderman's and R. Kamenetsky's did not—I do not recall off-hand—it was surely not out of principle. Today, of course, no self-respecting Bais Ya'akov girl, be her father a businessman or a pro-grammer, would risk attending college, lest her prospects for a *shiddukh* be impaired.

Nevertheless, in conceptual and axiological terms, the funda-mental problem of general studies remains. That being the case, I want to stress one point. The piece was published at a time when I was fresh out of graduate school and still engaged in a modicum of collegiate teaching. After moving to *Eretz Yisrael*, I heard occa-sional rumors that, now being firmly established in an institution wholly devoted to Torah, I had recanted.

I freely admit that, during the intervening years, confidence in culture—culture in Arnold's sense, "the study of perfection"—has been generally shaken, and this for at least three reasons. First, high culture—"the best that has been thought and said in the world," as Arnold defined literature—is less cherished than it once was. Interest in the humanities has waned, both within academia and outside of it, as the focus has shifted to more pragmatic and technological areas. Not only have priorities changed, but to most people the kind of spirit which animated an Arnold to posit literary culture as the "one dam restraining the flood-tide of barbarian anarchy," now seems hopelessly naive.

Second, the impact of the Holocaust has had a further eroding effect, perhaps paradoxically so. We were then, around 1960, much closer in time to the events. But, perhaps for that very reason, they were much less on our minds. This consciousness of that terrible era and, I might add parenthetically, the mini-industry which has lamentably grown up around it, has posed the terrible and terrifying question raised by one of the most literate men of our generation, George Steiner, in the preface to his book *Language and Silence*:

> We come after. We know now that a man can read Goethe or Rilke in the evening, then he can play Bach and Schubert and go to his day's work at Auschwitz in the morning. To say that he has read them without understanding, or that his ear is gross, is cant. In what way does this knowledge bear on literature and society, on the hope, grown almost axiomatic from the time of Plato to that of Matthew Arnold, that culture is a humanizing force, that the energies of the spirit are transferable to those of conduct?

Third, as contemporary culture has moved perceptibly away from our own mores, becoming increasingly vulgarized and inundated by permissiveness, hedonism, eroticism and violence, the need for distancing or possibly insulating ourselves from it and, by extension, from secular culture generally, has been felt more keenly. At a time when the penumbra of Victorian modesty still hovered over America, when, say, an actress of Ingrid Bergman's stature did not dare to set foot on America's shores for decades because of an extramarital affair with an Italian director, it was easier to ply the virtues of general culture than in today's climate of almost total *hefkerut* (moral anarchy) in the media.

THE COMPLEXITY OF EXPERIENCE

Nevertheless, I wish to reiterate emphatically that I continue to subscribe wholeheartedly to the central thesis of that early essay: the affirmation that, properly approached and balanced (and the caveats are there; there is need for much care and much caution), general culture can be a genuinely ennobling and enriching force.

I am not talking, mind you, about going to college *per se* (in *Eretz Yisrael*, even going to high school is an issue). Much of what now passes in many places for collegiate education is little more than sophisticated plumbing—at most, sharpening the mind and entitling its owner to a sheepskin and a union card, but barely affecting the spirit, barely touching the soul. I am talking about the spiritual value of general education, not just education for the sake of earning a living. In this respect, my fundamental position, the affirmative position, has not changed.

Quite the contrary, my personal experience over the last two decades has only reinforced an awareness of the spiritual significance of "the best that has been thought and said in the world." For what is it that such culture offers us? In relation to art—profound expressions of the creative spirit, an awareness of structure and its interaction with substance and, consequently, the ability to organize and present ideas; in relation to life—the ability to understand, appreciate and confront our personal, communal and cosmic context, sensitivity to the human condition and some assistance in coping with it; in relation to both—a literary consciousness which enables us to transcend our own milieu and place it in a broader perspective. Above all, culture instills in us a sense of the moral, psychological and metaphysical complexity of human life.

A good friend of mine had a nephew who attended Harvard Business School. After he graduated, his uncle asked him: "Tell me, what did you learn?" He replied, "I learned that you can only make money with other people's money." The uncle's response was, "If that's the case, you got a good education."

If I were pressed to encapsulate what I learned in graduate school, my answer would be: the complexity of experience. "The rest is commentary; go and study." With respect to the whole range of points enumerated above, I say again that my life experience, in the States or in *Eretz Yisrael*, within the public or the private sphere, has only sharpened my awareness of the importance of these qualities.

These elements—particularly the last—constitute, if you will, Centrist virtues. Centrism is as much a temper as an ideology, as much a mode of sensibility as a lifestyle. It is of its very essence to shy away from simplistic and one-sided approaches, of its very fabric to strive to encompass and encounter reality in its complexity and, with that encounter, to seek the unity which transcends the diversity.

If confronted by the question posed in Arnold's sonnet "To a Friend"—"Who prop, thou ask'st, in these bad days, my mind?"—I imagine none of us would give his reply:

> . . . But be his
> My special thanks, whose even-balanced soul,
> From first youth tested up to extreme old age,
> Business could not make dull, nor passion wild;
> Who saw life steadily, and saw it whole;
> The mellow glory of the Attic stage,
> Singer of sweet Colonus, and its child.

We do not have that kind of relationship to Sophocles. But we do, we ought, share the overriding desire to see life steadily and see it whole. And it is indeed true that, to that end, Sophocles, among others, is helpful. I am in no way intimating that that vision of life cannot be attained otherwise, or that one cannot be a *yerei Shamayim* or a *talmid chakham* without it. I am generally opposed to positing a single mold as the sole model for *avodat Hashem*, and I submit that, were it up to me, one could receive rabbinic ordination from *Yeshivat Rabbeinu Yitzchak Elchanan* even if, like R. Akiva Eiger, he did not have a B.A.

LITERARY, PSYCHOLOGICAL AND HISTORICAL SENSITIVITY

Speaking for myself, however, I can emphatically state that my general education has contributed much to my personal development. I know that my understanding of *Tanakh* would be far shallower in every respect without it. I know that it has greatly enhanced my perception of life in *Eretz Yisrael*. I know that it has enriched my religious experience. I know that when my father was stricken blind, Milton's profoundly religious sonnet "On His Blindness" and its magnificent conclusion, "They also serve who only stand and wait," stood me in excellent stead. I also know—and this has at times been a most painful discovery—that many of these elements are sadly lacking among the contemners of culture on the Right.

Psychological sensitivity in those circles is grossly deficient. Just recall, if you attended the funeral of a great rabbi, how abstract, repetitive and inane the eulogies were. When R. Aharon Kotler *zt"l* passed away, there was what was considered at that time a huge funeral downtown. There was a long row of eulogizers—*rashei yeshiva* and rabbis—but the only person who began to give an insight into the fire which animated that giant was Irving Bunim, a layman. When one's psychological sensitivity is lacking, the result is that much of Torah—whole *parashiyyot* and personalities in *Chumash*—are simply misread, in the sense of *gilui panim ba-Torah she-lo ke-halakha* (false interpretation of Torah), with a marvelous tradition of *midrashim* often distorted beyond recognition.

Historical sensibility is, at best, greatly constricted, and the mandate of "Remember the days of old, consider the years of many generations" (*Devarim* 32:7), which, as the Chatam Sofer pointed out, addresses itself to the reading and understanding of history, is largely ignored. This constriction has several ramifications. At one level, it limits the ability to understand properly many texts and contexts of Torah; at another, it jades the awareness of historical challenges—of which Zionism is perhaps the most prominent—and the responsibility to participate in the historical process at a public as opposed to a private level; at a third, there is often simply a distortion of reality.

This hit me in the face about ten years ago. I was asked to coordinate a program (run by *Yad Avi Ha-yishuv* in conjunction with several *kollelim* in Yerushalayim) to train rabbis who would serve in the Diaspora for a period of time. I decided to bring all the students together for a day of study at which they or their *rashei yeshiva* would give *shiurim* revolving around a certain idea. Since they wanted to become community leaders, I suggested that the conference deal with the topic of leadership.

I met with one of the students, a fellow who was considered a bastion of his *kollel*, and he said to me, "I don't understand—what is there to discuss? Why should we be wasting a day to deal with such a topic?" I asked, "Don't you think this is important for someone who is going to become a rabbi and a leader?" He replied, "It's very simple. A leader is someone who acts like the Chazon Ish." I asked, "Is that the only model of Jewish leadership?" He said, "Certainly." I responded, "Do you think that Moshe *Rabbeinu* spent his day exactly like the Chazon Ish?" He said, "Surely." I countered, "Well, there are verses in the Torah that tell us about his activities. . ." He answered that those verses, apparently, were all before *parashat Yitro*, but after *Yitro*—he was just like the Chazon Ish. I continued, "What about the Rambam?" He said, "Surely. How else would the Rambam spend his day?" I answered, "With regard to the Rambam, there are clear records; he tells us in his letters how he spent his time. Surely the Chazon Ish would never have spent his time treating the sultan's concubines in various harems. . ." But that passed him by completely.

Finally, the lack of historical sensitivity often produces the shortsighted use of power in dealing with the secular community for which the overall religious world in *Eretz Yisrael* today pays such a heavy toll.

This brings us to the last point I mentioned before, the question of less complex perceptions of the human condition. As opposed to what can emerge within a more Centrist context, an uncultured approach often tends to be superficial and simplistic. However, I am far from suggesting, God forbid, that whoever has not received a cultural exposure must, of necessity, think in these terms—but the tendency is there.

Centrism at its best encourages a sense of complexity and integration, and this in several respects. First, inasmuch as a person of this orientation looks to the right and to the left, he is more likely to reject the kind of simplistic, black-and-white solutions so appealing to others. Second, again by dint of his basic position, it is more complex, because it encompasses more of reality. It relates to more areas of human life, to larger segments of our communal and personal existence. Third, not only in quantitative terms but qualitatively, a Centrist approach is more inclined to perceive shadings and nuances, differences between areas and levels of moral and spiritual reality; more inclined to understand, for instance, what the concept of *devar ha-reshut* is all about;[2] more inclined to reject the popular myth that the answer to every single problem can be found in the *Shulchan Arukh* if only one knows how to deal with it. For those who lack a certain exposure, these insights are often more difficult to come by.

There are, in a somewhat related vein, other issues on which we differ because of our differing orientations. For example, subsequent to God's universal covenants with Adam and Noach, there was a special revelation to the Patriarchs and then to *Kenesset Yisrael*, the Congregation of Israel. Is the latter to be regarded as superimposed upon the basic categories of "the image of God," or is it something totally different? The Centrist instinct is to assume—even if both are correct—that the sharpening and heightening of the universal spiritual reality is part of what the sanctity of Israel is all about.[3]

Second, with regard to areas of practical Halakha, there are differences over how far and how fast one should push in order to arrive at a kind of foolproof practice. How high should the "fence around the Torah" be raised, even when raising it too high has an impact on other values, and even when raising it disregards the impact which it has upon the standing of the *kehilla*, the basic (and if it is basic, it is in some sense centrist) community as it has existed from generation to generation? The mentality which is totally immersed in certain specifics may often lack the spiritual energy to involve itself in other areas and might not give these considerations sufficient weight. Minutiae are, of course, critical to halakhic thought and experience, and the adherence to standards in their implementation is an essential ingredient of any form of serious Torah commitment. But these need to be viewed, and, within certain limits, defined, with reference to general spiritual and axiological factors.

Here we could deal with specific areas of halakhic decision-making, but whoever is involved knows that much of what today is considered as *yirat Shamayim* was thoroughly rejected by the *Rishonim*. For instance, the Rosh (*Sukka* 3:13) discusses the definition of an *arava* (willow), and says that the simple reading of the Talmudic discussion would indicate that it must grow on the banks of a river (at least according to many opinions). Then he says, "But I have not seen that our rabbis are concerned with this"—and we are dealing with a biblical commandment! His answer is not, "If that is the case, never mind what our rabbis did—we will be better and wiser;" rather, he suggests an alternate understanding.

To take another example, the *Kesef Mishneh* (*Hilkhot Terumot* 1:11) discusses the question of whether a gentile's fruits upon which he performed *meruach* (levelling) in *Eretz Yisrael* are rabbinically obligated in *terumot u-ma'asrot* (tithes and gifts). Although this is subject to a dispute among *Rishonim*, the prevalent practice had followed the Rambam's lenient opinion. He then writes about a contemporary rabbi who thought he was being pious by following the stringent opinion of other *Rishonim*, and persuading others to do the same. The *Kesef Mishneh* says categorically and vigorously: God forbid that we should change the long-standing practice of the *kehilla*, as it would be disrespectful to our predecessors and present them as sinners.

Here, again, we have an issue which to some extent divides us. This might perhaps be extended, but I do want to move on to the second major issue of which I spoke before, and this is the attitude toward Zionism and the State of Israel in general.

ATTITUDES TOWARD ZIONISM

Having quoted myself previously with regard to the question of culture, I will refer you now to another article I wrote, dealing with the topic of attitudes towards Zionism within the American Orthodox community.[4] In dealing with the differences between the adherents of and opponents to Zionism within the Torah world, I focused upon several major factors: conceptually, the extent to which man—and all of society collectively—should participate in the historical process; how partial successes or partial developments—half-way houses, if you will—were to be evaluated; how one perceived the specific reality of political Zionism; and to what extent was one ready and willing to work with secularists. All of these, I think, are significant factors in drawing lines between the pros and the cons.

But I think that in our context, another element may be added: in general, to what extent is one interested in the political order, the *polis*, and specifically, how much significance (if any) does one attach to the issue of Jewish sovereignty in *Eretz Yisrael*? Here, of course, there is a clear break between Centrists, who, animated by both Rav Kook and Rav Soloveitchik, stress the scope of Halakha and Torah as pervasive, touching upon every facet of human life, in the public sphere no less than the private, and those who are content to restrict themselves within their four cubits and care little about what flag flies above their yeshiva.

Speaking for myself, I am far from totally identifying with the official Zionist ideology. I have the privilege of being regarded in America as a bit odd for being a Zionist, and in *Eretz Yisrael* as being a little odd (at least within our world) for being suspect as not sufficiently Zionist. But, be that as it may, I would not go the full route with Rav Kook; I say freely that there are passages in which he writes of the importance of the state, its accomplishments and achievements, which bewilder me.

I was travelling not long ago with a Member of *Knesset* who is identified with *Gush Emunim*. He read a sentence to me, the general tenor of which was that the "ultimate happiness of man" is somehow the attainment of the state. He asked what I thought of this sentence. I answered, "I think it's terrible." We began discussing this further, and he let me in on the secret: this is a sentence from the latter parts of Rav Kook's *Orot*. As it turned out, this pronouncement was qualified in the very next line. First Rav Kook wrote that in secular, non-Jewish countries, the state is just a tool, but the state of *Klal Yisrael* becomes an end in itself, a sort of beatitude. In the next sentence, he said that as a result of the state, *malkhut Shamayim*, the kingship of God—which is the true "ultimate happiness of man"—is realized. Apparently, there are two levels of man's ultimate happiness.

Nevertheless, I do not share his assessment of the extent of the state's significance. I have reservations about the degree of emphasis which his disciples, his son among others, have assigned to the *gemara* in *Sanhedrin* (98a) which states that the clearest harbinger of the End of Days is when trees bloom and blossom in *Eretz Yisrael*. I also feel that there is there some excess in not only validating, but evaluating the importance of what, after all, are at most geo-political or socio-economic considerations.

But this is a question of degree. Surely, the basic awareness of what *malkhut Yisrael*, Jewish sovereignty, means—even in its very, very imperfect state—is part of my own being and something which I think needs to animate any person with historical vision and spiritual sensibility. That which relates to *Eretz Yisrael* and to the State of Israel should, for *spiritual* reasons, be close to our heart.

How this translates into practical educational policy, with an eye to the price that sometimes may be paid for this kind of excessive Zionist passion, is something which surely needs to be weighed. Be that as it may, we recognize the significance of the State of Israel, and I believe this is proper. As Centrists, we recognize it because, among other things, we have the capacity to relate to a broader spectrum of *Klal Yisrael*, and we have what is crucial: the ability to understand the significance of gradual steps, the historical consciousness, a developmental awareness.

I once noted that the law of "the four cups of redemption" at the *Seder* has a dual status. On the one hand, it is all a single mitzva. On the other hand, the *gemara* (*Pesachim* 110a) and the Rif say with regard to various laws (such as whether to pronounce a separate blessing on each) that "each one is a mitzva in its own right." If this be true of the cups, it is true likewise of the levels of redemption which those cups represent. Surely, we have been fortunate to witness some measure of *"ve-hotzeiti"* and *"ve-hitzalti"*

("I shall remove you" and "I shall save you"). Although these can be regarded only as first steps in the fulfillment of a larger process of redemption, they certainly also have a significance of their own—"each one is a mitzva in its own right."

"TORAH ONLY" OR "TORAH AND"

Both issues that I have mentioned, that of general culture and that of *Medinat Yisrael*, have in a very real sense—although they are diverse—a common denominator. It may be summed up by the phrase, "*Torah ve-*," Torah with something else.

Those who would subscribe to a position of "Torah only," in reality do not do so. The *gemara* in *Yevamot* (109b) says: "A person who has nothing but Torah, does not have Torah either," because that Torah is false, vacuous and invalid. Now, of course, the question is: What does one require besides Torah? Here there is room for different perceptions.

There is a remarkable comment by Rabbeinu Bachya ben Asher in his commentary on the Torah. In *parashat Nitzavim*, God tells us, "I have presented before you today life and goodness, and death and evil" (*Devarim* 30:15), followed by the injunction, "Choose life." Naturally, we understand that "life and goodness" refer to Torah, and "death and evil" to something else. Rabbeinu Bachya, however, understands that the entire phrase— "life and goodness and death and evil"—applies to Torah. There is Torah which is "life and goodness," and Torah which is "death and evil."

In this respect, Rabbeinu Bachya is simply following the tradition of *Chazal*:

Rava said: Any *talmid chakham* (scholar) whose inside is not like his outside is not a *talmid chakham*. Abbaye, and some say Rabba bar Ulla, said: He is called "loathsome" . . .

R. Shemuel bar Nachmani said in the name of R. Yonatan: What is the meaning of the verse (*Mishlei* 17:16), "Why is there money in the hand of a fool to purchase wisdom, though he lacks heart (i.e. understanding)?" Woe unto *talmidei chakhamim* who engage in Torah but have no *yirat Shamayim*. . .

R. Yehoshua ben Levi said: What is the meaning of that which is written (*Devarim* 4:44), "This is the Torah which Moshe placed (*sam*) before the Children of Israel?" If one is worthy, the Torah becomes for him an elixir of life (*sam chayyim*); if one is not worthy, it becomes for him a potion of death (*sam mita*). (*Yoma* 72b)

This is analogous to the familiar *gemara* (*Shabbat* 31a) about those who have the keys to the inner doors and not to the outer doors, and therefore have no access to the treasure which lies within. Likewise, there are similar statements in the *gemara* in *Ta'anit* and a number of other places about the need for *yirat Shamayim* to accompany learning.

What clearly emerges from the sources which I have cited and to which I have alluded is the sense that, while one seemingly would feel that Torah alone is sufficient ("Turn it over and turn it over, for everything is in it"—*Avot* 5:22), nevertheless there is something else which needs to be added. What is that something else? *Yirat Shamayim*, of course. But perhaps other elements as well.

Some feel that, inasmuch as "Torah is the best merchandise" (in the words of the Yiddish aphorism), why should anyone devote any time at all to anything but the "best merchandise?" In one sense, this notion seems eminently sensible. But do we really conduct ourselves in this way in all areas of life? If someone says he wants a piece of bread and butter, do we tell him, "Fool, why bread and butter? What's more important? Bread! So why put butter on the bread? Take two pieces of bread!" Of course not.

But the question is, what is the butter and is there such a thing within this sphere?

THE POSSIBILITY OF INTEGRATION

I believe that there is an analogue to butter, and there is much to be gained from it—even within the intellectual sphere itself, within learning proper, with reference to spiritual perception. Now, of course—and this cannot be reiterated too strongly—there are all kinds of caveats: the proper balance must be maintained, great care needs to be taken that improper or pernicious influences do not seep in, and we must always approach general culture critically, from a Torah perspective. But when that is done, the ability to incorporate something of general culture into the Torah world clearly exists.

There is a halakhic analogy upon which I would like to draw, by way of indicating what kind of process I think can take place here. Although one must separate *challa* only from dough made of the five grains, the *mishna* (*Challa* 3:7) tells us that if someone makes dough out of wheat flour and rice flour, he must take *challa* from all the dough, including the rice. The entire lump of dough becomes obligated in *challa*, even though rice is not one of the five grains. The *gemara* (*Zevachim* 78a) explains this on the basis of the law of *ta'am ke-ikkar* (taste is like substance): since the wheat imparts taste to the rice, the latter has the status of wheat. The *Yerushalmi* (*Challa* 1:1) offers a different explanation, based on the law of *gereira* (dragging or integrating). *Gereira* applies only to wheat and rice—if you make dough out of wheat and potatoes, even though the effect on taste would be the same, there is no such law. When mixed with wheat, only rice—because it is biologically very similar to the cereal grains—can become attached, appended, integrated into the wheat.

So we have here the wheat proper and that which is *nigrar*—

appended or incorporated—into the wheat. The same thing, I think, can apply within the spiritual order. There is Torah proper, and there is that which, properly integrated and related, can become *nigrar*. Not everything can be *nigrar*, but there are things which can be. Here there is "Torah and," but that "and," to the extent that it is related to Torah, is *metzuraf* (attached) to it.

Secondly, the concept of "Torah and" suggests that there are other values besides intellection, other human and Jewish goals, that there is a need to supplement, to give an integrated vision of human life. The *gemara* in *Avoda Zara* (17b), which I have quoted many times with reference to *Hesder*, speaks with great sharpness of someone who engages only in Torah and not in *gemilut chasadim* (acts of kindness): "It is as if he has no God!" Quite apart from learning—which is a cardinal, central value—there are other areas of human life that need to be dealt with. Surely, the creation and the sustenance of a viable and just society—*chesed* in the broader sense, as in "The world is built by *chesed*" (*Tehillim* 9:3)—needs to be perceived, and this too is a predominantly Centrist perception.

THEORY AND PRACTICE

Thus, the key issue distinguishing our approach from that of our colleagues on the Right is the question of whether to adopt an attitude of "everything is in Torah," or to append, balance and round out. With respect to this issue, I think that we stand on solid ground. We have a position which need not be viewed as being the sole position, nor even be regarded historically as the majority position, but surely it is a sound, solid and legitimate position. I believe, therefore, that the problem confronting Centrist Orthodoxy today is not, or ought not to be, primarily ideological.

Even if our position is, in certain respects, a minority view among halakhic Jews, judged by either historical or contemporary reference, this need hardly dismay us. On some issues, there is no question that the kind of the position that I have outlined here has been a minority view. The question of general culture is, after all, quite old, and it is true: this position was in the minority at the time of the *Rishonim* and certainly in recent centuries in Eastern Europe. But no one questions that it is legitimate. In other areas, with regard to the fullness of life as opposed to constriction, I think we stand on the high ground: historically, ours has been the majority view. Those who now present constriction as an ultimate ideal represent the minority view.

Be this as it may, I believe that the light by which we walk is a reliable guide—not the sole guide, but a thoroughly legitimate one. Our question, then, is: How well and how faithfully do we, as a community, walk by it? Our problem is not on the conceptual level, but rather on that of implementation, both operational and experiential. We will turn next to this question, the second component of our *cheshbon ha-nefesh*.

DIALECTICAL TENSION OR TEPID INDIFFERENCE?

Ideally, vibrant centrism should issue from the dialectical tension between diverse and, at times, even divergent values. Centrist Orthodoxy, specifically, can be powerful only when the concern for Torah remains passionate and profound, but is then supplemented by other elements. It can succeed when we can honestly state, by analogy with Byron's statement (in "Childe Harold's Pilgrimage"), "I love not man the less, but nature more," that, in comparison to others, we love not Torah less, but *derekh eretz*—in the full, rich sense of that term—more.

It is precisely here, I am afraid, that our *cheshbon ha-nefesh* begins. How much of our Centrism indeed derives from dialectical tension, and how much from tepid indifference? Is our commitment to *talmud Torah* truly as deep as that of the Right, but only modified in practice by the need to pursue other values? Do our students devote as much time and effort to *talmud Torah*, minus only that needed to acquire culture or build a state? Comparisons aside, let us deal with specific educational issues: What has all the time wasted on television, the inordinate vacations, a system of religious public schools in Israel which shuts down at one or two in the afternoon, to do with culture or Zionism?

Cannot one acquire both, in schools geared to the hilt for maximal Torah achievement? On the contrary, success in *talmud Torah* on the part of those who maintain a multiple vision requires greater tenacity, more devotion and more diligence, than among devotees of the monochromatic, who speak, in a phrase much beloved by the Right, of producing only *shemen zayit zakh*, the purest olive oil. But does that exist?

The children in Centrist summer camps today do not waste away their summers because they are busy mastering Bach or Euclid. They generally abstain from Torah study because their parents, or the community out of which they spring, do not consider *talmud Torah*, perhaps Judaism in general, as *that* important. So long as this is the case, we are indeed in serious trouble. The challenge which confronts us is how to build a community which is passionately committed to Torah, but understands the need for *gereira*. So far, this has proven to be a difficult and elusive task.

In part, it is the fault of the community; it is less committed, less involved, less engaged. But, we are here at a moment of *cheshbon ha-nefesh*: Is it only that? Are the community's leaders and educators blameless? A man who is a near and dear friend of mine, a *maggid shiur* in a certain yeshiva, once asked me: "How can a student in my yeshiva have any respect for the *rosh yeshiva*, how can he have any commitment to Torah, if every time he walks into the *rosh yeshiva*'s office, he finds him not bent over a *Gemara*, but reading *The New York Times*?"

Let me take another example, and I hope that the people involved will not take umbrage; we are speaking as friends. This year, a major rabbinical organization held its fiftieth anniversary celebration in Yerushalayim. In the course of the twelve days of this conference in *Eretz Yisrael*, they found time to meet with the Prime Minister, President, and Defense Minister; they found time for a fashion show, time to walk the streets of Tel Aviv with some of the mayor's assistants, time for all kinds of activities. But not one Torah institution was on the itinerary. The organizers' concern was with people who are on the move, people with power— the Belzer Rebbe was invited; he is powerful. I say this with pain; these are friends of mine. What can you say about this?

INSTILLING PASSION

I spoke before about a passionate concern for Torah. The key, indeed, is the passion—passion which is important in its own right as a component of *avodat Hashem*, and passion which holds the key to the development of other components, in the sense of "*Yirato kodemet le-chokhmato*" (*Avot* 3:9), where one's fear of Heaven is prior to his wisdom. In order to attain that passion, we as educators should be ready to sacrifice—and even sacrifice considerably—a measure of objective intellectual accomplishment. The sense that, indeed, the words of the Torah are "*chayyeinu ve-orekh yameinu*, our life and the length of our days," is far more important than the actual knowledge. Certainly, for so many of our students, who in the first place are not going to become *talmidei chakhamim*, love of Torah is far more important than knowledge of Torah.

The Lubavitchers like to relate that at a certain age, the Ba'al ha-Tanya decided he had to go to Vilna to learn from the Gra. En route, he was met by an older person (the Chassidim denote him as the prophet Eliyahu) who asked him, "Where are you going?" He said, "I'm going to Vilna to learn from the Gra." The elder said to him, "You know how to learn somewhat, but you don't know how to pray at all. Better go to the Mezeritcher Maggid."

Without passing judgment on this particular encounter, let us ask ourselves: What is the more acute problem in our Centrist community? I submit that, on a competitive basis, we might do better in the area of learning than in the area of prayer. I knew a man who was identified as an Orthodox rabbi but, ideologically, was essentially Conservative. Someone once asked him, "Why don't you identify with the Conservatives?" His response was, "How can I go to the Conservatives? They don't cry at *Ne'ila*" (the final prayer on Yom Kippur). Let us ask ourselves: Does our Centrist community cry sufficiently at *Ne'ila*?

It is only by instilling this kind of passion that we can avoid the lapse of Centrism into mere compromise. There are times when one must compromise, and this itself is an issue between us and the Right: How are we to gauge the qualitative as opposed to the quantitative element? They are the champions of the qualitative, *shemen zayit zakh*—adherents of the position which, in a magnificent sentence in his *Civil Disobedience*, Thoreau presented that, "It is not so important that many should be as good as you, as that there be some absolute goodness somewhere; for that will leaven the whole lump." We have a much greater commitment to the quantitative element, to reaching large segments of the community, even if we only reach them partially and the accomplishments are limited.

Even if we must, in a certain sense, compromise, it cannot be out of default. I remember years back reading a very perceptive remark of the Lubavitcher Rebbe; he said, "The problem with the Conservatives is not that they compromise—it is that they make a principle out of compromise." We cannot, God forbid, make a principle out of compromise, nor can we lapse into it by default. But if we are to avoid lapsing, then that passionate commitment must be kept burning. It is only when we can attain that passionate commitment that Centrism as a vibrant and legitimate spiritual force can be sustained. Only by generating profound conviction can we sustain ourselves from within and be inured to onslaughts from without: conviction of the overall importance of Torah, and of the worth—and there is worth!—of our own interpretation of it.

There are several lines in a poem written by an Irish poet, William Butler Yeats, which, as I survey the contemporary scene, often haunt me terribly:

> Turning and turning in the widening gyre
> The falcon cannot hear the falconer;
> Things fall apart: the center cannot hold;
> Mere anarchy is loosed upon the world,
> The blood-dimmed tide is loosed, and everywhere
> The ceremony of innocence is drowned.
> The best lack all conviction, while the worst
> Are full of passionate intensity.

I have no use whatsoever, in our context, for the comparative terms "best" and "worst," and I surely do not, with reference to the people I am talking about, present a categorical assertion that they "lack all conviction." But it is beyond question that good people in our camp lack the kind of passion and intensity with which they are being attacked.

Kana'ut (zealotry) is, among us, a dirty word. But I believe we should learn to distinguish between two senses of *kana'ut*. I mentioned R. Aharon Kotler *zt"l* before. In terms of the objective positions he maintained, he was far more liberal than his contemporary disciples. But he maintained his positions with a dynamism, a fire, an energy, a passion which is almost incredible. To have seen him simply, as *Chazal* say, "from behind" (*Eruvin* 13b), was an experience—he was a dynamo! There was within him a *kana'ut* not for extreme positions, but for *his* positions.

THE NEED FOR SPIRITUALITY

We must maintain our positions not only with a passionate conviction, but also with spirituality. This, I grant you, is an amorphous quality, and some people do not quite know what to make of it. It is even, particularly in *Eretz Yisrael*, regarded within our community with a great deal of suspicion. When you say someone is an *ish ru'ach*, a man of spirit, immediately people begin to raise an eyebrow—presumably he is a leftist, a poet, a bohemian artist or maybe a professor, but surely not one of "our people." However, in *Tanakh* it is Yehoshua who is described as an "*ish asher ru'ach bo*, a man possessed of spirit" (*Bemidbar* 27:18)—and he was the person who carried the mantle of Moshe *Rabbeinu*!

As amorphous and, perhaps, ambiguous as this quality may be, it is a central category. Admittedly, it can be divorced from our particular commitment. R. Soloveitchik was once visited by Alain de Rothschild, a man totally removed from the world of Torah and *mitzvot*. Afterwards, I asked R. Soloveitchik, "How did you find him?" R. Soloveitchik said, "You know, he's a spiritual person." And it meant something to R. Soloveitchik.

Here, then, is another quality which we sometimes lack. Perhaps a Centrist position, with its openness to the world and its multiple engagements, is inherently prone to this danger. The lack of spirituality, however, is very widespread on the Right as well. There is often an excessive focus on wealth and externals even among *benei Torah*; sometimes when they get together, they sound like stockbrokers. In all communities, therefore, there is room for a *cheshbon ha-nefesh*.

DIFFUSION AND DILUTION

O ur Rightist critics would contend that I am, in effect, trying to square the circle. At least insofar as the masses are concerned, the lack of either passion or spirituality is no accident, but the inevitable result of interest in the cultural and political orders. To an extent, I agree. Almost inevitably, diffusion does entail some measure of dilution. The pure Torah component within a *Torah im derekh eretz* approach is indeed likely to command less single-minded loyalty than the unitary goal pursued by the advocates of *shemen zayit zakh*.

But are we to start dismissing and rejecting *mishnayot* in *Avot* simply because they produce what someone has defined as inferior results? "Excellent is Torah with *derekh eretz*, for exertion in the both will eliminate the thought of sin" (*Avot* 2:2). The point of the *mishna* is precisely that one's commitment to Torah should be of the sort which obtains within a multiple context. Of course, within that context, we need to differentiate between the flour and the Torah: while it is true that "If there is no flour, there is no Torah, and if there is no Torah, there is no flour" (*Avot* 3:17), this is not a reciprocal relationship, axiologically speaking. The flour subserves the Torah, irrespective of the famous dispute of Rabbeinu Tam and Rabbeinu Elchanan whether Torah or *derekh eretz* is the primary component (*Tosafot Yeshanim, Yoma* 85b, and elsewhere). This dispute revolves around the question as to how one ordinarily is to arrange his life; but as far as values are concerned, no one could suggest that *derekh eretz* is primary as opposed to Torah.[5]

Even if we differentiate between flour and Torah, nevertheless, the substance of this *mishna* (and several others) is precisely that these need to interact at a public and a private level. So whatever degree of dilution is the result of subscribing to *Chazal*'s guidance, for that we bear no responsibility and need not trouble our conscience. Rather, the question is whether, beyond this dilution, the inclusion of a measure of secular culture or fealty to a secularly-oriented state is corrosive.

THE ASCENDANCY OF THE MORAL OVER THE INTELLECTUAL

Secondly—this too is an important question—we must ask ourselves just how this deficiency is to be measured against some of the moral and religious failings currently derivative from the pursuit of *shemen zayit zakh*: belligerence, arrogance, self-righteousness, occasional deviousness and chicanery. I very much believe that *shemen zayit zakh* can be produced with humble integrity. I am likewise convinced that *Torah im derekh eretz* can be pursued with passion and intensity. But that does not obviate the fact that, within our camp, there is room for improvement. And it is therein that our challenge lies.

Perhaps much of what I have said in relation to culture, quoting Arnold and Yeats and others, seems very rarefied. People may be asking themselves, "What does this have to do with us? We have to deal with children in elementary school or high school; this is not our concern." Nevertheless, I have related to culture at its apex, because the kind of vision which is maintained at the pinnacle has an impact, and should have an impact, upon what is done at lower levels. In this respect, the awareness of the evaluation of culture does have practical consequences for whatever level of education we are dealing with.

Granted that, our challenge is to see to it that indeed we maintain our position with depth and gusto. Given our constituency, of course, we cannot instill many of our students with the optimal level of love of Torah; we know from where they come. But, within our overall community, and surely within its leadership, such a level should exist. Woe unto us, if the only choice lies between tepid compromise and arrogant *kana'ut*.

A couple of years after we moved to Yerushalayim, I was once walking with my family in the Beit Yisrael neighborhood, where R. Isser Zalman Meltzer used to live. For the most part, it consists of narrow alleys. We came to a corner, and found a merchant stuck there with his car. The question came up as to how to help him; it was a clear case of *perika u-te'ina* (helping one load or unload his burden). There were some youngsters there from the neighborhood, who judging by their looks were probably ten or eleven years old. They saw that this merchant was not wearing a *kippa*. So they began a whole *pilpul*, based on the *gemara* in *Pesachim* (113b), about whether they should help him or not. They said, "If he walks around bareheaded, presumably he doesn't separate *terumot u-ma'asrot*, so he is suspect of eating and selling untithed produce. . ."

I wrote R. Soloveitchik a letter at that time, and told him of the incident. I ended with the comment, "Children of that age from our camp would not have known the *gemara*, but they would have helped him." My feeling then was: Why, *Ribbono shel Olam*, must this be our choice? Can't we find children who would have helped him and still know the *gemara*? Do we have to choose? I hope not; I believe not. If forced to choose, however, I would have no doubts where my loyalties lie: I prefer that they know less *gemara*, but help him.

If I can refer again to my experience over the last several decades, I think that one of the central points which has reinforced itself is the sense, in terms of values, of the ascendancy of the moral over the intellectual—with all my love for and commitment to pure learning. But, when all is said and done, you have to be guided not by what you love; you have to be guided by Torah. And the Torah tells us what is good:

He has told you, O man, what is good, and what the Lord requires of you: only to do justice, and to love goodness, and to walk modestly with your God. (*Mikha* 6:8)

An entire chapter of *Tehillim* (*mizmor* 15) is devoted to this subject:

> A psalm of David.
>
> Lord, who may sojourn in Your tent, who may dwell on Your holy mountain?
>
> He who lives without blame, acts justly and speaks the truth in his heart;
>
> Who has no slander upon his tongue, who has never done harm to his fellow, or borne reproach for his acts towards his neighbor;
>
> For whom a contemptible man is abhorrent, but who honors those who fear the Lord;
>
> Who stands by his oath even when it is to his disadvantage;
>
> Who has never lent money at interest,[6] nor accepted a bribe against the innocent.
>
> The person who acts thus shall never be shaken.

These are the criteria. *Chazal* similarly inform us:

> [Rabban Yochanan ben Zakkai] said to his students: Go out and see what is the good path to which a person should cling. . .
>
> Rabbi Elazar said: A good heart.
>
> [Rabban Yochanan] said to them: I agree with Rabbi Elazar ben Arakh, for his words encompass yours. (*Avot* 2:9)

If one must choose, surely a good heart is to be preferred.

But I would desperately hope that no such choice confronts us, and that we have the wherewithal—out of our Centrist perspective, out of our sensitivity to the moral and the intellectual, to the spiritual in every respect—and that we have the tools, the desire, the energy and the ability, in spite of all the difficulties— and I know that they are great—that exist in the field, to move towards building the kind of richer Torah reality that can and should animate us.

"DO NOT FEAR ANY MAN"

Although I have spoken of the problems of *machloket* (dispute) and attacks from the Right, I do not think that our primary task is to fight the Right, nor even to fend them off. Our primary task is to build within our own world: to build with courage, with conviction, with a sense of our own worth, with a sense that we stand for something important and vital.

This has practical implications. There is a prohibition in the Torah (*Devarim* 1:17), "Do not fear any man." Of course, this refers specifically to a judge, or, as the *gemara* (*Sanhedrin* 6a) says, to a student sitting before his teacher. In a broader sense, however, it has other implications. If an educator has a class or a school and knows that his students need to pursue a particular path—it is in their spiritual interest, in the interest of their growth as *benei Torah, yirei Shamayim* and *shomrei mitzvot*—but builds for them a different kind of curriculum because he is looking over his shoulder, he too violates the prohibition of "Do not fear any man."

There is no reason to have that fear or that anxiety. We must have the courage of our convictions, but first we must have the convictions. We need to have them for ourselves, in depth and in richness, and we need them to build upon.

One of the shibboleths constantly raised is whether our position is *le-khatchila* or *be-di'avad* (an ideal choice or a pragmatic default). I hear this all the time in *Eretz Yisrael* with regard to Hesder. If you ask me: Is our position *be-di'avad* or *le-khatchila*?—the answer is that it can be either. If one lapses into it, and certain compromises are made by default, then indeed it is *be-di'avad*. If it is the result of a rich, meaningful, profound and comprehensive commitment, if it grows out of the dialectical tension of trying to relate to the full gamut of spiritual goals which confronts us, if it is part of an effort to build intensively and extensively a worldview and a reality within our community—then indeed it is in every sense *le-khatchila*. And those who engage in it "shall go from strength to strength and shall appear before the Lord in Zion" (*Tehillim* 84:8).

NOTES:

1   "A Consideration of General Studies from a Torah Point of View," *Gesher* vol. 1 (1963), reprinted in *The Torah U'Mada Reader*, ed. Shalom Carmy (NY, 1985), and in Rabbi Lichtenstein's book, *Leaves of Faith*, vol. 1: *The World of Jewish Learning* (Jersey City, 2003).
2   See Chapter Two above.
3   See the appendix to Chapter One above.
4   "Patterns of Contemporary Jewish *Hizdahut*: Orthodoxy," in *World Jewry and the State of Israel*, ed. Moshe Davis (Jerusalem, 1977), pp.183-192; reprinted in Rabbi Aharon Lichtenstein, *Leaves of Faith*, vol. 2: *The Meaning of Mitzvot* (Jersey City, 2003).
5   See Chapter Two above, pp. 46-50.
6   The *gemara* (*Makkot* 24a) says this refers to one who has never lent money at interest even to a gentile.

GLOSSARY OF TERMS

Acharonim, later rabbinic masters (sixteenth century and onwards)

ahava, love

ahavat Hashem, love of God

Akeida, Binding of Isaac

Al chet, the litany of sins recited on Yom Kippur

al menat la'asot, in order to perform

amal, labor

amalah shel Torah, the labor of Torah

Amoraim, scholars of the *Gemara* (third to fifth centuries)

Anshei Kenesset Ha-gedola, the Men of the Great Assembly (approx. fifth to third centuries BCE)

anuss, coerced

apikores (pl. **apikorsim**), disbeliever, heretic

ara'i, transient

arava, willow branch taken on Sukkot

Aseh toratekha keva, Make your Torah permanent (*Avot* 1:15)

asmakhta, an implicit condition

av beit din, head of a rabbinic court

aveida, a lost object

avinu, our (fore)father

avoda, service

avoda ba-Mikdash, Temple service

avoda me-ahava, service from love

avoda she-balev, service of the heart

avoda zara, foreign worship, idolatry

avodat Hashem, the service of God

bakasha, petition

bal tosif, the prohibition of adding to *mitzvot*

balebatim, laymen

baraita, a tannaitic statement not included in the *Mishna*

be-di'avad, *ex post facto*, a second choice

Beit Ha-mikdash, Temple

beit midrash, Torah study hall

Be-khol derakhekha da'ehu, In all your ways know Him (*Mishlei* 3:6)

be-khol kocho, with maximal effort

bekiut, study with the goal of encompassing quantity

ben-Torah (f. **bat-Torah**), one who makes Torah study a central part of his life and embodies its values

ben-yeshiva, a yeshiva student

berakha, blessing

berit, covenant

Berit Bein Ha-betarim, Covenant between the Pieces

berit Noach, God's covenant with Noach, i.e. with humanity

berit Sinai, God's covenant with the Jewish people at Sinai

bittachon, trust

bittul Torah, taking time from Torah study

challa, the sanctified portion of dough that must be given to a Kohen

chas ve-shalom, God forbid

Chassidut, Hasidism

chazzan, prayer leader

Chazal, the talmudic sages

chesed, kindness

cheshbon ha-nefesh, soul-searching

chiddush, novel understanding

chillul Hashem, desecration of God's Name

chokhma, wisdom

chukkim, laws whose rationale is not readily apparent

Chumash, Pentateuch, the Five Books of Moses

daven, pray

derekh eretz, a multifaceted term which can mean decent behavior, gainful employment, or general culture

devar mitzva, obligatory actions or prohibitions

devar reshut, non-obligatory actions

deveikut, clinging to God

divrei chokhma, matters of wisdom

emuna, faith

Eretz Yisrael, the Land of Israel

frum, mitzva-observant

frumkeit, religiosity or observance

gadol ha-metzuveh ve-oseh . . . , a person who does something after being commanded is superior to one who does it without being commanded

galut, exile or diaspora

gedolei Yisrael, gedolim, great rabbis

Gemara, the amoraic section of the Talmud, commenting on the *Mishna*; **gemara**, a passage thereof

gemilut chasadim, acts of kindness

Ge'onim, post-Talmudic rabbinic leaders (eighth to eleventh centuries, Babylonia and N. Africa)

gereira (lit. dragging), integration

gerut, conversion

glatt-kosher, adhering to a high kosher standard

Gush Emunim, a right-wing spiritual-political movement in Israel

hadar, beauty, splendor

Halakha (adj. **halakhic**), Jewish law

ha-osek be-mitzva patur min ha-mitzva: a person who is engaged in performing one mitzva is then absolved from another

harbatzat Torah, dissemination of Torah

hashkafa, outlook or world-view

havayot de-Abbaye ve-Rava, Talmudic discourse, symbolized by the disputes of Abbaye and Rava, two prominent *Amoraim*

hefsek, interruption or separation

heise'ach ha-da'at, a lapse of attention

hekhsher, kosher certification

Hesder, a program in Israel where students alternate periods of yeshiva study with army service

hester panim, the hiding of God's face, a situation where God suspends His intervention in the world

ikkar, primary component

issur (pl. **issurim**), prohibition

Kaddish, a responsive prayer in praise of God, recited by the *chaz-*

zan or by mourners

kana'ut, zealousness

kashrut, laws of kosher food

kavod, honor

kavu'a, permanent or established

kedusha, sanctity

kefi kocho, according to the best of his ability

kefira, denial or atheism

kehilla, community

kemach, flour

Keriat Shema, the recitation of the biblical portion beginning, "Hear O Israel" (*Devarim* 6:4)

keritat berit, sealing a covenant

ketuba, marriage contract

keva, keviut, see *kavu'a*

kevod Shamayim, honor of Heaven

ke-zayit, an olive-sized portion

Kiddush, a blessing sanctifying the Shabbat, recited over wine

kinyan, mode of acquisition, or rights

kippa, skullcap

ki-veyakhol, as it were, as if one could speak such a way about God

Klal Yisrael, Kenesset Yisrael, the Jewish people, sometimes referring to them not as a collection of individuals but as a corporate, trans-historical entity

kodashim, sacred items

Kohen (pl. **Kohanim**), a priest, a descendant of the original high priest Aharon

kollel (pl. **kollelim**), a Torah study institution for married students (who receive financial support and are relieved of the burden of earning a living)

kollelnik (or **avrekh**), a kollel student

kove'a ittim la-Torah, one who sets aside times for Torah study

lamdan, a Torah scholar of attainments

le-havdil, to distinguish, a phrase generally used to separate between the sacred and the profane le-khatchila, *a priori*, first choice

le-ovdah u-leshomrah, to cultivate and to guard [the garden]; see *Bereishit* 2:15

Levi (pl. Levi'im), a member of the tribe of Levi of non-Aaronide descent; one who is assigned non-priestly functions in the Temple

lulav, palm branch taken on Sukkot

ma'amad Har Sinai, the revelation at Mt. Sinai

ma'aseh bereishit, creation

machloket, dispute

maggid shiur, Talmud instructor

malkhut Shamayim, Divine kingship

mam'it, one who does less

mamlekhet kohanim ve-goi kadosh, kingdom of priests and a holy nation

marbeh, one who does more

mattan Torah, the giving of the Torah

matza, unleavened bread

Medinat Yisrael, the State of Israel

megilla, scroll

Megillat Esther, the Scroll of Esther

me'ila, misusing that which has been consecrated to God

meisiach da'at, one who diverts his attention

melakha, labor

metzuveh, one who is commanded

mezuza, a scroll containing biblical passages affixed to doorposts

midrash (pl. midrashim), classic rabbinic exegesis of biblical verses, here generally referring to midrash aggada, non-legal rabbinic commentary on biblical passages

Mikdash, Temple

Mishna, the tannaitic stratum of the Talmud; a compendium of rabbinic teaching edited by R. Yehuda Ha-nasi (c. 200 CE); mishna (pl. mishnayot), a paragraph thereof

mishpatim, laws whose rationale is more apparent

Mitnagdim, opponents of Chassidut

mitzva (pl. mitzvot), commandment

mitzvot aseh, positive commandments (as opposed to prohibitions)

mizmor, psalm

mori ve-rabbi, my teacher and master

Musaf, the additional prayer service on Shabbat and holidays

mussar, ethical teaching, sometimes referring specifically to a system of ethical teaching founded by R. Yisrael Salanter in the nineteenth century

Ne'ila, the concluding prayer service of Yom Kippur

nigrar, appended or incorporated

Omer, the barley offering in the Temple on the second day of Pesach; refers also to the counting of forty-nine days from the second of Pesach to the festival of Shavu'ot

osek be-mitzva, one engaged in a mitzva

otzar, treasure-trove, storehouse

oved Hashem (pl. ovdei Hashem), servant of God

palterin shel melekh, palace of the king

parasha (pl. parashiyyot), section or passage (generally of Torah, referring to the weekly reading)

pareve, non-dairy and non-meat foodstuff

patur, exempt

Pesach, Passover

pesak, halakhic ruling

pesika, rendering a halakhic decision

pesul ha-guf, something which disqualifies or diminishes the item itself

R., abbreviation of Rabbi or Rav

rabbeinu, our master or teacher

rasha, wicked person

Ribbono shel Olam, Master of the Universe; the Almighty

Rishonim, medieval rabbinic masters (mid-eleventh to fifteenth centuries)

Rosh Ha-shana, Jewish New Year

rosh yeshiva, head of a yeshiva

Sanhedrin, supreme Jewish court in the classical period

Seder, festive Passover meal devoted to recounting the tale of the exodus

sefarim, religious books

Shabbat, the Sabbath

shalosh se'udot, three Sabbath meals

Shavu'ot, the Feast of Weeks

Shekhina, the Presence of God

shemen zayit zakh, the purest olive oil

Shemoneh Esrei, the central prayer of each daily service

shiddukh, a matrimonial match

shikhecha, forgetting

Shir Ha-ma'alot, a Song of Ascent (Psalms 120-134)

shiur, Talmud class

shofar, ram's horn

shomer (pl. shomerim), guard

sicha (pl. sichot), a talk or discourse, as opposed to a more formal shiur

siman, chapter

sugya, a section of the Talmud

sukka, temporary booth erected for the festival of Sukkot

Sukkot, Feast of Tabernacles

ta'amei ha-mitzvot, reasons for the commandments

tafel, minor or secondary

tallit, prayer shawl

talmid chakham (pl. talmidei chakhamim), rabbinic scholar

Talmud, see Mishna and Gemara

talmud Torah, Torah study

Tanakh, Bible

Tannaim, scholars of the Mishna (first century BCE to second century CE)

tefilla, prayer

tefillin, phylacteries

teruma, priestly agricultural gift

teshuva, repentance

Torah im derekh eretz, Torah and derekh eretz (see above), generally referring to the ideology developed by R. Shimshon Raphael Hirsch in nineteenth century Germany

torato umanuto, Torah is his main occupation

Tosefta, fourth century collection of beraitot

tum'a, impurity

tzaddik, righteous person

tzav, command

tzedaka, charity

tzelem E-lokim, image of God

tzitzit, four-cornered and fringed garment

umanut, trade or profession

Urim Ve-tumim, oracle using the stones on the high priest's breastplate

va-yetzav, and [God] commanded

Va-yetzav Hashem E-lokim al ha-adam, And the Lord God commanded the man (Bereishit 2:16)

ve-ha'arev na, prayer to "make the words of Your Torah sweet in our mouths"

viddui, confession

yerei Shamayim, one who possesses fear of Heaven

yeshiva, institution for Torah study

yeshiva bachurim, yeshiva students

yira, fear

yirat Shamayim, fear or awe of Heaven

yishuvo shel olam, the ordering or constructive development of the world

Yisraelim, Israelites (as opposed to Kohanim and Levi'im)

yissurin shel ahava, divine chastisements of love

Yom Ha-kippurim (or Yom Kippur), the Day of Atonement

zakhor, remember

zarim, outsiders, i.e. non-Kohanim

zekher la-Mikdash, in memory of the Temple

zekhira, remembering

Zikhronot, Remembrances, part of Musaf prayer on Rosh Hashana

GLOSSARY OF NAMES, BOOKS AND ACRONYMS

Avraham, Abraham

R. Avraham ben Yitzchak Av Beit Din, Provencal halakhist, twelfth century

Ba'al Ha-Tanya, R. Schneur Zalman of Liadi, first rebbe of Lubavitch, eighteenth century Lithuania

Ba'alei Ha-tosafot, the Tosafists, school of talmudic commentators founded by R. Tam, twelfth to fourteenth century France and Germany

R. Bachya ben Asher, exegete and kabbalist, thirteenth century Spain

R. Bachya ibn Pakuda, eleventh century Spanish moral philosopher

Bar Kokhba, second century leader of Jewish revolt against Rome

Chafetz Chayim, R. Yisrael Meir Ha-kohen, early twentieth century Lithuanian halakhist

Chatam Sofer, R. Moshe Sofer, nineteenth century Hungarian halakhist

R. Chayim *Or Zaru'a*, thirteenth century German halakhist

Chazon Ish, R. Avraham Yeshaya Karelitz, twentieth century halakhist, Israel

Chizkiyahu, King Hezekiah

Chovot Ha-levavot, The Duties of the Heart, a moral-philosophical work by R. Bachya ibn Pakuda

Eiger, R. Akiva, nineteenth century European talmudist

R. Elchanan (ben Yitzchak), twelfth century French Tosafist

Eliyahu, Elijah

Feinstein, R. Moshe, halakhic decisor, twentieth century U.S.A.

Hutner, R. Yitzchak, *rosh yeshiva* of Yeshivat R. Chaim Berlin, twentieth century U.S.A.

Ibn Ezra, R. Avraham, twelfth century Spanish exegete

Iyyov, Job

Kamenetsky, R. Ya'akov, *rosh yeshiva* of Torah Voda'ath, twentieth century U.S.A.

Karo, R. Yosef, sixteenth century halakhist, Turkey and Israel

Kesef Mishneh, commentary on Rambam's Code by R. Yosef Karo

Kook, R. Avraham Yitzchak Ha-kohen, twentieth century halakhist and thinker, pre-state Israel

Kotler, R. Aharon, *rosh yeshiva* of Lakewood, twentieth century U.S.A.

Maharal, R. Yehuda Loew of Prague, sixteenth century thinker and talmudist

Maharam (R. Meir) of Rothenberg, thirteenth century German halakhist

R. Meir Simcha of Dvinsk, late-nineteenth early-twentieth century Lithuanian talmudist

Meltzer, R. Isser Zalman, early twentieth century talmudist, Lithuania and Israel

R. Meshulam ben Ya'akov, twelfth century Provencal talmudist

Mezeritcher Maggid, R. Dov Baer, early leader of Chassidut

Mishkenot Ya'akov, talmudic work by R. Ya'akov of Karlin, nineteenth century Lithuania

Moshe, Moses

Noach, Noah

Or Zaru'a, halakhic compendium by R. Yitzchak of Vienna

Orchot Chayim, halakhic work by the late-thirteenth early-fourteenth century Provencal scholar R. Aharon ben Ya'akov Ha-kohen

R. Paltoi Gaon, ninth century head of Pumbedita yeshiva

Ra'ah, R. Aharon Ha-Levi, thirteenth century Spanish talmudist

Ra'avad, R. Avraham ben David, twelfth century Provencal talmudist

Ra'avan, R. Eliezer ben Natan, twelfth century German halakhist

Rambam (Maimonides), R. Moshe ben Maimon, halakhist and philosopher, twelfth century Egypt

Ramban (Nachmanides), R. Moshe ben Nachman, talmudist and exegete, thirteenth century Spain

Ran, R. Nissim ben Reuven, talmudist and philosopher, fourteenth century Spain

Rashi, R. Shlomo ben Yitzchak, talmudist and exegete, eleventh century France

Rashba, R. Shlomo ibn Adret, thirteenth century Spanish halakhist

Rema, R. Moshe Isserles, sixteenth century Polish halakhist

Rif, R. Yitzchak Alfasi, eleventh century North African halakhist

Rosh, R. Asher ben Yechiel, thirteenth century halakhist, Germany and Spain

Ruderman, R. Ya'akov, *rosh yeshiva* of Ner Israel, twentieth century U.S.A.

Salanter, R. Yisrael, founder of *Mussar* movement, nineteenth century Lithuania

Schneerson, R. Menachem Mendel, *rebbe* of Lubavitch *chassidim*, twentieth century U.S.A.

Sefer Ha-mitzvot, compendium of the 613 commandments by Rambam

Semag (*Sefer Mitzvot Gadol*), compendium of the 613 commandments by R. Moshe of Coucy, thirteenth century France

Shakh, R. Shabtai Hakohen Rappaport, seventeenth century

commentator on the *Shulchan Arukh*

Shaul, Saul

Shemona Perakim, ethical work by Rambam

Shemuel, Samuel

R. Shemuel Ha-naggid, halakhist and statesman, eleventh century Spain

Shlomo, Solomon

Shulchan Arukh, halakhic code by R. Yosef Karo

Soloveitchik, R. Chayim, late-nineteenth early-twentieth century Lithuanian talmudist

Soloveitchik, R. Yosef Dov (Joseph Baer), also called **the Rav**, talmudist and philosopher, twentieth century U.S.A.

R. Tam, R. Ya'akov ben Meir, twelfth century French talmudist and founder of Tosafist school

Taz, R. David Ha-levi, seventeenth century commentator on the *Shulchan Arukh*

Tosafot, see *Ba'alei Ha-tosafot*

Vilna Gaon (Gra), R. Eliyahu ben Shlomo Zalman, eighteenth century Lithuanian talmudist

Weinberg, R. Yechiel Ya'akov, twentieth century European talmudist

Ya'akov, Jacob

Yerushalmi, Jerusalem Talmud

Yeshivat Rabbeinu Yitzchak Elchanan, Rabbi Isaac Elchanan Theological Seminary (affiliated with Yeshiva University)

Yitro, Jethro

Yitzchak, Isaac

R. Yitzchak of Vienna, thirteenth century talmudist

R. Yona of Gerona, talmudist and moralist, thirteenth century Spain

Zevin, R. Shlomo Yosef, twentieth century Israeli talmudist and essayist

INDEX OF BIBLICAL,
RABBINIC AND
MAIMONIDEAN SOURCES

GENERAL INDEX

Abbaye, 36, 95, 135, 225, 237
Abortion, 6
R. Acha, 135
Achashverosh, 151, 168, 171, 177, 218
Adam
  command of, 1-2, 102, 105-06
  covenant of, 233
  curse of, 22, 27, 105, 111, 233
  mandate of, 1-3, 7, 8, 27
  sin of, 7, 8-9
Agag, King of Amalek, 126, 127, 128, 141, 186-7, 192, 200, 201
Ahavat Hashem. See Love of God
Akeida (Binding of Isaac), 122-24, 127, 159
R. Akiva
  bittachon of, 154-55
  on human grandeur, 9-10
Amalek
  eradication of, 126-27, 186-87
  remembrance of, 200-01
Amital, R. Yehuda, 26, 125
Amram, 22
Anger, 204
Anshei Kenesset Ha-gedola, 2
Aquinas, Thomas, 106
Arava, differing halakhic standards of, 233-34
Army service
  analogy to service of God, 55, 111, 166
  as a collective necessity, 43
  See also Hesder
Arnold, Matthew, 87, 205, 223, 226, 229, 248
Art, 10-11, 50, 226-27
Asa, King, 136
Assimilation, 178-81
Atheism, 194-96
Augustine, 138, 190
Avoda zara. See Idolatry
Avodat Hashem (service of God)
  balance and passion in, 212-14
  specialization in. *See* Spiritual specialization
  ubiquity of (*be-khol derakhekha da'ehu*), 1-9, 28-48, 86-89, 92-94, 106, 214-16
Avraham, 123, 124, 127, 146, 149, 151, 159

and the *akeida. See* Akeida
and love of God, 194
and Sodom, 108
and the work ethic, 13-14
command of, 22
covenant of, 21, 221
faith of, 144, 158, 166
R. Avraham ben Yitzchak *Av Beit Din*, 87, 92

Ba'al ha-Tanya. See R. Schneur Zalman of Liadi
Bach, J. S., 227, 242
R. Bachya ben Asher, 142, 143, 237
R. Bachya ibn Pakuda. *See* Chovot Ha-levavot
Bacon, Francis, 194
Balance
  as an element of *teshuva*, 215-16
  vs. Extremism, 212-16
Balebatim. See Laymen
Bar Kokhba, Shimon, 155
Be-khol derakhekha da'ehu. See Avodat Hashem
Ben Azzai, Shimon, 117
  specialization in Torah of, 83-84, 98-99
Berakha (blessing), and ownership, 4-5
Bergman, Ingrid, 227
"Beyond Tragedy," 154
Bittachon (trust in God), 134-61
  after destruction of the Temple, 149-52
  and education, 155-56
  and human effort, 138-39
  and medical intervention, 134-37
  and miracles, 139-40
  contemporary, 152-55
  faith within, 140-47
  historical view of, 149-52
  in *Tehillim*, 147-49
  love of God within, 140-47
Blessing. *See* Berakha
Bradley, F.H., 99
Brothers Karamazov, The, 119
Browning, Robert, 90
Buber, Martin, 56
Bunim, Irving, 230
Byron, George Gordon, 15, 241

265

RABBI AHARON LICHTENSTEIN is a leading Jewish educator, scholar and thinker.

Born in France in 1933, he escaped just before the German invasion and arrived in the United States in 1941. He was educated at Yeshivat Rabbi Chaim Berlin under the tutelage of Rabbi Yitzchak Hutner *zt"l* and Rabbi Ahron Soloveichik *zt"l*, and continued at Yeshivat Rabbenu Yitzchak Elchanan, where he was granted rabbinic ordination by his mentor, Rabbi Joseph B. Soloveitchik *zt"l*. After receiving his Ph.D. in English Literature from Harvard University, he taught both Talmud and Literature at Yeshiva University, New York, and headed its *kollel*.

Since moving to Israel in 1971, he has headed·Yeshivat Har Etzion in Alon Shevut, a highly regarded advanced Torah institution, whose students, believing the defense of Israel to be a moral, national and halakhic imperative, also serve in the Israeli military. In addition, he is Rector of Herzog Teachers' College and *Rosh Yeshiva* of Yeshiva University's Gruss Kollel in Jerusalem.

Rabbi Lichtenstein's views on religious, social and personal issues are widely sought both in Israel and the Diaspora, and his influence is extended by his many disciples who serve as rabbis, educators and communal leaders worldwide. A tireless pedagogue, he lectures extensively and has published dozens of articles in the areas of Talmud, Jewish Law and Jewish Thought.

RABBI REUVEN ZIEGLER is Editor-in-Chief of Yeshivat Har Etzion's Virtual Beit Midrash (*http://www.vbm-torah.org*), which offers weekly courses, without charge, to thousands of students around the world. As Director of Archives at the Toras HoRav Foundation, he co-edited Rabbi Soloveitchik's *Out of the Whirlwind* and is currently preparing additional volumes based on Rabbi Soloveitchik's manuscripts.